Fabric Painting Made Easy

OTHER BOOKS AVAILABLE FROM CHILTON

Robbie Fanning, Series Editor

Contemporary Quilting Series

Contemporary Quilting Techniques, by Pat Cairns
Fast Patch, by Anita Hallock
Fourteen Easy Baby Quilts, by Margaret Dittman
Machine-Quilted Jackets, Vests, and Coats, by Nancy Moore
Picture Quilts, by Jane Hall
Precision Pieced Quilts Using the Foundation Method, by Jane Hall and Dixie Haywood
The Quilter's Guide to Rotary Cutting, by Donna Poster
Quilts by the Slice, by Beckie Olson
Scrap Quilts Using Fast Patch, by Anita Hallock
Speed-Cut Quilts, by Donna Poster
Super Simple Quilts, by Kathleen Eaton
Teach Yourself Machine Piecing and Quilting, by Debra Wagner
Three-Dimensional Appliqué, by Jodie Davis

Creative Machine Arts Series

ABCs of Serging, by Tammy Young and Lori Bottom
The Button Lover's Book, by Marilyn Green
Claire Shaeffer's Fabric Sewing Guide
The Complete Book of Machine Embroidery, by Robbie and Tony Fanning
Creative Nurseries Illustrated, by Debra Terry and Juli Plooster
Creative Serging Illustrated, by Pati Palmer, Gail Brown, and Sue Green
Distinctive Serger Gifts and Crafts, by Naomi Baker and Tammy Young
The Fabric Lover's Scrapbook, by Margaret Dittman
Friendship Quilts by Hand and Machine, by Carolyn Vosburg Hall
Gifts Galore, by Jane Warnick and Jackie Dodson
How to Make Soft Jewelry, by Jackie Dodson

Innovative Serging, by Gail Brown and Tammy Young
Innovative Sewing, by Gail Brown and Tammy Young
Owner's Guide to Sewing Machines, Sergers, and Knitting Machines, by Gale Grigg Hazen
Petite Pizzazz, by Barb Griffin
Putting on the Glitz, by Sandra L. Hatch and Ann Boyce
Serged Garments in Minutes, by Tammy Young and Naomi Baker
Sew, Serge, Press, by Jan Saunders
Sewing and Collecting Vintage Fashions, by Eileen MacIntosh
Simply Serge Any Fabric, by Naomi Baker and Tammy Young
Soft Gardens, by Yvonne Perez-Collins
Twenty Easy Machine-Made Rugs, by Jackie Dodson

Know Your Sewing Machine Series, by Jackie Dodson

Know Your Bernina, second edition
Know Your Brother, with Jane Warnick
Know Your Elna, with Carol Ahles
Know Your New Home, with Judi Cull and Vicki Lyn Hastings
Know Your Pfaff, with Audrey Griese
Know Your Sewing Machine
Know Your Singer
Know Your Viking, with Jan Saunders
Know Your White, with Jan Saunders

Know Your Serger Series, by Tammy Young and Naomi Baker

Know Your baby lock
Know Your Pfaff Hobbylock
Know Your Serger
Know Your White Superlock

Teach Yourself to Sew Better Series, by Jan Saunders

A Step-by-Step Guide to Your Bernina
A Step-by-Step Guide to Your New Home
A Step-by-Step Guide to Your Sewing Machine
A Step-by-Step Guide to Your Viking

Fabric Painting Made Easy

Nancy Ward

Craft Kaleidoscope

CHILTON BOOK COMPANY

Radnor, Pennsylvania

Designed by Adrianne Onderdonk Dudden
Drawings by Marianne Russell
Black-and-White photos by Chuck Gallagher
Color photos by Mark Jenkins
On the cover: The dinosaur jeans feature a Bright-Line transfer by Dizzle.
The fish fabric on the fish vest is by Hoffman Fabrics of California.
The writing on the napkin was stitched with Viking stitch #1 on cassette M.

Library of Congress Catalog Card No. 92–56580

ISBN 0-8019-8341-x

Manufactured in the United States of America

1 2 3 4 5 6 7 8 9 0   2 1 0 9 8 7 6 5 4 3

Dedicated with love to my folks,
Doris *and* **Vince Ward**

Contents

Foreword

This morning while transferring a wet load to the dryer, I noticed one of my husband's collar stays had fallen out—you know, one of those little white plastic doodads that stiffen the point of a collar. *Hmm*, I thought, *how could I use that in fabric painting?*

That's how I know Nancy Ward's book is successful. I've been content to sew till today; now I want to paint everything. But I'm a beginner. I have found the choices available in fabric and craft stores totally baffling. Where to start? What to buy first?

Nancy's book is written for people like me. She explains not only the properties of paint, but discusses specific brands. She knows from her years of teaching that beginners buy a color they like and then are too often disappointed by the results because it wasn't the appropriate type of paint.

Nancy is also practical. She discovered that the backing on paperbacked fusible web was parchment paper, which you can buy by the roll in the grocery store and use like a Teflon pressing sheet.

She saves and recycles everything, including test strips of paint, old pantyhose, containers, egg cartons, you name it (collar stays?). And she has lots of design ideas for those of us who think we can't draw.

I like to laugh while I'm learning and Nancy Ward is a stand-up comedienne in a real-person's paint smock (i.e., a garbage bag with holes cut for neck and arms). "What you can't do," she says, "is mix paint in the cup you'll be drinking coffee from tomorrow" and "Don't use the dinner table to dry things flat unless you're looking for an excuse to go out to eat."

Best of all, I hate to clean up and she shows me how to make it easy. Learning that plastic film sticks to a wet surface is worth the price of the book—merely wipe the counters and sink with a damp sponge and cover all with plastic film.

Robbie Fanning
Series Editor

Acknowledgments

I owe a deep debt of gratitude to the administration of Monterey Peninsula College, particularly Jim Chub and Myrna Mertz. With their support and encouragement, I had the ideal teaching situation.

The students were outstanding—I greatly appreciated their enthusiasm and participation. Special thanks are due Gladys Keller, Margaret Royalty, and Terri Tanaka.

Thank you hardly seems adequate for the Chilton editors who had to wade through the thousands of words I stuffed into this book. Tim Scott, Allison Dodge, and Robbie Fanning read, reread, and then read again all those words.

Marianne Russell's talents can be seen on just about every page of this book. I admire her talents. I value her friendship.

Joyce Whipple and I have been friends longer than either of us admits to being alive. I hope each of you has a friend like Joyce.

Sisters and brothers are another pleasant addition to our lives. Sally or Mike always seem to come up with the right suggestion when I get stumped.

Needless to say, my children grew up in a house piled high with projects. I used to tell them that waiting for me to "finish just this one thing" developed patience. My heartfelt thanks to the most patient people I know—Jack, Dave, Tim, Joe, Andy, and Kate.

Recognition is due the many manufacturers and companies who answered dozens of questions and provided products for this book. I could not have written the book without their assistance: A Homespun Heart, Aleene's, Art's International, Banar Designs, Inc., Beacon Chemical Co., the Bead Shop, Beadery Craft Productions, Blueprints Printables, Carnival Arts, Inc., Cerulean Blue, Ltd., Clover Needlecraft, Inc., Coats & Clark, W.H. Collins, Colortex, Craft Stop, Creative Machine, DecoArt, Deka, Delta Technical Coatings, Inc., Delta/ Slomons, Dritz, Duncan Crafts, Dupey Management Co., Dylon USA, EZ International, Galacolor, Golden Touch, Inc., Great Copy Patterns, Grumbacher, HTC, Hoffman California Fabrics, Ivy Imports, J. & P. Coats, James River Corp., Jo Sonja's Artist's Colors, Jones Tones, Kwik.Sew, Marvy Uchida of America, Corp., Mary's Productions, Open Chain Publishing, Palmer Paint Products, Pelle's, Pellon Division of Freudenberg Non Wovens, Plaid Enterprises, Polymerics, Precision Valve Corp., Putnam Company, Quilter's Rule International, Quilting Creations by D.J., Rowenta, Rupert, Gibbon & Spider, Seitec, Sew-Art International, Shafaii, Siphon Art, Solar-Kist, Stretch & Sew, Sulky of America, Sure-Fit Designs, Tandy Leather, Testor Corp., Therm O Web, Tolin' Station, Treadleart, Tulip Productions, Viking Sewing Machine Co., Wearable Wonders, Wilton Enterprises, Works of Heart, Wrights/Boye, and Y & C.

Trademarks

The following are trademarks or registered trademarks:

™ PRODUCTS

Aleene's™

Aleene's™: Budget School Glue™; Hot Stitch Fusible Web™; Jewel-It™; OK To Wash-It™; School Glue™; Stick Glue™; Stop Fraying™; Tack-It Over & Over™; Transfer-It™; Fine Polyester Glitter™

Beacon Chemical Co.™

Beacon™: Fabric Tac™; Gem Tac™; BeDazzler™ Liqui Fuse™

blueprints-printables™

Brush Plus™

Co-Motion™

Co-Motion™ Stamp 'N' Iron™ Fabric Transfer Ink

Createx Colors™

DecoArt™

DecoArt™ Dazzling Metalics™; DecoWriter Tips™; Dimensions™; Glo-it Luminescent Paint Medium™; Hot Shots™; Transparent Medium™

Delta/Slomons™

Delta: Cool™; Glitter™; Swell™; Starlight Dye™ by Delta; Fabric Dye™ by Delta; by Delta Liquid Hearts™; by Delta Liquid Stars™; Stencil Magic® By Delta; Stencil Magic® Stencil Paint Cremes by Delta; Stencil Magic® by Delta Repositionable Stencil Adhesive Spray; Photo To Fabric Transfer™ by Delta

Distlefink Designs, Inc.™

Dizzle®: Brite-Line™; Glitterlooks™; Magic Sticker Paint™; Paint Blocks™

Dye Ties™

Dye∗Namite™

Dylon™

FabricARTS™

FabricARTS™ Water-Based Resist

Fabric Painters' Drying Sheet™

Fashion Show®: Basic Fabric Soft Paint™; Country Fabric Soft Paint™; Fabric Soft Paint™ Extender; Glitter Fabric Soft Paint™; Jewel Fabric Soft Paint™; Neon Fabric Soft Paint™; Pearl Fabric Soft Paint™; Sparkle Fabric Soft Paint™; Picture This™

Fashion Patches™

Founder's™

Founder's™ Stikit Again & Again™

Fray Check™

Galacolor® Extender™

Galacraft's Magic™ Transfer Medium

Galafetti™

Gleams™ Ceramcoat® Acrylics

Glitter Webbing™

Heat N Bond™

"Hera"™ Marker

HTC Trans-Web™

Inkadinkado® Fabric Transfer Ink™

Jones Tones™

Just Enough™

Liquid Appliqué™

Liquitex®: Liquitex® Liquigems™; Liquitex® Opalescents™; Liquitex® Marble Ease™

Marble-Thix™

Palmer® Paint Pots™

Paper Maid® Kitchen Parchement™

Pelle's See-Thru™ Stamps

Pellon® Heavy-Duty Wonder-Under™; Pellon® Wonder-Under™

Polymark™

Presist™

Iron-On™ Fabric Transfer Ink (Ranger Industries product)

Scribbles® products with ™: Scribbles® Matchables™; Scribbles® Brush 'N Soft™

Second Impressions™

Sew-Art international™

Speed Stitch™

Sequin Art™ Glue

Sponge Painter™

Sticky Stuff™

Stitchless™ Fabric Glue

Sure-Fit Designs™

Sure Stamp™

The Fabric Pattern Transfer Kit™

Tulip™

Tulip™: Big and Easy™; Brite Ideas™; Brush Top™; Christmas Textured™; ColorPoint™; Color Switch™; EasyFlow™; Fashion Suede™; Glitter™; Happy Chalk™; Jumpin'Jeans Denim™; Secret Recipes™; Soft Glitter™; Soft Lite Paint™; Soft Sparkling Tints™

Tumble Dye™

Ultrasoft 2000™

Webbing™

®PRODUCTS

Armo®

Binny & Smith®

Boye®

Ceramcoat® by Delta

Clotilde, Inc.®

Cloud Cover®

Color Dazzles®

Crayola®

Crayola Craft®

Daisy Kingdom®

DecoArt™: Fashion Tape®; Heavy Metals®; So-Soft Fabric Paints®; Shimmering Pearls®

Deka®

Deka®-Silk; Deka®-Silk Resist; Deka®-Permanent Fabric Paint; Deka®-Perm Air; Deka®-IronOn Transfer Paint; Deka®-Fun; Deka®-Flair; Deka®-Marbling Medium

Dizzle®

Dizzle® Pre-Shaded® Transfers

Dritz®

Easy Way Appliqué®

EmbossArt®

FabricMate®

Fashion Show®

Fasturn®

Fastube®

Fine Fuse®

FolkArt®

Grumbacher®

Helmac®

Jacquard®

Jo Sonja's®

Lint Pic-Up® by Helmac®

Liquitex®

Lumière®

Magic® Goo Gone

Magic Wand®

Marvy® Uchida
Neopaque®
Palmer®
Paper Maid®
Paper Maid® 20 Below® Freezer Wrap
Pellon®
Plexi® 400 Stretch Adhesive
Presist®
Pressure-Fax® Transfer Pen
Preval® Power Unit
Quilter's Rule®
Rowenta®
Scribbles®
Simplicity®
Singer®
Singer® Sewing Library®

Stitch Witchery®
Stitch-n-Tear®
Sulky®
Sulky® of America
Sure-Stamp®
Tandy Leather Company®
The Beadery® Craft Products
Treadleart®
Tuf-fuse®
Tulip™: Puffy®; Slick®
Unique Stitch®
U.Tee.it®
Viking Sewing Machine Co.®
Wilton® Enterprises, Inc.
Wrights®
Y & C®

Introduction

As a teacher, I see my students' projects develop from an idea to completion. As an author, I'm not a part of that process. I won't be there to give a boost when you need encouragement. And I won't be there to nag (and boy, do I nag!) when it's time to move along with your project.

You'll have to give yourself the praise you deserve and keep yourself moving. I'll miss being there. But you can drop me a line (in care of Chilton) and let me know how you're doing. I'd love to see a picture or two.

I won't even pretend that this book has a complete listing of all the many wonderful products available for fabric painting. Not only are there literally hundreds of excellent supplies and tools on the market, but also manufacturers are constantly introducing new products. So, when you find a product that's not mentioned in this book, give it a try. (And let me know about it!)

Fabric
Painting
Made
Easy

1

Fast and Easy, and a Lot of Fun

Fast and easy are two words that get thrown around a lot to describe crafts projects. I've gotten tangled up in some of those so-called fast and easy projects. The only easy part was dumping the thing in the trash after I had spent hours creating a disaster.

I won't even suggest that every fabric painting project can be done in a snap. But there are all sorts of projects that can be done in less than 15 minutes, and even more that take less than a half hour. That's the kind you want to start with. Save the more involved ones until you've had some practice with the quickies.

One of my favorite quickies is described in Chapter 5 (see Figs. 5-41 through 5-44). A quilting stencil, some glue, and glitter create an almost instant design on a shirt. If you don't like glitter, use a marking pen with the stencil. (Now that's really fast and easy!)

There are many products available that are intended specifically to make fabric painting easy. A prepainted or dyed transfer can be ironed on a shirt in about 5 minutes. That's not almost instant, that *is* instant. You can add other decorations to that transfer if you wish.

You certainly don't need sketching or drawing talents to use these transfers. There are literally hundreds of transfers and patterns and designs.

If you're as devoid of drawing skills as I am, you'll thank your lucky stars there is such a wonderful assortment. If I had to depend on my drawing abilities, I'd be limited to ducks. I do make a dynamite duck out of a capital S (Fig. 1-1).

Don't feel that using a drawing done by someone else diminishes your involvement in a project. That transfer (or pattern or design) is just a supply.

Fig. 1-1

Use transfers whenever they suit your purpose. It's really the same as using a clothing pattern for a sewing project.

One type of fabric painting that can cause frustration is adding a fine line of paint around an appliqué. If you're a cake decorator, you've got an advantage. When you think about it, you'll agree that methods used for frosting decorations are similar to those used for outlining with paint. If you haven't had that type of experience, I don't recommend outlining for your first project. It's not difficult; it just requires some practice.

Fabric painting isn't burdened with a lot of rules. But some things are important to remember. I call them the Unbreakable Rules of Fabric Painting.

The Unbreakable Rules of Fabric Painting

1 **Prewash all fabrics.** Do not use any type of softener or bleach when prewashing. New

fabric has a finish that keeps paint, glue, or fusibles from bonding to the fibers. That finish has to be removed. Softeners and bleach affect the way paint, glue, or fusibles bond to fabric.

2   Press fabric after prewashing. Paint collects in all those ridges and wrinkles. The color of the dried paint will not be even.

3   Do not use treated or coated fabrics. (Permapress fabrics, fabrics treated with Scotchguard, water-repellent fabrics; and polished cottons, for example, have permanent finishes; washing does not remove them. Permanent finishes prevent paint, glue, or fusibles from bonding to fabric.)

4   Do not use acrylic or acrylic-blend fabrics. There's a good chance paint will slide right off these fabrics. Rather than take the chance, don't use them.

5   Follow manufacturer's instructions. If you don't, colorfastness and durability of finished items will be affected.

After reading these rules, you can see why they're important. Regardless of how little time a project takes, you don't want all the paint going down the drain the first time the fabric is laundered. Be sure to read my Unbreakable Rules of Painting in Chapter 3, which tell you how to mix, use, store, and clean up your paint and brushes.

Another rule to follow: Please use care when selecting and applying decorations to clothing worn by young children. You know how they love to stick anything in their mouth. Small objects (buttons, beads, jewels, stones, etc.) are even more appealing to children if they have the challenge of pulling them off the garment. Use only decorations and products that are appropriate to the child's age.

About This Book

My purpose in writing this book is twofold: to provide instructions for specific projects and to provide information about tools and supplies used for fabric painting. These supplies are not limited to paints. I've divided these supplies into categories and listed them in the appendixes (see table of contents).

To help you get ready for your first project, I've written Chapter 2 on designing your project, and Chapter 3, which describes paints, resist, and fabric markers.

Keep in mind that the projects I've included (Chapters 4, 5, and 6) are just the beginning. Use them as the basis for experimenting and creating your own techniques.

You'll learn how to appliqué and outline in Chapter 7. And if you make a mistake (I prefer to call this a "creative experience"), take heart—you're not alone. Chapter 8 tells you how to avoid mistakes and how some mistakes can be made to look as if they were part of your plan all along.

The Answer Box (Chapter 9) is the opposite of a question box. This is where you can find the answers to all your questions. If these answers were scattered throughout the book, you'd spend ages trying to remember where you saw them. Instead, you can look in this alphabetical listing when you run across a term you're not familiar with.

Before you begin your first project, I recommend that you read the Cleanup Tips (Chapter 9). Drying Paint (also in Chapter 9) is another subject you should read up on. The way you dry your project can be crucial to its success.

I think it's time we get to the fun part! After you read Chapters 2 and 3, pick a project and gather the supplies you need. Happy painting!

2

Designing Your Project

Don't fret if you aren't able to draw the designs you want to paint. All the paint in the world will dry up before I reach a level beyond lousy when it comes to drawing a design. Fortunately, there are all kinds of supplies and equipment that allow me—and you—to make use of the talents of others.

Literally hundreds of designs can be ironed on, traced, transferred, or photocopied. They're available by the sheet, packet, booklet, or book.

You don't have to use the complete design. Combine sections of different designs, or combine types of designs (iron-on transfer with traced design). Do what you want, the way you want to do it. It is, after all, your creation.

Other than iron-on transfers, which must be used as-is, you can use an image of the original design or a reversed image. You can repeat a design all in the same direction, or in combinations (Fig. 2-1).

Iron-on transfers leave an instant image on fabric. They're available in every size, shape, and type. Some are for single use; others for multiple use. (See Transfers and Transfer Supplies, Chapter 9).

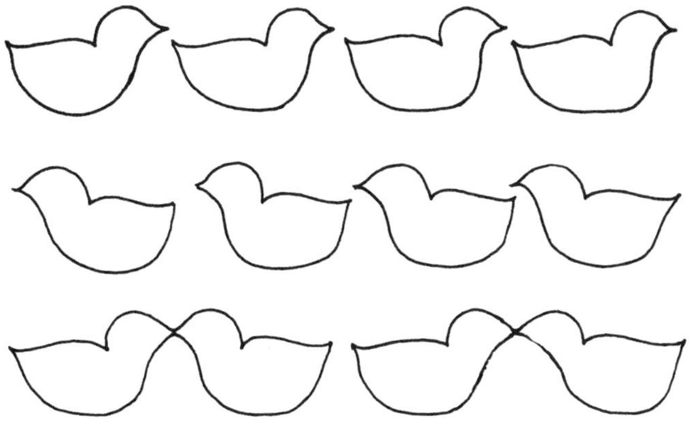

Transfer pens and paints extend the usability of multiple-use transfers. You can use them to color in a transfer design before pressing it on fabric, or to make your own transfers.

Most iron-on transfers can be painted or embellished after application. Some manufacturers recommend using a glaze coating over unpainted iron-on transfers. Glaze coatings can also be used over painted or glittered iron-on transfers on outerwear (such as denim jackets). The coating will project your handiwork from the elements (see Coatings in Appendix B). Read instructions before beginning.

Transfers and transfer supplies are listed by brand name in Appendix D.

Tracing and Transfer Hints and Supplies

The most common supply used for reproducing a design on fabric is transfer paper. Designs are drawn or traced on the paper and transferred to fabric. Test your paper before you use it. (Some papers require use of special pens.) See also Transfer Paper under Transfers and Transfer Supplies in Chapter 9.

Transfer paper can sometimes be one big pain. The tracing doesn't look anything like the original drawing, or the transfer ends up being a mess of unconnected lines. To prevent these problems, don't make short, jittery strokes when tracing. Relax your hand and fingers. If you put a stranglehold on the pencil, the position of your hand will change. Most tracing problems are caused by your inability to see where you will be tracing because your hand covers a portion of the design. Hold the pencil as far away from the point as possible. The

Fig. 2-1

closer you get to the point, the tighter you grip the pencil.

When transferring a design, place your fabric on a hard surface. It's important that both fabric and transfer are stable, flat, and wrinkle-free. If necessary, tape your fabric to the work surface.

Place transfer on fabric. Apply tape across the full length of the bottom edge of the transfer paper (Fig. 2-2). After transferring your design, flip the paper back. (Don't let the fabric shift or move.) If not all lines are visible, flip the paper back down over the fabric and redraw.

As long as the fabric did not move, and the paper was taped securely to the fabric, the transfer will be exactly where you wanted it. On the other hand, if everything moved every which way, remove your markings and start over. Trying to fix it would drive you up the wall. Remove paper when all markings are the way you want them.

Some transfer papers are transparent; some are not. When using transparent paper to trace a design placed under the paper, use a lead softer than a number 2. With a softer lead, you won't have to push so hard to make the markings, and there'll be less chance of tearing the paper. Also, mistakes are easier to erase.

Chalk transfer paper is not transparent, and so it cannot be used for tracing. Draw around the outline of the design on the uncolored side of the paper. Place the colored side of the paper on your fabric. Redraw the design, using a stylus, seam marker, or non-working ballpoint pen. An image of the design is transferred to the fabric. For a reversed image turn the design over on the paper.

If the design is printed on a lighter-weight paper, it isn't necessary to redraw the design on the back of the transfer paper. Place the paper with the design on top of the uncolored side of the transfer paper. Go over your design with a stylus. Turn the design over on paper for a reversed image.

EZ Crafts Transfer Paper and Pressure-fax Transfer Pen work slightly differently. This paper and pen allow you to make a "rub-off" transfer. The transfer paper is transparent. Trace your design, using the transfer pen. Place paper on fabric, traced side down. Rub over the back of the paper. (Use the back of a plastic spoon.) The image will be reversed when transferred to fabric. You'll be able to use the EZ transfer at least twice, usually more. Complete directions are included with the paper and pen.

If you don't want to take the time to trace, photocopy your design onto EZ transfer paper. Place the transfer paper on fabric, copy side down. Press for 20 seconds. I found a dry iron at cotton setting worked best. Test before using. Photocopies made from EZ paper may not transfer well on fabrics with a high synthetic content. (See The Wonderful Photocopy Machine below.)

The Marvy Uchida Fabric Pattern Transfer Kit contains transfer rice paper and a fabric/transfer pen. The removable marking pen is used to trace the design onto the transparent rice paper. Either side of the tracing can be placed on either side of the fabric when you redraw the tracing. This is handy because you can use the image either way (original or reverse). The paper is washable and reusable. Test pen on fabric before use.

Stencil plastic and template markers can be used for tracing. Stencil plastic is available with a clear or gridded surface. The best use of these products is for basic, uncomplicated designs, such as those found in coloring books. Printed fabric, especially with a large floral pattern, is another source of designs suitable for stencil tracings and transfer paper. Use a template marker for tracing. It won't smear on the plastic. (Fabric markers do.) Cut the design from plastic after marking. You can easily cut the plastic with regular scissors. A craft knife is necessary only if the design is intricate (lots of zigs and zags). Place either side of stencil on right or wrong side of fabric and trace around edges. Cookie cutters are excellent stencil/designs; you can easily draw around them.

Fig. 2-2

Transfer Pens and Paints

These products can be used to touch up purchased transfers for extended use or for making your own iron-on transfers.

Trace designs on Tracing Vellum (made by Sure-Fit Designs) with Sulky Iron-on Transfer Pens and you've made a reusable transfer that can be ironed on fabric three to six times (more if you use a light touch with the iron when transferring). Tracing Vellum comes on a roll in 18″ and 24″ widths, which makes it handy to use.

White ink (Sulky Iron-on Transfer Pen) is opaque and perfect for use on dark fabrics, especially denim. When used on cooking parchment paper, all of the white ink transfers to fabric. (The transfer will not be reusable.) But what you get is an iron-on transfer that looks exactly like the purchased ones. You can also use transfer pens to touch up purchased transfers that got crinkled in the envelope.

Deka IronOn paint can also be used on Tracing Vellum, cooking parchment paper, or any non-slick paper. Transfer paint can be used to fill in larger areas of iron-on transfers. One restriction: it must be used on fabric having at least a 60% synthetic content.

The Wonderful Photocopy Machine

I'm a big fan of photocopy machines. Owning one is right at the top of my wish list. A stack of Dover design books and a half hour at the copier keeps even the fastest painter busy for days.

If the design you like is too big (or small) for your project, enlarge (or reduce) it to fit your need. Most copy centers have machines that can reduce or enlarge.

Whenever you have one of those little gridded 2″ drawings often found in magazine craft instructions and you're supposed to explode it to a 24″ drawing, enlarge the thing on a copier.

First enlarge the small drawing as large as the copy paper is wide. Then cut sections (gridded areas) apart. Enlarge each section independently, at the same scale. Paste the enlarged sections to a piece of paper. The copy center may have a machine that is large enough to make a copy of the paste-up. That's sure a lot faster, and less frustrating, than enlarging it by hand.

A photocopy eliminates the need to trace. Place on fabric, copy side down, and press with a dry iron at cotton setting. Be sure to use an up-and-down pressing motion; do not slide the iron. A reverse of the image is transferred to the fabric. The copy center can give you instructions for making copies that will not be reversed.

Just remember that everything on the photocopy transfers: page numbers, wording, titles. Cut out any part of the copy you do not want transferred before pressing on fabric. You will have to answer a lot of questions when a page number is on the front of a shirt (especially since it will probably be reversed)!

Clover Charcopy Tracing Paper can be photocopied on the uncolored side. Place the colored side on fabric and retrace the design. Use the "tape-across-the-bottom" method explained on page 4. The Hera Marker (Clover) works well with this paper. You can also use a stylus or nonworking pen. The chalk tracing on the fabric will be the exact image, not a reverse.

Cut 8½″ × 11″ sheets of both Charcopy and cooking parchment paper. Cover the colored side of Charcopy with cooking parchment paper. Use lift-off tape to secure papers together. Use the single-feed paper tray of the machine. Copies are made one at a time. Fabric must be washed to remove marking made with Charcopy Tracing Paper if you make an error.

Cooking parchment paper can be used for copying. Cut 8½″ × 11″ sheets (or size used in copier). Use the single-feed tray of the machine. Copies are made one at a time.

Place on fabric, copy side down. Press. Let cool. Slowly remove paper. The design (reversed) will be slightly raised on the fabric; cooking parchment paper does not absorb ink like standard copier paper.

Tolin' Station makes a vellum paper for copiers. It's available in both 8½″ × 11″ and 11″ × 17″ sheets. Press on fabric like cooking parchment paper. This paper can be used on all fabrics, but works especially well on silk.

After pressing, let fabric cool before removing vellum paper. Use a fine-line applicator and outline the design with Resist. As soon as the Resist dries, you're ready to paint. Of course, this isn't limited to silk; use it on any fabric.

This paper can also be used for "rub-off" transfers, and with either transfer pens or china markers. Directions are included in package.

Copying on Fabric

Lightweight fabric can be photocopied. Cut an 8½″ × 11″ piece of freezer paper and organdy or batiste. Use a fabric that is at least 50% cotton. Both paper and fabric must be the same size.

Press fabric to plastic side of freezer paper (Fig. 2-3). Then it's off to the copy center.

Insert the fabric/paper sheet into the single-feed paper tray of the copier, fabric side up. (Copies

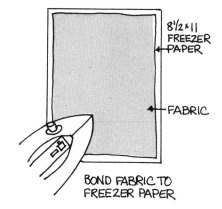

BOND FABRIC TO
FREEZER PAPER

8½ × 11
FREEZER
PAPER

FABRIC

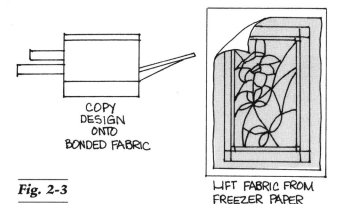

COPY
DESIGN
ONTO
BONDED FABRIC

LIFT FABRIC FROM
FREEZER PAPER

Fig. 2-3

must be made one at a time.) Copy your design. When you remove the fabric from the paper, you've got a perfect reversed image of the design on your fabric.

You must use a layer of paper (and freezer paper is the easiest to use) under fabric. It doesn't have enough body to go through the machine. Heavy fabric is too thick; it gets stuck in the rollers of the machine. If you want to reuse the freezer paper for another copy, wipe off the ink residue with a dry cloth.

I use fabric copies as patterns for stitched (hand and machine) and glued beads and sequins designs. Stained glass designs are excellent for this type of embellishment. (Paisley designs from printed fabric aren't too bad either!) The completed design can be stitched, glued, or attached with lift-off tape to clothing.

Copying on Freezer Paper

When you want to copy a design onto freezer paper, keep the paper side up in the tray. Press fabric to the plastic side of the paper, or cover the plastic side with a piece of parchment paper. Tape parchment paper to the plastic side of the freezer paper. This is a fast way to create freezer paper stencils (see Stencils in Chapter 9).

Copying on Paper-Backed Fusible

If you want to handle two jobs at one time, press paper-backed fusible web (light or regular-weight) to the wrong side of lightweight fabric before copying.

Copy design on either fabric or fusible backing. Cut excess fusible backing and paper along outer edges of design. Copying on backing produces an exact image on the fabric; copying on fabric produces a reverse image.

One advantage of copying on the fabric is that all lines of the design will be on the fabric and can be used as a guide for painting, markers, or embellishments.

Now you have your own no-stitch appliqué, ready to be fused to fabric. Paint or embellish, if desired.

The appliqué can be painted before fusing. Use a paint that can be heat-set. Translucent paint is my choice, especially one with crystals or sparkles. Metallic paint, applied with a fine-line brush, accents lines of the design. Markers don't do a bad job either. (See Heat-Setting, Chapter 9).

Be sure to read Chapter 7, in which I explain fusing and stitching of appliqués and outlining with paint.

If your copy center is concerned that glue from the fusible web might get on the rollers of the machine, copy on any of the parchment papers mentioned earlier in this section on photocopying. That copy can be transferred to the paper backing of the fusible web as follows: Cover ironing board with cooking parchment paper. Place fabric wrong side up on ironing board. Cover with fusible web, paper side up. Place copy face down on paper backing.

Press as directed for fusible. The copy will transfer to the paper backing of the fusible web while the web fuses to the appliqué fabric. The fusible will be bonded to the wrong side of the fabric. Cut out design. Fuse appliqué to background fabric (shirt, pants, etc.). Paint or embellish, if desired.

Transfer Mediums

There are three brands of liquid coatings that can be used to transfer the image from a photocopy to fabric. Each works somewhat the same.

These solutions are not limited to transferring black-and-white photocopies. Color photocopies can also be used.

The solutions are often used with photocopies of photographs (quilt blocks in memory quilts, grandchildren's photos, etc.). These supplies protect the surface of the copy. Paint and embellishments can be added, if desired.

The transfer medium is spread on the front of

the photocopy. When dry, the paper is dampened from the back of the photocopy. Transfer medium is brushed over the copy for added protection. Follow manufacturer's instructions.

Launder according to manufacturer's instructions.

Copyright Laws

Please observe copyright laws when using published designs. Using designs for personal use is permitted. Using designs on items that will be sold or displayed requires permission from the publisher and/or designer. All Dover Publications contain information concerning use of their designs.

3

Fabric Painting—What It Is and What It Does

This chapter is about paint and paint-related supplies, the main components of fabric painting projects. Some types are suitable for several techniques. Some are limited in use.

Refer to Appendix B for addresses and mail-order information for brands of paint listed in this chapter. Appendix C has a detailed description of tools used for applying paint.

You've already read the Unbreakable Rules of Fabric Painting in Chapter 1. The Unbreakable Rules of Painting are just as important.

The Unbreakable Rules of Painting

1   Shake paint before opening container. Paint settles. Usually the stuff at the bottom of the container is what makes the paint work. If you don't shake, the good stuff stays at the bottom of the barrel.

2   Unless paint is applied directly onto fabric from tip, pour or squeeze paint from the container (bottle, jar, or tube) onto a non-stick surface or into a mixing container. Non-stick surfaces are plastic plates, freezer paper, parchment paper, or plastic food wrap. Wax paper is not a non-stick surface (when it's used with fabric paint).

3   Do not put brushes, spoons, stirring sticks, etc., into paint container.

4   After pouring paint from container, clean paint from lip and tightly cover. Store container in a cool place, out of direct sunlight. Paint

thickens when exposed to air. The longer and the more frequently the top or lid is off, the thicker the paint becomes. The larger the mouth of the container, the greater the exposure to air.

5   Mix and blend additives and colors on non-stick surfaces listed in #2 or in mixing container. Blending and mixing is easy if you separate the glops of colors or additives. Pull small amounts of the blending color into the edge of the color you want darker. (It's easier going from light to dark than from dark to light.) Don't use the dump-and-stir, "ice cream soup" method. You usually end up with a grungy brown or gray color. Instructions for some additives tell you to dip the end of your brush into the additive before filling the brush with paint. Separated globs make that easier.

6   Follow manufacturer's instructions if mixing different types of the same brand together in the one container. Not all paints made by a manufacturer are compatible. Read instructions on container before mixing. If in doubt, don't mix!

7   Using different brands on the same project (Tulip with Delta, for example) is OK as long as they aren't in contact with one another. Use one brand in one part of the design and the other elsewhere. (Brands and types can be intermixed when decorating gift wrapping paper.) The formulas used by different companies usually are not compatible. Mixing brands together in the same container can be a disaster (like the paint falling off a shirt the first time it's laundered).

8 Label (color, paint type, additive) leftovers of mixed paint. Mystery paints often produce results that are not satisfactory.

9 Store paint in an air-tight container (glass or plastic). Keep it in a cool place, out of direct sunlight. Storage affects the life of the paint. Storing containers on the windowsill, next to the furnace, or in the garage (especially if you live in a cold climate) is a killer for paint. Paint doesn't fare well in sunlight or in excessive heat or cold. (See also the section on storage at the end of this chapter.)

10 Clean brushes or rollers immediately after use. Even disposables are worth the few seconds used for cleanup. Dried paint can be impossible to remove from any brush. *To clean bristle brushes,* rinse paint from brush. Pour a small amount of a nontoxic brush cleaner into your cupped palm (I like Brush Plus). Vigorously stir cleaner with brush in a circular motion, pushing bristles into your palm. Rinse. Reshape bristles. Store with bristles up. *To clean sponge (foam) brushes and rollers,* rinse paint from brush or roller. Apply small amount of a nontoxic brush cleaner or liquid dishwashing detergent to brush or roller. Squeeze a small amount of cleaner or detergent on sponge. Squish the cleaner or detergent into the brush to remove paint. Rinse thoroughly in clear water. Store upright.

11 Utensils and containers used for preparation or consumption of food should not be used to mix or store paint. Keep items used for mixing and storage of paint separate from those used for food. Scrub counters thoroughly to remove all traces of paint.

12 Keep all paint and paint-related items out of the reach of small children. The colors and sparkle of paint, glitter, and sequins are more than any child can ignore. Preventing an accident is much easier than dealing with one.

Fabric Paint and Fabric Dye

There are vast differences between fabric paint and fabric dye. That doesn't mean one is better than the other; but it does mean one might be more suitable than the other for a particular technique.

Fabric paint sits on, or coats, fibers of fabric; it does not penetrate or soak into fibers. Fabric paint adds texture, from nominal to heavy, to fabric. It is available in a variety of types, always in liquid (fluid to thick) form. Migration (ability to flow over fabric) of fabric paint ranges from none (thick paints) to complete (fluid paints). Additives enhance fabric

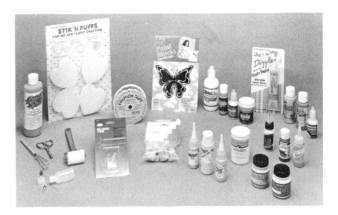

Fig. 3-1

paint's properties. Thinning with water increases migration, while use of additives reduces migration. There is a wide range of suitable application methods. Most fabric paint is non-toxic. Soap and water can be used for fabric paint cleanup (before it dries); it is colorfast and permanent when dry. Heat-setting, after drying, is sometimes required for colorfastness and permanency.

Fabric dye is absorbed by fibers of fabric. It penetrates fibers and does not add texture. Migration is complete. Applicaton may be limited to dipping or immersing. Fabric dye requires specific additives to "fix" the dye for colorfastness and permanency. Fabric dye comes in liquid or powder form, can be toxic, and requires specific procedures for use and disposal.

With the exception of Visionart, Just Enough, Tumble Dye, Dye Ties, PaintStik, and Stencil Magic, the products used in this book are fabric paint. Delta Fabric Dye, Delta Starlight Dye, and Grumbacher Permanent Fabric Dye are fabric paints.

Although Visionart, Just Enough, and Tumble Dye are liquid dye, they are nontoxic and do not require procedures normally needed with powdered or other liquid fabric dyes.

Dye Ties are used only for tie-dyeing. The dye solution in the ties is dried and activated in hot water. Follow all directions on package.

PaintStik and Stencil Magic are solid oil paints. Odorless turpentine or turpentine substitute is required for cleanup.

Warnings are included on labels of paint and dye products that require safety procedures. Do not ignore these warnings.

Types of Fabric Paint

Paint types vary drastically. Knowing what those differences are makes it easier to select the correct paint for a project. Following are thumbnail descriptions of each type of paint:

Soft Paint

- Does not add stiffness to fabric
- Most types not suitable for dimensional application
- Most types require being brushed, or pushed, into fabric
- Often labeled "brush-on" or "brushable"
- May be suitable as glue substitute
- May require heat-setting
- Some types can be sprayed with water after application
- Application with paint bottle or with tool suitable for outline and detail painting, or with syringe, brush, roller, print block, or spreader

Hard/Stiff Paint

- Adds stiffness to fabric
- Not suitable for large painted areas
- Suitable for dimensional outlining
- Most types suitable as glue substitute
- May require special laundering or drying
- Application with paint bottle or tool suitable for outline and detail painting, or with syringe, brush, print block, or spreader

Textured Paint

- Contains strands, shapes, or particles
- Base is either transparent or colored
- Will not retain raised shape on surface of fabric
- Adds texture to fabric
- Available in soft or hard/stiff types
- May not be suitable for large painted areas
- Most manufacturers recommend application by brushing or spreading

Glitter Paint

- Usually adds heavy texture to fabric
- Available in soft or hard/stiff types
- Available in dimensional and non-dimensional types
- Some types can be used for large painted areas
- Application varies according to type and brand

Stretch Paint

- Greater flex properties than other paint types
- Stretches with fabric
- Dimensional and non-dimensional types available
- Application varies by type and brand

Dimensional Paint

- Remains raised on surface of fabric after application
- Retains shape when dry

Fig. 3-2

- Some soft paints suitable as dimensional paint
- Hard/stiff type not suitable for large painted areas
- Puff or Swell types require heat to expand
- Shiny types may require heat for good bond
- Slick types may melt when ironed
- Some dimensional paints not suitable for machine drying
- Application with paint bottle or tool suitable for outline and detail painting, or with syringe, brush, spreader, or print block

Non-dimensional Paint

- Will not retain raised shape on surface of fabric
- Flattens into surface
- May add texture to fabric
- Available in soft or hard/stiff types
- Application varies by type and brand

Fluid Fabric Paint

- Spreads over fabric
- Dries soft; usually dries fast
- Adds little or no texture to fabric
- Usually can be heavily diluted with water
- Many types require heat-setting
- Not suitable for dimensional use
- Most can be sprayed with water after application
- Addition of water or extender changes shade
- Use of covering white or opaque white increases opacity (see Additives, below)
- Thickener changes density
- Application with paint or specialty bottles, dropper, brush, roller, print block, stamp, spreader, heavy spray, or light mist, or by dipping or immersing, or with refillable marker

Liquid Fabric Dye

NOTE: The following description applies to Vision-art, Just Enough, and Tumble Dye, but not to other fabric dyes.

- Can be highly concentrated
- High dilution rate
- Additives may be necessary to control migration
- May migrate rapidly when brushed
- Quickly absorbed where applied
- Dries soft
- Does not add texture to fabric
- May require heat-setting
- Application with speciality bottles, dropper, brush, roller, or by dipping or immersing, or with refillable marker

Application Methods

Instructions on the paint container often recommend a method of application for that paint. See Appendix C for brand names and suggestions on where to get the following items, used for applying paint. Under each kind of applicator is a list of the types available.

Bottles

- Paint bottles with "writer" tip
- Specialty (pull-top or squirt-type bottle)
- Fine-line applicator bottles (½ oz. to 16 oz.), used with removable metal tip

Brushes

- Disposable sponge (foam), ¼" to 4" widths
- Synthetic bristle, suitable for acrylic paint or fabric paint, available in numerous types and sizes
- Natural bristle, suitable for silk painting, ½"–2" width

Equipment for Dipping or Immersing

- Plastic bags
- Pans or buckets used as containers

Droppers

- Glass or plastic tube with a squeeze top

Print Blocks

- Sponge, rubber, wood, or plastic blocks
- Found objects

Refillable Markers

- Purchased product for use only with fluid fabric paints and liquid fabric dye

Rollers

- Sponge (foam) type
- Rubber brayers
- Plastic or wooden rollers used for wallpaper seams

Containers for Spraying or Misting

- Containers available with or without adjustable nozzle
- Removable propellent container

Spreaders

- Purchased product used for fabric paints
- Plastic putty knife
- Expired charge card

Stamps

- Purchased stamps, available with foam, wood, or clear plastic base

Syringes

- Plastic syringes with tapered or straight tip, also called injectors

Properties of Paint

Paints do not have identical properties. If you know what the following terms mean, you can select the right paint for a particular project.

Transparency

The color or print of the background fabric is clearly visible when paint is transparent. Depending on technique, transparent paints can blend with the background, creating a shaded color. Additives increase the transparency of some paints; follow manufacturer's directions. Transparent paint will not cover the subtle shadings of a preshaded iron-on transfer.

Translucency

The color or print of the background fabric is somewhat visible when paint is translucent. Depending on technique, translucent paints can blend with the background, creating a third color. For example, when you paint a blue background with yellow translucent paint, you will get a blended green effect. Additives increase translucency of some paints; follow manufacturer's directions.

Opacity

The color or print of the background fabric is completely covered when you use opaque paint. For example, opaque paint will completely cover the color of a denim jacket. Additives can be used to increase the opacity of some paints. Follow manufacturer's directions.

Additives

Additives enhance the basic properties of a paint. Directions on the container will explain how it is used and what it does. Don't use an additive unless it's recommended on the paint container. Don't mix additives of one paint brand with paint of another brand. Following are descriptions of the different types of additives.

Covering White or Opaque White

♦ Increases opacity of paint

Extender

♦ Creates lighter or pastel shades
♦ Does not change consistency of paint
♦ Can increase transparency ot translucency
♦ Can be used to increase "softness" of paint

Textile Medium

♦ Bonds paint to fabric
♦ Increases coating ability of paint
♦ Depending on brand, is either brushed on fabric or added to paint
♦ May require heat-setting

Thickener

♦ Depending on amount used, changes consistency of paint from fluid to very thick

Water

♦ Creates lighter or pastel shades
♦ Changes consistency of paint
♦ Follow manufacturer's recommendations for satisfactory results; many paints cannot be diluted with water
♦ Distilled water is recommended if tap water contains high amounts of minerals

Resist

See also Appendix B for names of brands and manufacturers.

In this book I use the terms "Resist" (capital *R*) and "resist" (lowercase *r*). Resist with a capital *R* is used to denote products labeled Resist and used traditionally. A lowercase *r* is used to denote products not normally used as resist (glue, for example). See Resist in Chapter 9 for more information.

Resist is applied to areas of fabric where you do not want paint. Fabric absorbs Resist so paint cannot coat fibers. Traditional Resist is often associated with silk painting. It can, however, be used for any paint technique and on any fabric. Gutta is not recommended for beginners.

Following are descriptions of the different types of Resists.

Solid Resist

♦ Crayons (fabric type and standard)
♦ Must be heat-set before paint is applied

Traditional Resist (Liquid)

♦ Available in clear, metallic, and colors
♦ Clear is removed by laundering; metallic and colors remain in fabric and are colorfast (unless noted to contrary by manufacturer)
♦ Usually applied with metal-tipped, fine-line applicator bottle; must be pushed into fibers
♦ Usually not suitable for use on sweatshirt fleece or heavy wovens
♦ Requires proper storage

Other Traditional Resist Products (Presist)

♦ Comes in liquid form
♦ Applied with fine-line applicator, brush, roller, stamp, or block print
♦ Is removed quickly and easily in water
♦ Lines not as sharply defined as with Resist
♦ Can be substituted for washable glue resist
♦ Suitable for all fabric types and weights
♦ Requires proper storage

Non-Permanent Glue

♦ Comes in liquid
♦ Use only glues that are water-soluble when dry
♦ Suitable for all application methods used with Presist
♦ Lines not as sharply defined as with Resist or Presist
♦ Not suitable for intricate designs
♦ Removed in laundering
♦ Suitable for all fabric types and weights

Paint Used as Resist

Pre-test before beginning project; paint selected must coat fibers completely; suggested brands and types listed in Appendix C.

Fabric Coatings

See Appendix B for brand names and manufacturers.

Certain techniques, paints, and markers require that a coating be added to the fabric. The coating is applied either by brush or by dipping fabric into liquid. Four types of coating are listed here.

Antifusant

Antifusant is applied to fabric before painting or using marker to reduce or prevent the spread of paint or markers across fabric. Depending on brand, it is either permanent-finish or removed in laundering.

Glaze Coating

Glaze coating is used as a protective coating over paints, markers, glued glitter, and unpainted iron-on transfers. It also adds texture to fabric. It is applied after paint or markers are heat-set. Dilute the glaze coating as directed on the bottle, then apply in a thin coat with a soft brush or with a spray bottle.

Mordant

Mordant increases the ability of paint to bond to fabric and improves its colorfastness. To make a mordant solution, alum (powder or granules) or aluminum sulfate powder is added to water. Fabric is rinsed in solution and dried before marbling. Mordant is removed in laundering. See Marbling in Chapter 9 for more information.

Textile Medium

Textile medium can be used as a substitute for antifusant when markers are used. Textile medium gives a permanent finish, which will not rinse out. It may add texture to fabric and may require heat-setting. See also Additives, earlier in this chapter.

Permanent Markers

See Appendix B for brand names and manufacturers. Following are descriptions of the different kinds of markers:

Fast-Dry Markers

♦ Dry almost immediately when applied to fabric
♦ Seldom blend with adjoining colors
♦ Rarely smudge
♦ Heat-setting recommended

Slow-Dry Markers

♦ Long drying time
♦ Blend with adjoining colors
♦ Will smudge when wet
♦ Heat-setting recommended

Decorative Markers

See Liquid Appliqué, Appendix B.

♦ Raised or puffed appearance after heat-setting
♦ Requires 12 hours drying time before heat-setting

Enamel Markers

♦ Excellent for outerwear, cloth shoes, and banners

♦ Can be used with stencils on several types of surfaces (fabric, wood, etc.)
♦ Follow manufacturer's directions

Transfer Pen

See Sulky Iron-On Transfer Pen, Appendix B.
♦ Suitable for use on fabric or paper
♦ Opaque white suitable for dark fabrics
♦ Must be heat-set when used on fabric

Using Antifusant with Markers

Antifusant is recommended when markers are used on fine wovens. Pretest for other fabrics. Textile medium can be substituted for traditional antifusants; follow instructions on the bottle.

Storing Paint, Resist, and Markers

Storing Paint

Paint is not extremely fragile, but storage rules do apply. Direct sunlight, extreme heat or cold are paint killers. See the Unbreakable Rules of Painting at the beginning of this chapter.

If properly capped and stored after opening, paint can remain good for 6 to 12 months. Run a wire into the tip after painting to keep the paint in the tip from drying up (see Chapter 7).

I think the least complicated way to store anything is in plastic boxes. I put my paint containers in plastic boxes, which I stack on shelves. The shelves are in a very crowded workroom, out of direct sunlight.

I put only one type of paint in each box. A glop of paint from each container goes on the cap of that container. That way I know at a glance which colors I have of a certain type, and the exact color of the paint when dry.

If you prefer storing "writer-tip" bottles upside down, punch holes in a piece of cardboard that has been cut to fit a box. Push bottle, tip down, into the holes. Jones Tones makes cardboard storage boxes intended specifically for this type of storage.

Storing Resist and Presist

These products require special care in storing. Sunlight and heat will destroy a bottle of Resist. Some manufacturers recommend keeping it in the refrigerator in very warm climates. At the very least, keep it in a covered box in a cool spot.

Storing Non-Permanent Glues

These products do not require special storage. I just keep them in plastic boxes (what else?) on one of the many shelves used for all the other plastic boxes.

Storing Permanent Markers

Unless the manufacturer tells you differently (see barrel), put all markers with the same type tip in separate plastic bags or boxes. One glance will tell you what colors you have (or need) in a particular tip.

I make it a habit to push the cap of the marker on the table top after replacing it. When I hear the click, I know the cap is on good and tight. More markers meet their doom from loose caps than from overuse.

4

Painting without Tools

Painting without tools is no-stress painting: twist, tie, dip, tape, and soak to your heart's content. The designs will be abstract. To duplicate the design in two or more items, paint all items at one time.

I know you've heard this advice before, but please read all instructions before you begin a project. If you see a term you don't understand, look in Chapter 9. Consult Appendix A for recommended products.

I give Basic Instructions first for each technique. Then under Variations, I give a few of the many ways basic instructions can be altered for a different look or design. Refer to Basic Instructions for information when doing a variation.

Tinting—Basic Instructions

NOTE: Before beginning this technique, please read about Cleanup Tips, Dish Drainers, Drying Paint, and Heat-Setting in the alphabetical listings in Chapter 9.

Remember, all fabrics are not created equal. (When I use the term "fabric," I mean fabric or garment.) If you like adventure, go for it. If you don't appreciate surprises, use a "tester" shirt or scrap yardage for pretesting.

Supplies

- Fabric or garment to be tinted
- Paint: see Tinting, Appendix A
- Plastic bucket or large pan
- Plastic gloves (optional)
- Dish drainer

Getting Ready

1. Remove all labels from clothing.
2. Determine how and where paint will be dried.
3. Place dish drainer in sink.
4. Put fabric in bucket. Add enough lukewarm water to cover item (use a measuring cup to measure the water as it is added to the bucket). Remove item; wring it out over bucket and set it aside.
5. Add paint to water in bucket (refer to the dilution rate given in Appendix A) as appropriate for amount of water added to bucket.
6. Stir paint and water in bucket thoroughly.

Painting

1. Shake out all folds and wrinkles from fabric.
2. Drop fabric into bucket, pushing down so it's completely submerged in paint/water mix.
3. Leave item in bucket 5–10 minutes; stir frequently.
4. Remove item from bucket, then place in dish drainer in the sink.
5. If you have a double sink, fill empty side with lukewarm water. If not, fill bucket with lukewarm water. NOTE: Paint/water mixture can be reused, but results with second use will not be as satisfactory, and colorfastness may be affected.
6. Drop fabric into lukewarm water. NOTE: Don't put item into sink or bucket when the water is running because the running water causes streaks.
7. Plunge fabric up and down in water.
8. Hold fabric over sink (or bucket); squeeze (don't twist or wring) excess water from item (Fig. 4-1). NOTE: Color is slightly darker

Fig. 4-1

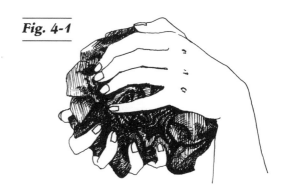

when wet. If fabric is slightly darker than you want, it is not necessary to do steps 6 and 7. If fabric is much darker than you want, rinse more than once.

9 Dry flat, on hanger or on line.

Cleanup

1 Pour paint/water mix down drain; pour 2 more quarts of water down drain.

2 Wipe off all surfaces with soapy water.

Laundering

1 Heat-set before laundering (required for all brands).

2 Do not launder item for at least 5 days.

3 Launder according to paint manufacturer's instructions.

TINTING—VARIATIONS

Uneven Tinting

Variation A. Do not wet item before putting into paint/water mix.

Variation B. Do twist and wring when removing from paint/water mix and after rinsing (Fig. 4-2).

Variation C. Do run water directly on portions of item when rinsing.

Variation D. Follow steps 1–8 under Painting, above. Cover counter with freezer paper, shiny side up. Place fabric on freezer paper. Sprinkle salt over item. Salt pulls the color out, producing a spotty look (Fig. 4-3). Use large grain (kosher or rock) or DekaSilk salt. You can salt randomly or in a design.

You can use open-back cookie cutters for design outline. Place cookie cutters on fabric. Shake a thin layer of salt inside shape (Fig. 4-4). (The outer edges of the salted design will not be sharp and defined.) Shake salt off fabric when paint is dry.

For clothing, insert shirt board inside shirt. Apply salt to back or front of shirt. When paint is dry, shake off salt. Turn shirt over, repeat on other side.

For yardage, salt right side; dry flat. When dry, shake item over sink to remove salt.

Variation E. Use combinations of Variations A through D.

Two-Color Tint

Apply first color. Wring and twist for uneven tinting. Tint with second color immediately. It is best if one color has a greater paint-to-water ratio than the other color. For example, if you use paint diluted with six parts water for one color, use paint diluted with less water for another color.

Shading

Variation A. Fill an empty "paint writer" bottle (that's the kind with the little nozzle top) with tint mixture. Use tint to enhance a design, fill in spaces, or as the only color added to fabric. This process can be done before or after other painting. If done immediately after painting, the wet paint will run and smear around the outside edges.

Variation B. Use undiluted paint in a "paint writer" bottle to make random lines across the

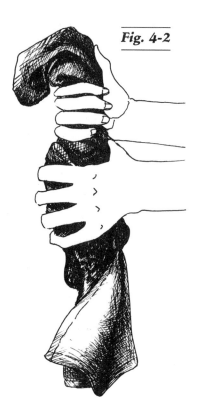

Fig. 4-2

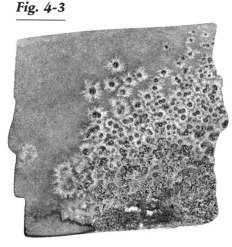

Fig. 4-3

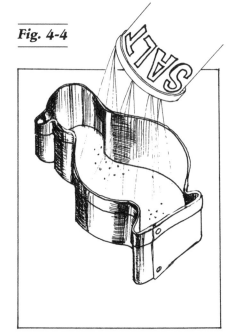

Fig. 4-4

front and back of the shirt (Fig. 4-5). Twist and wring the shirt to spread the paint (Fig. 4-6). This method is most effective if done immediately after tinting. If you want to use soft glitter paint, wait until the fabric has started to dry. Glitter paint can't be diluted.

Variation C. Mist or spray another tinted color on base color. Mist produces muted areas of second color. Spray will produce more defined areas of second color. Second color will run into first if it is still wet. Second color will be more pronounced if first color is dry.

Variation D. Tint fabric; do not dry. Wrap a nylon band around neck edge of shirt (Fig. 4-7). Tightly twist shirt. Tie nylon bands around shirt about every 3″ to hold twist (Fig. 4-7, middle). Loop nylon band at neckline over hook of hanger. Hang from shower head. (It will be drippy.) Pour 4 ounces of water on shirt, at neck edge and across shoulder line. Dry 8 hours. Remove bands; untwist. Dry flat or on hanger.

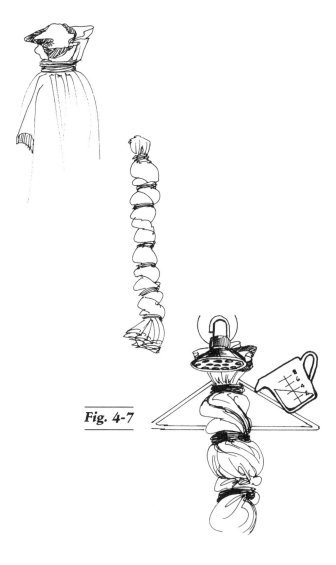

Fig. 4-7

Fig. 4-5

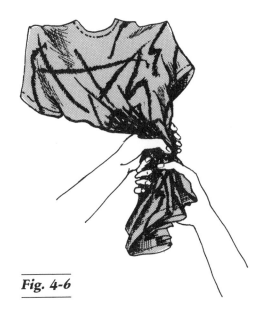
Fig. 4-6

Antique Patina

This technique is used by quiltmakers to create an "old" look on new fabric, usually with brown paint. Follow all steps listed for Tinting—Basic Instructions. Refer to Antique Patina, Appendix A, for paint brands and color. Paint/water amounts listed in Appendix A produce a very light tint. Use more paint if you want a deeper tone.

Mix paint/water mixture thoroughly. Fabric can be wet or dry before tinting. If the fabric is dry, tinted color will be more streaked. Color will be uneven if fabric is wrung out and twisted when removed from paint/water mix.

Rinsing is usually not necessary, unless the color is much darker than you want. Pretest.

Paint must be heat-set after dry.

Overtinting of Printed Fabric

The colors of printed fabric are slightly changed when tinted (Fig. 4-8). This is particularly handy when you need a specific shade of fabric for quilt

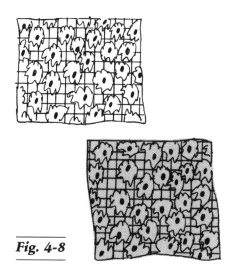

Fig. 4-8

making. Follow directions for Antique Patina, using the color of your choice. You can add more paint to the water for a deeper tone. Pretest.

Dyeing—Basic Instructions

NOTE: Before beginning this technique, please read about Cleanup Tips, Dish Drainers, Drying Paint, and Heat-Setting in the alphabetical listings in Chapter 9.

Fabric paint is great to use for dyeing fabrics—colors are permanent when dry, paint is nontoxic, and cleanup is fast. Colors are deeper because less water is added to the paint.

The procedure is the same as in Tinting—Basic Instructions. Read those instructions before beginning.

Supplies

The supply list is the same as for Tinting. For Paints to use, see Dyeing, Appendix A.

Getting Ready

See Tinting—Basic Instructions, above.

Painting

See Tinting— Basic Instructions, above. For medium tone, leave item in bucket 2–5 minutes. For deep tone, leave item in bucket 2–10 minutes. Pretest when you want an exact color.

Cleanup

See Tinting— Basic Instructions, above.

Laundering

See Tinting— Basic Instructions, above. Heat-setting is required for all brands.

DYEING—VARIATIONS

Any variation given for Tinting above, can be used. *Caution:* Darker colors of paint will cover original color of fabric, or previously applied paint. Paint is diluted with less water then in tinting; fabric will absorb color quickly.

Variation A. Tint item. Dry.

For *clothing*, fold sleeves to front, then fold shirt in half. Fold in half again. Roll from neck to hem (Fig. 4-9). Paint absorption is greater on top edges of the folds; the result is painted bands on the shirt. If you want more paint on shirt front, fold back together for first fold.

For *yardage*, fold yardage in half, selvage to selvage, then fold in half, cut edge to cut edge. Continue folding in this manner until yardage cannot be folded easily. Fold fabric wrong sides together when you want more paint on the right side of the fabric.

Add 1″ paint/water mixture (dye bath) to a flat-bottom container. Dip rolled edges of garment or yardage in dye bath (Fig. 4-10). The paint will be absorbed on these edges. Lay on flat, unfolded side in dish drainer. Leave until paint has stopped dripping. Dry flat or on hanger.

Variation B for Clothing. Tint garment. Dry. Fill spray bottle with dye bath mix. Use shirt board insert. Spray or mist dye bath randomly on shirt back. Dry flat or on hanger. Turn shirt to front and

Fig. 4-9

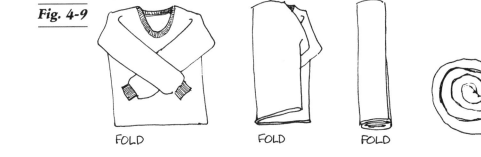

FOLD   FOLD   FOLD   ROLL

Fig. 4-10

spray. Dry flat or on hanger. You can stuff with plastic bags before spraying or misting.

Variation B for Fabric. Tint fabric. Dry. Fill spray bottle with dye bath mix. Cover foam board or cardboard with plastic wrap or freezer paper, shiny side up. Place fabric right side up on board. Spray or mist randomly. Dry flat on hanger or on line.

Variation C. Dye 2-yard piece of fabric; do not dry. Gather one end of yardage into a 2″ wad. Wrap a nylon band around wad to hold it in place (Fig. 4-11). Twist yardage so tightly that it forms a circle. Hold circle shape, and wrap a nylon band around second end of yardage (see figure). Loop both bands over the hook of a hanger. Wrap additional bands around yardage to keep fabric twisted. The more you twist and loop, the more interesting the finished results will be. Pour 4 ounces of water over bends and twists. (This can be a drippy mess, so do it outside or in the tub.) Hang hanger on line or shower hook. After 8 hours, remove bands. Finish drying on line or hanger.

Paint in a Bag— Basic Instructions

NOTE: Before beginning this technique, please read about Cleanup Tips, Dish Drainers, Drying Paint, and Heat-Setting in the alphabetical listings in Chapter 9.

I was going to call this method "No Mess/No Stress." All you do is chuck all the stuff into a plastic bag and shake. I prefer the zippable, freezer bags because they're durable and can be reused.

If you are doing more than 1 yard of fabric or you are doing large-size sweats, use a 2-gallon zippable plastic bag or a small garbage bag. And again, don't hesitate to combine this method with other No-Tool Painting methods. Paint coverage will be random, unlike the complete coverage obtained with dyeing.

Basic instructions for 1 yard of fabric are given first, followed by instructions for T-shirts and sweats.

Supplies

- ♦ Paint: see Paint in a Bag, Appendix A. Use tinting paints for lighter shades; dyeing paints for darker shades. For 1 yard of fabric, you need 4 ounces paint/water for moderate coverage.
- ♦ 1 yard fabric
- ♦ Plastic bag large enough to hold fabric and paint easily
- ♦ Plastic gloves (optional)
- ♦ Dish drainer

Getting Ready

1 Prepare paint/water mixture.
2 Place drainer in sink.

Painting

1 Pour half of paint mix in bag.
2 Drop fabric in bag.
3 Pour second half of paint mix in bag.

Fig. 4-11

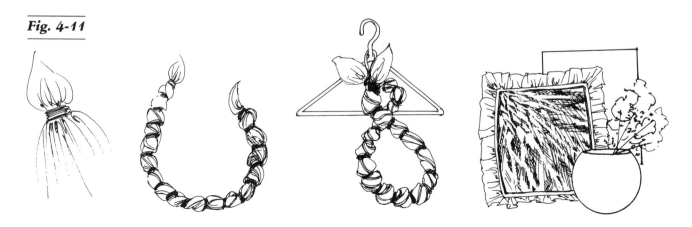

4 "Zip" bag, or tie it closed. Check for leaks. Shake and squash bag to disperse paint mix. Not all of the fabric will be painted.

5 Hold bag over drain. Cut hole in corner of bag. Excess paint will run down drain. (Don't cut a hole if you want to reuse bag).

6 Open bag and dump fabric into dish drainer.

7 Arrange fabric in drainer so painted areas are not touching unpainted areas. Fabric will have irregular blotches of paint (Fig. 4-12). Leave until dripping has stopped.

8 Dry flat on hanger or line.

Fig. 4-12

Cleanup

1 Immediately wipe off all surfaces with hot, soapy water. Pour 2 quarts water down drain.

2 If you want to reuse the plastic bag—and if you didn't cut a hole in the corner—wash it in hot soapy water; rinse; dry.

Laundering

1 Heat-set when required (recommended for all paints).

2 Do not wash for 1 week

PAINT IN A BAG—T-SHIRT, SWEATSHIRT, SWEATPANTS (adult size medium)

Follow basic instructions for fabric. For the T-shirt, you need 4 ounces total paint and water. For the sweatshirt, you need 6 ounces total, and for the sweatpants, 6 ounces total.

PAINT IN A BAG—LARGER PIECES OF YARDAGE

Use a plastic bag large enough to hold item and paint. A clear bag is best. A sweater storage bag, with a zipper, works very well. Shake bag gently, not vigorously, if it's not leak-proof; otherwise you'll end up with a newly decorated kitchen. Add one-third of your paint/water to bag before putting item in bag. Pour second third on item in bag, shake and squash. Then add last third and shake and squash. It isn't necessary that those thirds are exact measures. That last portion is to paint uncovered areas. Dry flat, on hanger or line. Heat-set. Do not launder for 1 week.

PAINT IN A BAG—VARIATIONS

Variation A. Spray clear water on portions of fabric before placing in bag. Paint will run into dampened areas, creating a muted color around outer edges of paint.

Variation B. Thoroughly dampen fabric before placing in bag. Wring excess water from fabric. Paint saturation will be more even. Color will be muted.

Variation C. Tint or dye before or after placing fabric in bag. (Tinted or dyed fabric can be wet or dry.)

Variation D. Use as background for other methods. Read Tinting—Variations, Overtinting of Printed Fabric (page 17) before beginning.

Ties Used with Liquid Resist—Basic Instructions

NOTE: Before beginning this technique, please read about Cleanup Tips, Heat-Setting, Resist, Shirt Boards, and Tying the Ties in the alphabetical listings in Chapter 9.

Don't think tie-painting is limited to brightly colored, "spiky" circles. That's just one of the many designs that can result when you tie fabric (clothing or yardage) in a bundle. This method, using liquid resist, is an entirely new approach.

This technique is done in two stages. First, resist is applied to the fabric, which must be dried overnight. Second, after the resist has dried, the fabric is tinted or dyed.

Supplies (for resist)

NOTE: Do not mix tint or dye solution until after resist has dried.

♦ Sweatshirt
♦ 2–4 ounces washable glue (see Ties Used with Liquid Resist, Appendix A)
♦ Plastic bag (type used for newspapers is great), large enough to hold tied bundle and glue resist. Don't add glue to bag until after bundle is tied.
♦ Four 36″ lengths of covered floral wire or other tie materials if you prefer
♦ Shirt board insert

Getting Ready

Remove all labels from clothing

Tying Tie Bundle

1 Crease line down center front of shirt, from neck to hem.
2 Crease line across center front of shirt from underarm seam to underarm seam.
3 Grab shirt at the point where the two crease lines cross, with thumb and first finger of right hand (Fig. 4-13).
4 Make a circle with thumb and first finger of your left hand. Slide this circle down shirt front from point held by right hand. Stop about 1″ below neck ribbing.
5 Hang onto the gathered bundle with your left hand. You can put some fabric from the bottom half of shirt front into the bundle if you want. The tip will move slightly down.
6 Tightly wrap a piece of the covered wire twice around the base of the bundle, leaving a 3″ tail of wire (see figure).
7 Hold the tail toward the point of the bundle, and begin wrapping the length of wire toward the point. (Wrapping over the tail will lock it in place). Pull the wire as tight as you can. It's usually easier to use the first length to wrap the bundle from base to tip. That stabilizes the bundle. Then wrap remaining ties over first tie.

Fig. 4-13

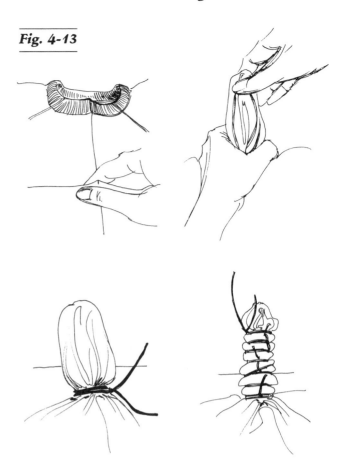

8 Before adding more wrap, check the placement of the tie. The base should be spaced evenly between the underarm seams. The point should be slightly above, or at, the junction of the center front and underarm seam. This is the time to make changes.
9 Wrap should not be continuous; there should be at least ¼″ spacing. You want open areas so the resist can penetrate the fabric.
10 Add new lengths of wire as needed. Lock the end and beginning of each piece of wire as described in step 7. Tuck end of last piece under wrapped wire, to hold it in place.

Applying resist

1 Check the size of your bag to see if it's large enough for tie.
2 Add 2 ounces of glue to bag.
3 Put tied bundle into bag (Fig. 4-14). Squish the glue over the bundle. You want glue only on the bundle. If glue is getting on the shirt, put a nylon band around the top of the bag to hold it closed. A thin, even coat of glue should cover all sides of the bundle. Add more glue to the bag, if needed.

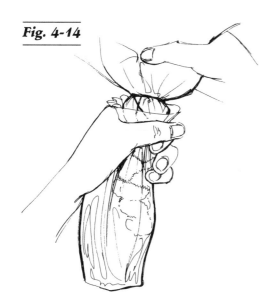

Fig. 4-14

Fig. 4-15

4 Hold the top of the bag so the opening is just large enough to pull the bundle out. Pull the bundle out through the opening. This removes excess glue and pushes glue into fabric.

5 Slide shirt board inside shirt, leaving shirt on flat surface. Dry for about 10 minutes. Glue will lose its shine, but is not dry.

6 Remove ties. Pull bundle open.

7 Leave shirt board insert in place until glue is completely dry. I usually let it sit overnight.

Cleanup

1 Immediately wipe up any glue spills with a soapy cloth or sponge.

2 Dispose of glue bag.

Tinting or Dyeing

Do not tint or dye fabric until glue is completely dry. Drying can take 12 hours.

Follow Tinting—Basic Instructions or Dyeing—Basic Instructions. If shirt is left in paint/water mix more than 5 minutes, the glue resist will soften and tint will seep into resist areas (which is fine, if that's what you want). Dry flat or on hanger.

Laundering

1 Heat-set before laundering.

2 Do not launder for at least 5 days. Launder shirt right side out, in warm water. Dry at regular heat cycle. Resist will be removed in first or second laundering.

TIES USED WITH LIQUID RESIST— VARIATIONS

Variation A: T-shirt. The technique is the same, but you will need less glue resist (Fig. 4-15).

Variation B: Sweatpants. Place tie in knee area, along the side of the pants. A second tie can be placed closer to the bottom cuff of the pants.

Variation C. Do not dry shirt after tinting or dyeing. Stuff shirt (T or sweat) with plastic bags and hang on hanger. Pour 2 to 4 ounces darker tint color, or dye bath on shirt along neck, shoulder line, and down sleeves. The second color can be sprayed or misted, rather than poured.

Variation D. Tint or dye shirt (T or sweat). Allow tint or dye to dry. Tie front or back of shirt, then coat tied bundle with resist. After resist has dried, overtint or dye with second color.

Variation E. After resist has dried, repeat tie and resist steps on shirt back. Dry resist, tint or dye.

Variation F. Hold peak of bundle and twist fabric (Fig. 4-16). Wrap tie around twisted base, to hold twist in place. Wrap tie to peak, tightening the twist. Use enough tie material to hold the twisted bundle.

Variation G. Instead of spending time tyeing ties, use plastic curtain rings (or any other kind of plastic ring). Rings come in sizes from tiny to big. Just pull the fabric through the ring (Fig. 4-17). Use three or four sizes of rings, from large to very small. The big ones go on first; following rings decrease in size.

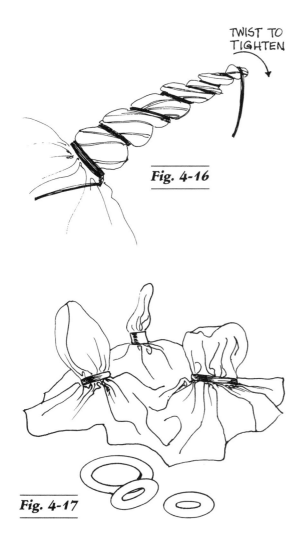

TWIST TO TIGHTEN

Fig. 4-16

Fig. 4-17

Variation H. Silk can be tie-painted quickly with beautiful results. Use small rings (even the teeny ones used for knitting). Dip the bundles into paint suitable for silk and fine wovens. Dry flat. Remove ties. You can add a second color of paint to unpainted areas if you are using white silk. Apply paint with a brush to areas surrounding tied designs, or place another series ot ties on the fabric and dip. Dry flat. Heat-set.

You can use resist (washable glue or Presist) instead of paint for the first dipped ties. Allow resist to dry before removing ties and applying paint either with a brush or by dipping ties.

Variation I. You can have more than one resist bundle. Keep bundles tied until all resist is applied. It may be necessary to apply resist with a brush or cloth if bundles are close together. It just wouldn't be possible to dip each bundle into the glue bag.

Variation J. Create beautiful quilt blocks with ties and resist. Blocks can be all the same color, or multiple colors. Combine plain or patterned fabric blocks with the tinted or dyed blocks. Muslin is a good fabric choice. Tear or cut blocks to size. Ties

can be centered or offset in the block. Use covered wire, narrow rubber bands, or pearl cotton for ties. Dry flat.

Variation K. You can make whole quilt tops quickly with ties and resist. Combine small and large bundles over quilt top. Use rings or ties to hold the bundles. Apply resist with a brush or cloth, if necessary. Leave all ties in until resist is dry. The top and back can be of different colors or prints. Overtint or dye in the same or different colors. Hand- or machine-quilt to enhance the irregular designs created with the ties.

Solid Resist with Tint or Dye—Basic Instructions

NOTE: Before beginning this technique, please read about Cooking Parchment Paper, Freezer Paper, Heat-Setting, Pretesting, Resist, and Stencils in the alphabetical listings in Chapter 9.

Get out the crayon box and plan to have fun. If you can't remember the golden rule of coloring, it's simple: All strokes go in the same direction.

NOTE: This technique is done in two stages. First, crayon is applied to fabric and pressed. Second, fabric is tinted or dyed, if desired.

Supplies
- T-shirt
- Plastic quilting stencil or stencil that has narrow channels outlining design
- Repositionable glue (spray or liquid) or glue stick
- Freezer paper
- Crayons
- Cooking parchment paper
- Iron and ironing board
- Supplies listed in Tinting or Dyeing, Basic Instructions, this chapter

Getting Ready: Crayon Resist
1 Press freezer paper to wrong side of shirt, under area where stencil will be placed (Fig. 4-18, step 1). Turn shirt right side out, after paper has cooled.
2 Apply enough repositionable glue to the back of the stencil to hold stencil in place (Fig. 4-18, step 2).
3 Place shirt on a firm surface. Smooth wrinkles; shirt must be flat (Fig. 4-18, step 3). Pin shirt to cardboard or foam board.
4 Position stencil on shirt. Insert end of crayon into cut lines of stencil (Fig. 4-18, step 4). (If channel is narrow, you may have to sharpen your crayon before you start.) Crayon stencil

1. STABILIZE

2. GLUE

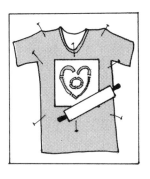

3. ADHERE

4. APPLY CRAYON

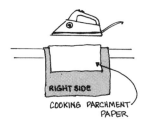

5. PICK UP EXCESS

6. PRESS

Fig. 4-18

Tinting or Dyeing

Follow Basic Instructions for Tinting or Dyeing. Cover crayoned areas with parchment paper when heat-setting.

Laundering

Do not dry items with crayon resist in a hot dryer.

SOLID RESIST WITH TINT OR DYE— VARIATIONS

Variation A. Use more than one color of crayon for the stencil. For example, if the stencil is composed of hearts and flowers, use different colors for each flower and for the hearts.

Variation B. Crayon resist methods can be used with stencils that have large cut-out areas. Bond freezer paper to the wrong side of the fabric. Apply repositionable glue (spray or liquid) to back of stencil. Attach stencil securely to the fabric. You can use different color of crayons, just as if you were coloring a picture. Don't leave any space between colors. Just remember, the wax does spread when melted. Don't use a heavy layer around the outer edges, or the wax will creep under the stencil. Pretest.

Variation C. Cut a stencil from freezer paper (Fig. 4-19; see Stencils in Chapter 9). Bond a stabilizing layer (freezer paper or Totally Stable) to the wrong side of the fabric. Bond the freezer paper stencil to the right side of the fabric. Color inside the openings of the stencil. See Variation B for caution about crayon spreading when melted. Cover with cooking parchment paper; press. Remove freezer paper after crayon has cooled.

Variation D. Crayon shavings can be used as a resist on all fabrics. It's a very effective technique

design. Stroke in one direction only. The layer of crayon should be even and reasonably heavy.

5 Remove stencil. Check design to make sure all lines are evenly colored. Recolor where necessary. Remove any crayon particles from shirt (Fig. 4-18, step 5).

6 Place shirt on the ironing board. Cover crayoned design with cooking parchment paper (Fig. 4-18, step 6). (Since you memorized the Cooking Parchment Paper Rule, I really didn't have to say that.) Press with a hot iron. Don't remove freezer paper until shirt has cooled.

Fig. 4-19

on silk (Fig. 4-20). Bond freezer paper to the wrong side of the fabric. Apply crayon shavings, and cover with cooking parchment paper. Press. The shaving will spread quite a bit when pressed.

Brush or roll paint over the right side of the silk after crayon has cooled. I leave the freezer paper in place and cover the fabric with cooking parchment to heat-set. (I hear all those shrieks of horror from silk painters!)

Variation E. "Rubbings" are described under Resist in Chapter 9. Children love making rubbings (and so do I!). Use Lego pieces, coins, bottle tops—anything that will make an impression when the crayon is rubbed on the covering fabric. First, arrange items on the shiny side of freezer paper (Fig. 4-21). Next, cover the items with fabric and rub the fabric with crayon (you may need to help a child with this step). Now remove the fabric from the collage. Place cooking parchment paper under and over the fabric, and press. (Of course, an adult must do the pressing.) Remember, do not press over the items used to make the rubbing—only over the crayoned fabric which has been covered with parchment paper.

Variation F. Another children's favorite is having their colored pictures transferred to fabric.

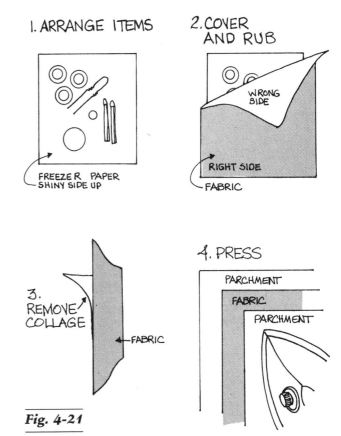

Fig. 4-21

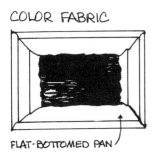
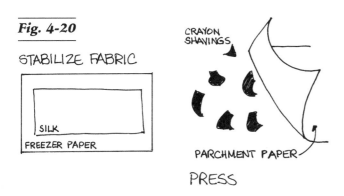

Fig. 4-20

STABILIZE FABRIC

SILK
FREEZER PAPER

CRAYON SHAVINGS

PARCHMENT PAPER

PRESS

COLOR FABRIC

FLAT-BOTTOMED PAN

Have the child color a picture with crayons (crayon strokes must be heavy). Have the adult turn the picture face down on the fabric and press (of course, the picture will be reversed). Remove paper with colored picture from fabric. Cover the fabric with cooking parchment and press again. If you used a lightweight fabric, place a layer of cooking parchment under the fabric before you do any pressing. These rubbings on aprons, T-shirts, quilt blocks, pillows, or place mats make great gifts for grandparents.

Marbling—Basic Instructions

NOTE #1: Before beginning this technique, please read about Drying Paint, Heat-Setting, and Marbling in the alphabetical listings in Chapter 9.

NOTE #2: The time required for this technique is longer than for others. Fabric must be rinsed in mordant solution, dried, and pressed before marbling.

Read Marbling in Chapter 9 before beginning projects. Supplies, terms, and techniques are explained in greater detail there. See Appendix A for suggested paints.

Marbling offers one advantage over any other painting technique: You know exactly what the design will look like before it is placed on the fabric.

If you don't like what you see on the size (the medium on which the paint floats), rearrange it. If the paint gets so mixed up that producing a suitable design is impossible, dump everything out and start over. The laundry starch or unflavored gelatin (Variation A) used to make the size are relatively inexpensive.

Supplies

♦ 8" square lightweight woven fabric (cotton, poly/cotton, silk)
♦ Alum (pickling type found in spice department of grocery store, powder or granule) and water
♦ 8" or 10" square disposable pie or cake pan cookie sheet (used for rinsing platform)
♦ Liquid laundry starch (used as size)
♦ Newspapers
♦ Paint in two or three colors (see Appendix A)
♦ Assorted items for pattern making, such as wide-tooth combs, knitting needles, eye dropper, wooden skewers (see step 3 of Painting, below)
♦ Small plastic plate

Getting Ready

1 Dissolve 2 tablespoons alum in 1 quart warm water. Stir well. Soak fabric in alum solution until thoroughly saturated. Squeeze out excess solution. Wait till dry; then press. Fabric should not be wrinkled.
2 Shake starch bottle. Starch must be thoroughly blended.
3 Add starch to 8" or 10" square pan. Depth should be at least 1".
4 Cut newspaper into strips 2" wide and 6" long (you will use these in steps 1 and 7 under Painting).
5 If necessary, thin paint with water to achieve proper consistency.
6 To test consistency of paint, pour a small amount of starch into a small paper or plastic plate. Drop one or two drops of paint on starch. Drops should be about ¼" across. Do not touch surface of starch with tool used to drop paint. Paint should float on surface of starch and spread ½" to 2" across. Increase or reduce water ratio to paint, if necessary.
7 Cover work surface with sheets of newspaper.

8 Place rinsing platform next to pan of starch on counter.

Painting

1 Skim surface of starch with newspaper strips (Fig. 4-22). Slightly curve strips to fit inside round pans. The lower edge of the strips should be perpendicular to the top surface of

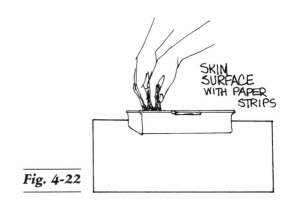

Fig. 4-22

the starch. Discard strips after skimming surface of size.
2 Drop paint on starch in pan, using skewers, knitting needles, or eye dropper. For this project, drop colors randomly (Fig. 4-23).
3 Use one or two tools (wide-tooth comb, skewers, etc.) to drag paint across starch (Fig. 4-24). Don't break the surface of the starch with tool.

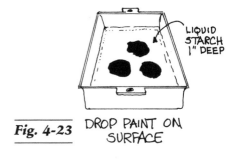

Fig. 4-23 DROP PAINT ON SURFACE

Fig. 4-24 DRAW PATTERNS

4 When pattern is to your liking, gently drop fabric on paint, Fabric should lie flat on surface of starch (Fig. 4-25). Lumps and bumps will not receive paint and will leave white spots.

Fig. 4-25 FLOAT FABRIC

5 When you can see paint on wrong side of fabric (about 5 seconds), pick up fabric and place it paint side up on rinsing platform. Fabric should be smooth and flat.

6 Place rinsing platform in sink, resting on one end. Pour lukewarm water over fabric, removing excess paint and starch. The marbling pattern will not be disturbed (Fig. 4-26). You're only removing excess paint. Leave on rinsing platform until dripping has stopped. Dry flat.

7 Remaining starch can be used for a second marbling. Skim all paint from surface with newspaper strips. Add more starch to pan, if necessary.

Cleanup

1 Small amounts of starch can be poured down kitchen sink.

2 Clean all tools and equipment.

Laundering

1 Heat-set (don't rinse out remaining starch until after heat-setting).

2 Rinse in warm water.

3 Do not launder for 1 week.

4 Launder according to paint manufacturer's instructions.

Application

1 Cut marbled fabric in circle.

2 Fuse or stitch to T-shirt or sweatshirt (see Chapter 7).

MARBLING—VARIATIONS

Variation A. Another inexpensive size is made with unflavored gelatin. Dissolve 2 ounces unflavored food gelatin in hot water. Add 1 quart lukewarm water, and stir well. The amount of size can be increased for a larger pan.

Gelatin size tends to thicken as it sits. Because the paint does not have to be as thin as for starch, it can be manipulated into shapes, such as flowers, trees, stars, or hearts.

Variation B. Use square disposable pans when marbling quilt blocks. Disposable planter liners are excellent pans to use for long, narrow pieces of fabric (belts, scarves, ties, etc.)

Variation C. Tumble Dye can be misted on size right from the bottle. It can also be dropped on size. An interesting and easy method is to mist Tumble Dye onto the size, then add drops. The design is instant.

For a departure from traditional marbling, mist or spray with other fluid dye or paint brands, or those that can be highly diluted. The results are

Fig. 4-26

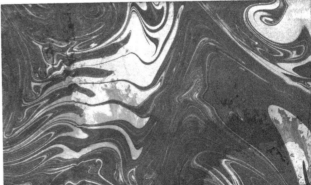

truly interesting (Fig. 4-27). The thin overall layer of paint produces designs that are less definite than those resulting from drops (stones) of paint.

Variation D. Freezer paper stencils (negative or positive) can be bonded to fabric before marbling. Be sure all edges are well bonded. Don't remove stencil until marbling is dry to touch.

Variation E. Plain old shelf paper can be turned into beautiful marbled gift wrap. Use the biggest pan you can find for this.

Variation F. After you've tried different methods with woven fabrics, use T-shirt-weight cotton or poly/cotton knits.

Remember, marbling is like any other technique. Experiment. Try out every idea you think up. If nothing else, you'll know what doesn't work. And that's not all that bad.

Fig. 4-27

5

Painting with Tools

This chapter deals with techniques that use a tool—something you hold in your hand—to apply the paint. Tools run the span from spray bottles to sponges to brushes to rollers to spreaders to anything that can be used to apply paint to fabric.

The format for instructions is the same as in Chapter 4: basic instructions are given first, followed by instructions for variations.

Read all instructions for a project before beginning. Chapter 9 explains in an alphabetical listing the terms used in these instructions. Also, the word "fabric" is used to mean yardage or a garment.

Mist Painting with Rings— Basic Instructions

NOTE: Before beginning this technique, please read about Cleanup Tips, Heat-Setting, Shirt Boards, and Spray/Mist Bottles in the alphabetical listings in Chapter 9.

I love this technique. It's so fast and easy, and the results are terrific. Use it for a basic tie-painted look on a sweatshirt, or jazz it up for a "Night at the Ball" top.

Supplies

♦ Pastel-colored sweatshirt, adult size small
♦ 20 plastic rings, sizes ½" to 2" (you can substitute wooden or metal rings)
♦ Hanger with skirt loops
♦ 24" piece of wire (20–30 gauge)
♦ Spray bottle with adjustable nozzle, pump-type mist bottle or aerosol container (see Spray/Mist Bottles, Appendix C)
♦ 4 ounces paint/water (see Misting and Spraying in Appendix A). NOTE: Carnival Arts Spray Dye-Namite can be substituted for mixed paint (see Variation G).

Getting Ready

1 Prepare area where misting will be done.
2 Remove clothing labels.
3 Pull shirt fabric through rings (Fig. 5-1). You may want to place the rings to make a specific design. For example, you could align them from left shoulder to right hem, down the center front, or in horizontal lines. Or place the rings in a random pattern.
4 Pull fabric or push rings so rings are tightly positioned. Rings secure the bundle and also act as a paint blocker. Stacked rings hold the bundle even more securely. Paint will not seep under tightly placed rings.
5 Loop a piece of wire (garden twist tie or covered wire) through one of the rings. Bring each end of the wire around the skirt loops on a hanger so that the shirt dangles from the bottom of the hanger (Fig. 5-2).

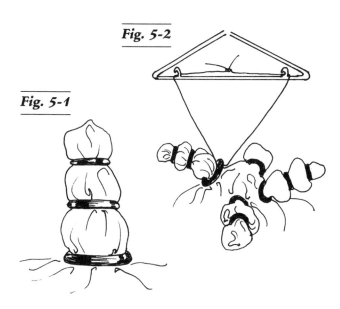

Fig. 5-2

Fig. 5-1

6 Mix paint, and fill bottle (adjust nozzle to mist).

7 Test-mist on paper towel.

Painting

1. Evenly mist all exposed areas of the shirt. Rotate the hanger without touching wet paint. Do not separate gathers or pleats formed by the rings.

2 Leave on hanger until paint does not come off on your hands (30 to 60 minutes). Remove wire loop.

3 Pull rings off. Hang shirt on hanger until paint is completely dry (Fig. 5-3).

Fig. 5-3

Cleanup

1 Clean up work area with a damp sponge immediately after misting.

2 To clean spray bottle, fill with soapy water and shake. Empty and fill with clear water. Spray water through nozzle until all paint residue is gone. If necessary, clean nozzle with the point of a pin. NOTE: Excess paint can be stored in the spray container. Be sure to label it and store in an out-of-the-way spot.

3 Put rings in a jar of soapy water as soon as they are removed from shirt. Cover jar and shake. Soak about 10 minutes; then wipe off paint. Dry metal or wooden rings with paper towels.

Laundering

1 Heat-set if required; I recommend heat-setting in all cases.

2 Do not launder for 1 week.

3 Launder according to paint manufacturer's instructions.

MIST PAINTING WITH RINGS— VARIATIONS

Variation A. There are all kinds of ways this technique can be used with T-shirts (Fig. 5-4). Use white or colored T-shirts. If your colored shirt has

Fig. 5-4

a neck rib and sleeve cuff in a contrasting color, use that color paint for misting. Use a paint/water mix totaling 2 to 3 ounces. Stack rings whenever you want larger, non-painted sections. Teeny rings (the kind used as knitting markers) create small color bursts or symmetrical designs. Medium-sized rings can be pulled from sleeve cuff to neckline. They can also be used if the shirt is twisted before the rings are pulled over shirt body. If you use a larger ring, pull it from sleeve cuff to center front of the shirt. Pull one or several large rings from bottom hem to underarm seam.

Rings can be pulled onto a single layer (front or back) or double layer (back and front together).

Use any of these methods to apply rings in combinations. You can use a different color paint with each method. Each color will be a different shape on the fabric, ranging from small to large sizes.

Variation B. Mist sweat-pants to coordinate with your sweatshirt. The pull-and-tug method of applying rings is the same for pants. Pull the rings up the leg, from the bottom cuff, or pull fabric from the side of leg. Space stacked groups of rings for bands of paint and background color. Use white or colored pants.

Variation C. Complete all steps under Getting Ready and Painting in the Basic Instructions. Repeat painting steps, placing rings in new areas. Mist, using a second paint color.

Variation D. Outline designs in dimensional paint, or brush a soft glitter paint across design areas (Fig. 5-5). You can brush transparent paint across designs for a wash effect.

Variation E. Misting with rings is especially effective on printed or pastel yardage. When yardage will be used to make clothing, select a basic pattern without darts and gathers. Lay pattern pieces on right side of yardage, leaving at least 1″ space between each pattern piece. Mark cutting line with permanent marker. Cut out each piece, ½″ beyond the marked line (Fig. 5-6, Steps 1–3). Stay-stitch curved edges.

Put rings on cut pieces (Fig. 5-6, Step 4). For a symmetrical design, lay fronts, side by side, right side up. Duplicate ring placement on both front pieces. Use notches on garment pieces as references for placement of rings. If the back has a center seam, repeat this method for a symmetrical design on the back pieces. Your type of fabric will dictate the size of rings. Remove rings when paint is dry to the touch. Finish drying flat. Press.

Cut pieces along marked cutting line. Stitch garment. You can embellish the garment with paint, beads, or sequins (Fig. 5-6, Steps 5–7).

Variation F. This is an effective technique to use with silk (clothing or yardage). Because most paints migrate quickly through silk (or any fine wo-

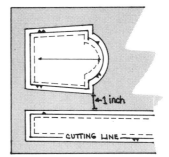

1. LAY OUT PATTERN

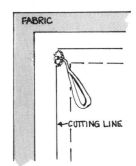

2. MARK CUTTING LINE

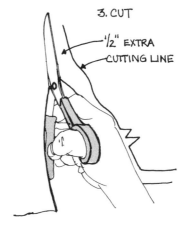

3. CUT

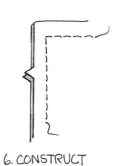

4. RING AND PAINT

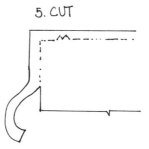

5. CUT

6. CONSTRUCT

7. EMBELLISH

Fig. 5-6

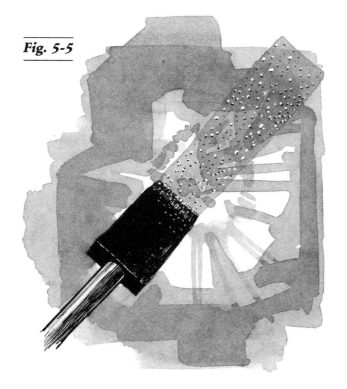

Fig. 5-5

ven fabric), a very light mist will cover a large area. You can apply Resist before misting. Mist colored fabrics for a two-tone effect.

Variation G. Carnival Spray Paints in the aerosol container are all ready to go. Spray in a well-ventilated area. You can remove the rings almost immediately. Follow directions on can for heat-setting.

Variation H. Use large rings widely spaced and a light color Carnival Dye-Namite for the first spraying (Fig. 5-7). Do not remove rings when paint is dry. Form bundles in the sides and put small rings on the points of the large bundles. Spray with a second color. You can use a third color, too, if you want.

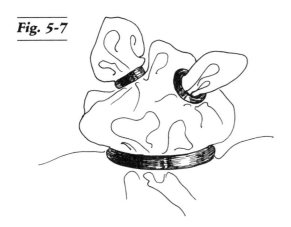

Fig. 5-7

Variation I. You can mist your fabric with rings for quilt making, by the block, or the whole top at once. If you mist individual blocks, you can place the rings in the same way on each block, or randomly. Pin blocks right side up to paint-proof board for misting. Remove from board when paint is dry to the touch. Then remove rings, and dry flat. Press before stitching.

For a whole quilt top, you can mist in a single, center design, or a combination of designs. Use one hoop of an embroidery hoop in the size needed as the first ring of a single design. Grab the center of the top, and pull it through ring. You can pull the fabric so the hoop is evenly placed along the outer edges of the yardage. For additional rings, use embroidery hoops or any rings that are the correct size. Leave rings in place until paint is dry to the touch. Remove rings, then finish drying on the line. Press before stitching.

Use varying sizes of rings in a random or evenly spaced placement for combination designs. Leave rings in place until paint is dry to the touch. Press before stitching.

Spray Painting with Two Colors—Basic Instructions

NOTE: Before beginning this technique please read about Cleanup Tips, Drying Paint, Heat-Setting, and Spray/Mist Bottles in the alphabetical listings in Chapter 9.

Supplies

♦ White T-shirt, adult size large
♦ Two colors of paint, 2 ounces paint/water each (see Misting and Spraying in Appendix A). You can substitute Carnival Arts Dye-Namite, Webbing, or Glitter spray paints.
♦ Two spray bottles with adjustable nozzle (see Spray/Mist Bottles in Appendix C). You can use one bottle, but using two is easier and faster.
♦ Hanger
♦ Plastic bags (the kind used by grocery or retail stores); don't substitute newspapers or paper bags

Getting Ready

1 Determine where spraying will be done; then prepare area
2 Mix paint with water, and put mixture in spray bottles. (If you are using only one bottle, mix lighter color first. Have a container handy to store excess of first color when you are ready to mix second color).
3 Adjust bottle with lighter-color paint to semi-mist position. Test-spray on paper towel.
4 Adjust bottle with darker color paint to heavy stream position. Test-spray on paper towel.
5 Put shirt on hanger. Stuff bags into shirt; you want a lumpy, bumpy shirt. Use one or two straight pins in hem to hold bags in shirt.

Painting

1 Hold the bottle of lighter color paint 6″ to 8″ from the shirt. Spray, leaving spaces between sprayed areas (Fig. 5-8). The lumps of the bags create an uneven pattern. If you are using one bottle for both colors, immediately empty first color into another container. Fill spray bottle with second color. Adjust spray to stream; test spray on paper towel.
2 Hold bottle of darker color 3″ to 4″ from shirt. Spray a heavy line of paint around neck ribbing (don't spray ribbing) and across shoulder line on front and back of shirt. Paint should be heavy enough to run down shirt. Spraying around hems of sleeves is optional.
3 If paint does not run down shirt, spray water over areas of dark paint.
4 Leave shirt on hanger and bags in place until paint does not rub off on your hand.
5 Remove bags. Complete drying on hanger or line.

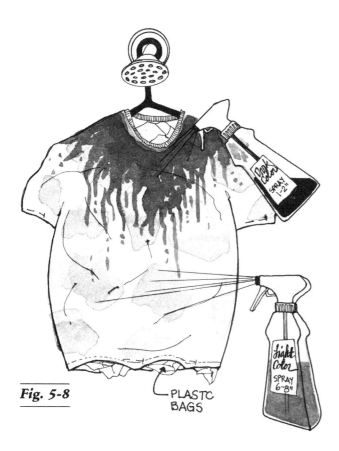

Fig. 5-8

PLASTC BAGS

Cleanup

1 Clean up work area immediately after spraying.
2 Rinse bottles with clear water. Fill with soapy water. Shake. Spray soapy water through nozzle. Rinse. Use point of pin to clean out nozzle, if necessary.

Laundering

1 Heat-set if required; I recommend it in all cases.
2 Do not launder for 1 week.
3 Launder according to paint manufacturer's instructions.

SPRAY PAINTING WITH TWO COLORS—VARIATIONS

Variation A. For sweatshirt, follow basic instructions, increasing paint/water mix to 3 ounces of each color.

Variation B. You can spray sweatpants to coordinate with your sweatshirt. Increase paint/water mix to 4 ounces of each color. Spray heavily with second color around waistband to create lines down legs.

Variation C. Use two colors, one at a time, for semi-mist spray. Use light color first; follow with medium shade. Colors can overlap. Use third color (dark) for stream spray around neck and shoulder.

Variation D. Mist with diluted Delta Starlight Fabric Dye, an opaque paint. Use a stream spray of transparent or light-colored paint around misted areas.

Variation E. Create a pattern with stream spray. Your pattern can be diagonal, horizontal, or vertical lines across misted areas. Leave at least 2″ space between lines. Use tape to mark lines for accurate placement of spray.

Variation F. Mist, with rings, using a medium paint color on white shirt. Let dry. (See Mist Painting with Rings—Basic Instructions.) Stuff bags into shirt, mist unpainted areas with a light color. Stream-spray, using a dark or metallic color for third color.

Using Fabric Stamps— Basic Instructions

NOTE: Before beginning this technique, please read about Antifusant, Fabric Markers, Freezer Paper, Pretesting, Shirt Boards, Stamps, and Stamp Pads in the alphabetical listings in Chapter 9.

For all stamping projects, I recommend bonding a layer of freezer paper or Totally Stable to the wrong side of the fabric.

Supplies

♦ T-shirt, adult size (see Variation I for fabric that is 60 percent or more synthetic)
♦ Stamp(s) of your choice
♦ Paint, approximately 1 ounce (see Fabric Stamps—Ink for Pad, in Appendix A)
♦ Freezer paper or Totally Stable
♦ Stamp pad (purchased or homemade)
♦ Marking chalk or removable marker

Getting Ready

1 Remove clothing labels if back neck will be stamped.
2 Mark shirt for placement of stamp(s). You could print a large stamp at center neck; small stamps around hems of sleeves.
3 Press freezer paper or Totally Stable inside shirt as a "shirt board."
4 Prepare a stamp pad (see Chapter 9).
5 Do a test-stamp on your fabric, on a hard surface.

Stamping

1 Stamp on markings. NOTE: If some stamp prints are incomplete or have light-colored areas, retrace lines of design with a fine-tipped marker.

2 Dry shirt flat. Remove shirt board insert when paint is dry.

Cleanup

1 Stamp on a wet sponge to remove excess paint from stamp. Clean remaining paint from stamp with a soft toothbrush. Store stamp on its back.

2 If pad is one you inked, the ink can be left on pad. Store in "zipper"-type plastic bag. Expell air before closing. Use within 3 days; rinse paint from it at that time. Purchased pads should be in tightly closed box. They are not rinsed out—use until all ink is gone.

Laundering

1 Heat-set after 24 hours.
2 Do not launder for 1 week.
3 Launder according to manufacturer's instructions.

USING FABRIC STAMPS— VARIATIONS

Variation A. The pockets of T-shirts are great places for stamp designs. Slide a piece of plastic wrap inside the pocket before stamping (Fig. 5-9). You can also stamp around the hem of sleeve cuffs, or around the bottom hem.

Variation B. If you have selected a small stamp a "shower" of stamps is very attractive on T-shirts (Fig. 5-10). Stamp repeatedly from the middle of one sleeve across the shoulder and into the center front. Stamp another series of designs beginning about 6″ above the bottom hem and about 4″ from the side seam. Stamp to the hem and about 6″ around to the back of the shirt. Have a slight curve to the outer edges of the series.

Variation C. Color stamped designs with permanent fabric marking pens. You may need to ap-

ply an antifusant before stamping. Stabilize fabric before using markers.

Variation D. Use Marvy Uchida's Liquid Appliqué for a puffed effect. Squirt a quarter-sized blob of this paint on a piece of freezer paper (plastic side). Use a sponge roller to roll the paint out so that the roller is evenly coated with paint. Roll over the stamp to ink it.

I ink a stamp pad with the Liquid Appliqué when I use the embroidery stitch stamps from Works of Heart. Those designs are perfect to use on crazy quilt pieces.

The layer of Liquid Embroidery is not as thick when applied by a stamp as when applied directly from the barrel on fabric; the puffed effect is minimal. Dry overnight before applying heat.

Variation E. After Liquid Appliqué is dry to the touch, color your design with marker. Dry overnight before applying heat.

Variation F. Larger stamp designs can be painted or filled in with soft transparent paint. Use a fine liner brush for small areas.

Variation G. Pelle's has a wide variety of quilt block stamps. Creating a miniature quilt is superfast with stamps (no stitching of tiny pieces; hand-quilting optional). Mini–stamped quilts are great as pillow covers or wall decorations. One friend made a stamped quilt for her daughter's doll.

Variation H. Try stamping silks and fine woven fabrics. You may need to apply an antifusant coating before stamping. Pretest before beginning project. Heat-set stamped prints before using another paint technique over your stamped design.

Variation I. If your fabric has a synthetic content of at least 60 percent, use Deka IronOn Paint as the stamping ink. Sulky transfer pens can be used on all fabrics. Stamp the design onto paper to transfer to the shirt. (The design will be reversed.)

IronOn Paint or Sulky Transfer Pen can be used to color the design stamped on paper, before transfer. Or you can paint or color the design with another type of paint or marker after you have transferred it to the shirt.

Use any absorbent (no shine) paper as the transfer paper. Tracing Vellum (see Chapter 9), typing paper, and computer paper all work well. The transfer sheet can be as large as the entire front (and/or back) of a shirt. Repeat designs can be used in strip form. Templates can be cut for neck lines.

Allow paint to dry on paper. Place the painted side of the paper on the right side of the fabric. Press, following paint manufacturer's instructions. Remove paper. The painted transfer can be used at least three more times.

Fig. 5-9

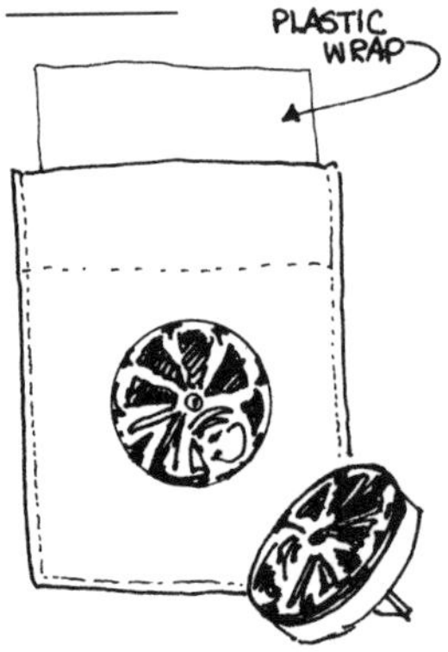

PLASTIC WRAP

Fig. 5-10

Block Printing— Basic Instructions

NOTE: Before beginning this technique, please read about Antifusant, Cleanup Tips, Drying Paint, Glitter Drift, Heat-Setting, Print Blocks, Shirt Boards, Stamps, and Stamp Pads in the alphabetical listings in Chapter 9.

In these basic instructions, you will use a purchased plastic block with paint. You will print a design down the sleeves of a shirt and from neck ribbing to cuff ribbing; and down the sides of pants legs, from waist to cuff. This technique is more time-consuming than some other fabric-painting techniques because it takes time to mark block placement and to allow the paint to dry between applications.

Supplies

♦ Sweatshirt and pants, child's size medium (if you are using fabric that is more than 60 percent synthetic, see Variation G)
♦ Purchased block of your choice
♦ Paint-proof cardboard or foam board to use as a "shirt board"
♦ Paint, approximately 3 ounces (see Print Blocks in Appendix A). Pretest with block.
♦ Disposable brush
♦ Small, flat pan or piece of freezer paper
♦ Toothbrush

Getting Ready

1 Remove clothing labels.
2 Cut cardboard or foam board pieces to fit inside shirt sleeve and pants leg. The board should be wide enough so fabric is taut but not stretched. You can tape pieces of board together to get the required length. Remove boards and paint-proof (see Shirt Boards in Chapter 9 for an explanation).
3 Fold sleeves in half so that the fold line extends from neck ribbing to cuff ribbing. Press line with warm iron.
4 Fold legs in half along side seams, if any. The fold line will extend from waistband to cuff. Press line with warm iron.
5 If pressed line is not easily seen, mark line with chalk or disappearing marking pen.
6 Fold sleeve in half, cuff to neck. Fold in half again. Press fold lines with warm iron. Open. Using your block as a measure, determine how many prints can be made along the outer fold line. Use pins to mark sections (Fig. 5-11). Prints will be centered on pressed lines between pin markings.

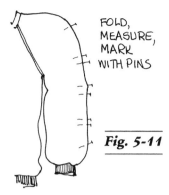

FOLD, MEASURE, MARK WITH PINS

Fig. 5-11

7 Repeat measuring procedure for pants leg.
8 Slide cardboard or foam core pieces into one sleeve and one leg, taking care not to disturb markings for print placement. If fabric is not taut and smooth, secure with pins. You will print one sleeve and one leg first. You will print the second sleeve and leg after paint from the first printing is dry. Don't remove boards until paint is dry.
9 Protect work areas.
10 Pretest selected paint with block and fabric. You can pat the paint on the surface of the block, or use a stamp pad. Use whichever method gives the best impression.

Painting

1 Squeeze a small amount of paint in a small pan or on a piece of freezer paper. Pat side of disposable brush in paint. Pat paint on surface of plastic block. Center block on pressed (marked) line and between pin markings (Fig. 5-12). Print all markings on one arm and leg.

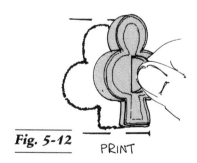

Fig. 5-12   PRINT

2 Apply a new coat of paint to your block for each print.
3 Leave boards in place until paint has dried.
4 Print the second arm and leg after the first has dried.

Cleanup

1 Clean up your work area between first and second printings.
2 Clean paint from block between first and second printings as well. Use a toothbrush to get paint out of grooves. Clean brushes.

Laundering

1 Heat-set if required.
2 Do not launder for 1 week.
3 Launder according to paint manufacturer's instructions.

BLOCK PRINTING—VARIATIONS

Variation A. For adult-size shirt and pants, double the paint amount. Follow Basic Instructions.

Variation B. Using an appropriate-size block, print ½″ to 1″ below the neck ribbing of a T- or sweatshirt (Fig. 5-13). Use a shirt board as described under Getting Ready, above.

For a dressy look, print with a glitter paint. Add jewels around the design.

Variation C. Coordinate block prints with purchased iron-on glitter appliqués (Fig. 5-14). Select like designs and combine them throughout the shirt. You might use floral blocks between bow-shaped iron-on glitter appliqués around the neck, sleeves, and hem.

Variation D. Use small block prints around hems of shirts, sleeves, and skirts and on shirt pockets.

Fig. 5-14

MIX WITH IRON-ON APPLIQUES

Fig. 5-13

PRINT AROUND NECK, ADD JEWELS

Variation E. Spread or pat an even layer of glue suitable for glitter (see Glues Used with Glitter, Appendix D) on block. Print with glue. Immediately sprinkle glitter over glue (Fig. 5-15). Allow glue to dry, preferably overnight. Remove excess glitter. (See Glitter Drift, Chapter 9.) Do not launder for 2 weeks.

Fig. 5-15

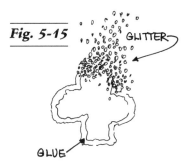

GLITTER

GLUE

SPARKLE SPRINKLE

Variation F. Squeeze a quarter-sized glop of Liquid Appliqué (Marvy Uchida) on a piece of freezer paper. Roll out with a sponge roller. The coating of paint (Liquid Appliqué) must be evenly distributed over the surface of the roller. Roll the paint over the block and print on fabric. Wait at least 12 hours before puffing the design. Puffing will be minimal to moderate, depending on the amount of paint left on fabric after printing.

Variation G. Roll Deka IronOn paint over the surface of the block. Print on paper. When dry, transfer the design to fabric. Transfer can be used at least three times. IronOn is intended for synthetic blends containing at least 60% synthetics. When used on other fabrics, the colors are not as deep or colorfast.

Variation H. Silk and fine woven fabrics print beautifully. Pretest, and use antifusant (see Chapter 9) if necessary. Stabilize the fabric before printing. You can tint or dye the fabric before or after printing, if you wish. Heat-set between techniques.

Printing with Found Objects—Basic Instructions

NOTE: Before beginning this technique, please read about Cleanup Tips, Design Placement, Drying Paint, Print Blocks, and Shirt Boards in the alphabetical listings in Chapter 9.

Supplies

- T-shirt, adult size large
- Chore Girl or similar product for cleaning pans
- Paint, 1 ounce for "flower" block, ½ to 1 ounce for brushed stem (see Print Blocks in Appendix A)
- 2 small flat pans for paint
- ½″ disposable paint brush
- Shirt board
- Fine or extra-fine glitter (optional)

Getting Ready

1 Try on shirt; mark design placement.

2 After taking shirt off, mark with removable marker where each flower will be.

3 Insert shirt board.

4 Arrange Chore Girl in flat circle shape, seams in back.

5 Prepare work area.

6 Test-print on a paper towel. Decide whether you want heavy paint saturation on each print, or some prints with heavy saturation and some with light. Dipping the block in paint for each print will result in heavy saturation.

Practice using the sponge brush for painting "stems" on a paper towel. Dip the side of the brush in paint. Pat off excess paint. Position tip just under flower. Pull brush away from flower. There should be a slight curve to the stem (Fig. 5-16).

Fig. 5-16

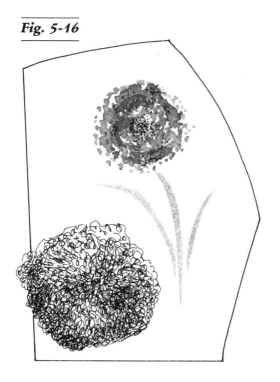

Leaves are even easier than that. Lay side of sponge brush in paint. Pat it a couple of times on paper to remove excess. Bend the brush in a curved shape. Position the tip away from the stem, and press brush on fabric.

Now don't worry too much about precision when you're doing these stems and leaves. Remember, this is a flower printed with a pan cleaner. All you want to do is give an impression of a stem and leaves. One big swing does it for the stem (no short strokes—go for it!). Don't worry about floppy leaves, either—even real ones get that way.

7 For your "flower block," pour paint in pan. Print all the flowers before putting the paint for the stems in second pan.

Painting

1 Dip flat side of Chore Girl in paint; then print. Print half of the markings. Sprinkle glitter on wet paint (optional).

2 Print second half of "flower" markings. Sprinkle glitter on wet paint (optional).

3 Add paint used for stems and leaves to the pan.

4 Paint stems and leaves.

5 Dry flat. Don't remove shirt board until paint is dry.

6 Wait at least 4 hours before removing excess glitter.

Cleanup

1 After printing, put Chore Girl in soapy water to soak. Rinse in warm water. You won't be able to get all the paint out, but you can use it again for printing.

2 Wipe up any paint spills.

3 Clean brush.

Laundering

1 Heat-set if required.

2 Do not launder for 1 week, 2 weeks if you used glitter.

3 Launder according to paint manufacturer's instructions.

PRINTING WITH FOUND OBJECTS— VARIATIONS

Variation A. Substitute a Kiwi shoe polish applicator for the Chore Girl. It can be just a nice round circle, or it can become a flower or a smily face. Sprinkle glitter over wet paint for sparkles; overlap circles of several colors for an abstract design.

Variation B. Use an opaque paint for the circle print (see Variation A). When dry, overprint with a transparent paint, using a larger square or rectangle (use the bottom of a small cardboard box). Try using translucent crystal or a soft glitter paint for a special touch on the second print.

Variation C. Drop a dime-sized amount of paint (of a second color) into the center of the wet paint of the printed flower shape you made in basic instructions, above. Use either a soft glitter or opaque paint. Sprinkle on the center for additional sparkle (Fig. 5-17). Use the tip of a toothpick to pull the paint (and/or glitter, if used) toward the edges of the flower print.

Fig. 5-17

Variation D. Outline flower shapes with dimensional paint after flower print is dry. Don't try to make an actual flower shape. The outline should be more of a circular shape or one with four or five rounded petals.

Variation E. Add small jewels or dots or pearlized paint for dew drops on the flowers.

Painting with a Brush— Basic Instructions

NOTE: Before beginning this technique, please read about Freezer Paper, Pretesting, Shirt Boards, and Tapes in the alphabetical listings in Chapter 9.

I was going to write instructions for painting a preshaded transfer. But the instructions that come with the transfers are so good, it didn't seem to make much sense to waste space telling you how to paint them.

What is not a waste of time is teaching you how to paint a transfer of this type. Try it at least once. It's the best possible introduction to painting with a brush. Some of the many brushes available are shown in Fig. 5-18.

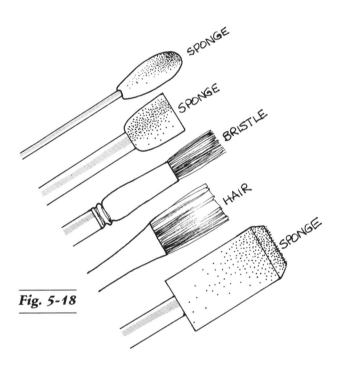

Fig. 5-18

Supplies

- T-shirt, adult or children's size
- Piece of foamboard or cardboard that is wider and longer than the shirt (or use your ironing board).
- Straight pins
- 1″ clear package or silver duct tape (masking tape may leak)
- Brush (wide soft flat or 1″ sponge)
- Paint, approximately 3–4 ounces (Do not use stiff/hard types. If in doubt, paint a 2″ square on tester shirt. Let dry; check stiffness.)
- Piece of freezer paper or plastic wrap that is larger than shirt

Getting Ready

1 Turn shirt inside out, and lay it on the board, back up.

2 Press freezer paper or Totally Stable to wrong side of shirt back. Turn shirt right side out when cool.

3 Form uneven pleats across shirt front. Begin at left sleeve and work across body and right sleeve. Pin pleats in place.

4 Position strips of tape across the pinned pleats. Tape strips do not have to be placed evenly (Fig. 5-19).

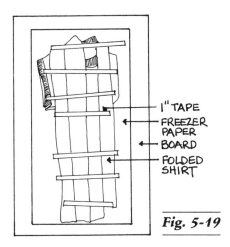

Fig. 5-19

5 Remove pins.

6 Mix paint, if additives or water are used.

Painting

1 Brush paint across top of pleats, over folds (Fig. 5-20). Don't brush into the fold of the pleat.

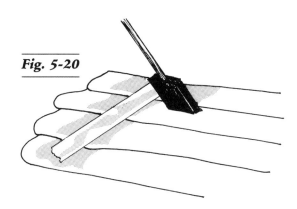

Fig. 5-20

2 Vary the amount of paint on your brush for a streaked effect.

3 Dry flat.

4 Remove tape when paint is dry.

Cleanup

1 Clean brush immediately. (See The Unbreakable Rules of Painting in Chapter 3.) Store upright.

2 Wipe off work area.

Laundering

1 Heat-set if required; I recommend it if paint has been diluted.

2 Do not launder for 1 week.

3 Follow paint manufacturer's instructions when laundering.

PAINTING WITH A BRUSH— VARIATIONS

Variation A. Fold shirt front in half. Crease center front line. Insert shirt board inside shirt. Tape a strip 3″ from either side of the center crease (Fig. 5-21). Tape lines serve as a block on either side of the pleated area.

Arrange even, narrow pleats between the two taped lines. Pin pleats down as you form them. (Don't be concerned if not every pleat is exactly the same size.) Tape across pleats. Leave large spaces between tape sprips. Remove pins.

Use a 4″ sponge brush to brush paint down pleats (Fig. 5-22). Paint from below neck ribbing to bottom hem. Remove tape when paint is dry. You

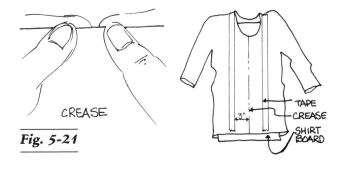

Fig. 5-21

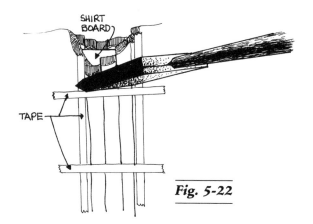

Fig. 5-22

can place jewels, beads, or studs on unpainted strips down shirt front (Fig. 5-23). See Embellishments in Chapter 9 for methods of attaching these items.

Fig. 5-23

Variation B. A fan-shaped brush leaves an interesting impression when the side of the brush is pressed on fabric (Fig. 5-24). Metallic, pearlized, or glitter paints applied in this way work well on all fabrics, from silk to sweat fleece. You can group the fan shapes tightly, arrange them in a random manner, or join them side by side to form rounded shapes.

Pretest the paint on a tester shirt or scrap fabric; if there is too much, or it is too runny, you won't get much of a fan shape.

You can stick a rhinestone or a loop of cross-locked beads in the center of the curved bottom for a different look. A spot of glue or paint holds the cut ends of beads.

Variation C. The flat side of a sponge brush (any size) leaves an uneven rectangular imprint when laid on fabric. Uneven rectangles can be arranged in a pattern or combined with round sponge block prints. Use a flat pan with short sides to load the brush with paint.

Glitters and stiff dimensionals tend not to release easily from the brush, but you can sprinkle glitter over wet paint for an embellishment.

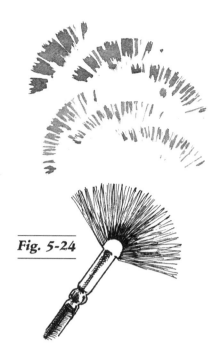

Fig. 5-24

Painting Silk and Fine Wovens—Basic Instructions

NOTE: Before beginning this technique, please read about Blank Clothing and Accessories, Edge Finishes, Heat-Setting, Refillable Markers, and Resist in the alphabetical listings in Chapter 9.

Supplies

- Blank silk scarf (or silk yardage)
- Piece of freezer paper larger than scarf
- Piece of cooking parchment paper larger than scarf
- Iron and board
- 2–4 ounces paint for 9″ × 45″ scarf. More than one color can be used. (See Painting Silk and Fine Wovens in Appendix A.)
- Brushes: wide, soft, flat brush or 1″ sponge brush; also ¼″ sponge dauber (see Brushes in Appendix C)
- Crayons for resist
- Curved or straightedge ruler (optional)
- Dark marker

Getting Ready

1 Use a dark marker (pencil is too narrow and light) to draw outline of scraf on paper side of freezer paper. Draw or trace your design within that outline (Fig. 5-25, step 1). Use French or dressmaker curves and a ruler for guides.

2 Turn paper over; cover with scarf. Marked design should be visible through the fabric

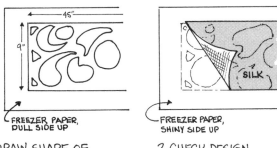

1. DRAW SHAPE OF SCARF DESIGN

2. CHECK DESIGN FOR VISIBILITY

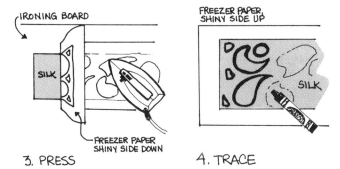

3. PRESS

4. TRACE

Fig. 5-25

wide and heavy enough to penetrate fabric when melted. Children's crayons may be substituted for fabric crayons. Fabric crayons will produce a deeper color.

5 Cover scarf with cooking parchment paper. Press with iron at wool setting. Wax in crayon should melt into fabric. Let cool.

6 Mix paint, if additives or water are used.

Painting

1 If the design has small areas surrounded by wax, use a dauber to apply paint within those areas (Fig. 5-27). Saturate the dauber tip with paint, lay on fabric in center of waxed area. The paint will spread within the waxed area.

2 For larger areas, saturate either a soft, flat brush or a 1″ sponge brush with paint. Lay the end next to a waxed line and pull away from that line (Fig. 5-28). The paint will spread across, and away from, the line when the brush touches the fabric.

Work across, and away from, the line until the area is painted. Work quickly. Don't stop working in the middle of an area. If you do, you'll have what is called a hard edge (Fig.

(Fig. 5-25, step 2). If it is not, darken design lines on paper side.

3 Place scarf on ironing board, wrong side up. Straighten side and end hems (or raw edges if you are using yardage). Position plastic side of freezer paper on scarf. The marked outline of the scarf should align with the side and end hems (or raw edges) of the scarf. Press plastic side of paper to scarf, with iron set at silk (Fig. 5-25, step 3). After cooling, turn over so fabric side is up.

4 Trace design on scarf with crayon (Fig. 5-25, step 4; Fig. 5-26). Crayoned lines must be

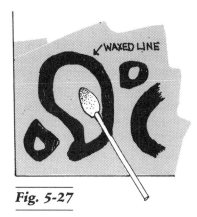

Fig. 5-27

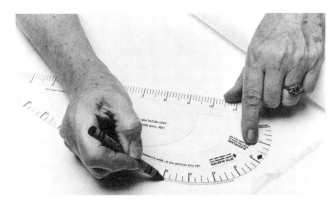

Fig. 5-26

Fig. 5-28

5-29). The paint can run only so far across the fabric. When it comes to a halt in dry fabric, the paint dries very quickly, which is not necessarily bad. In fact, it's very effective—if you wanted that as part of the design (see Variation A). But when you want a smooth, fluid look to the paint, a hard edge is frustration time. And that's when the design plan suddenly changes from no hard edges to hard edges all over the scarf.

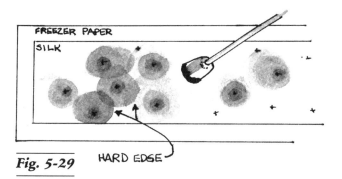

Fig. 5-29

3 You can finish your edges by applying paint or Resist before removing freezer paper from scarf. Or make self-fringe: Mark the lines before removing freezer paper from scarf. Both methods are explained under Edge Finishes in Chapter 9.

4 If you heat-set the paint before removing the freezer paper from the scarf, the paint on the wrong side of the scarf will look slightly flattened. Remove freezer paper when cool. If some should stick, soak the scarf in cool water after heat-setting to remove any bits and pieces. Whether on freezer paper or not, heat-set at cotton setting. Cover the wrong side of the scarf with cooking parchment paper if freezer paper was removed. Press on the cooking parchment paper or freezer paper. Turn scarf over, cover with cooking parchment paper and press.

Cleanup

1 Clean brushes immediately.
2 Wipe off work area.

Laundering

Hand-wash, line-dry.

PAINTING SILK AND FINE WOVENS—VARIATIONS

Variation A. I love hard edges. I think the shapes and overlaps of color are beautiful. Press

freezer paper to the wrong side of a scarf. Mark the scarf, either in an organized or disorganized way, with a chalk marker. (All you need is a dot you can easily see.) Leave at least 1″ between marks. The paint will spread in an irregular, circular shape about 1″ across.

Dip the end of a square-ended dauber in paint. The bottom half of the dauber should be saturated with paint. Place the dauber on the marked dot, pressing into fabric. Continue "painting" all marked dots in this way, dipping dauber in paint as necessary. Apply paint to dots randomly (move back and forth from one end of the scarf to the other end).

There will be areas where the original color of the scarf is visible. Paint those areas with another color paint, using either the pointed or square-ended dauber. This second color can be applied before the painted dots (the first color) are dry. If the first color is still wet, it will blend along the edges with the second color. If the first color is dry, it will have a hard edge, and there will be little blending with the second color.

Getting fancy is pretty easy with this mark-and-press type of painting. You can use either a refillable marker or a fabric marker instead of chalk to do the dot marking. Use a dark color for the dots. Press a light color on the dot with the dauber (pointed or square-end). Apply a dark color around the edges of the light color, using a dauber or refillable marker. Fill the surrounding areas with the light color, or a third color. The result is a series of indefinite shapes of overlapping colors. The darker colors will show through the lighter colors.

Outline shapes with permanent metallics or colored Resist, or use it as a squiggle line over the paint. Push Resist into fabric, just as you do before painting. Heat-set when all paint and Resist are dry, either on or off the freezer paper. The Resist will remain in the fabric.

Variation B. Substitute cotton, rayon, or a poly/cotton blend for silk. The paint will not run quite as much on these fabrics.

Variation C. Don't stop at a scarf. Use one of these techniques on a basic blouse (silk, cotton, or poly/blend) that you make or purchase. If you sew the blouse, paint yardage before cutting and stitching. The cutting lines can be marked (permanent marker) on the fabric before painting. Leave at least 1″ space between pattern pieces.

Variation D. Photocopy selected design (see Chapter 2). For a 45″ scarf you will need to use just over four 8½″ × 11″ copies to cover length. Stabilize silk or other fine woven fabric with freezer paper. Transfer copy to silk by pressing. Paint design as desired. Heat-set.

Painting with a Roller— Basic Instructions

NOTE: Before beginning this technique, please read about Blockers, Rollers, Shirt Boards, Stencils, and Tapes in the alphabetical listings in Chapter 9.

Supplies

- ◆ Sweatshirt, Adult size large
- ◆ Two or three 12″ doilies
- ◆ Spray repositionable glue (see Glues/Adhesives in Appendix D)
- ◆ Sponge roller (see Rollers in Appendix C)
- ◆ Paint, 2 ounces (see Stencils in Appendix A)
- ◆ Freezer paper for rolling out paint
- ◆ Shirt board

Getting Ready

1 Don't spearate the doilies. Leave two or three stuck together when you take them out of the package. These will be used as one layer.

2 Inspect the doilies; usually all the holes in the design are not punched through. Do the punching out over a large piece of paper (to save picking up paper bits).

3 Spray the back of the doilies with glue. (Remember: don't separate—treat them as one.) Wait 10 minutes and spray again. Let dry 10 minutes before placing on fabric.

4 Center doilies on shirt front. Press down with the back of a plastic spoon or a wallpaper roller.

5 Mix paint if additives are used.

6 Position shirt board behind area where paint will be applied.

7 Put paint on a piece of freezer paper. Roll out, filling the roller evenly with paint.

8 Pretesting is a good idea. Use the same kind of doily that will be used for this shirt.

Painting

1 Beginning at center, roll paint over doilies (Fig. 5-30). Don't roll paint beyond the outer edges of the doily. Fill roller as necessary for an even coat of paint.

2 Leave doilies in place until paint is dry.

3 Remove shirt board.

Cleanup

1 Clean roller immediately.

2 Wipe off work area.

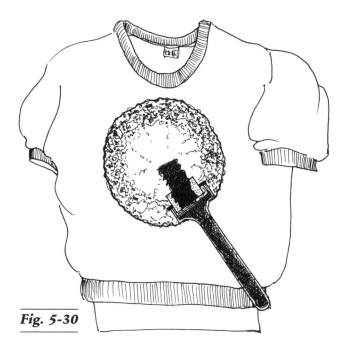

Fig. 5-30

Laundering

1 Heat-set if required.

2 Do not launder for 1 week.

3 Follow manufacturer's instructions.

PAINTING WITH A ROLLER— VARIATIONS

Variation A. Doily designs look great on everything from T-shirts to jean jackets, from silk to sweat fleece. The method is exactly the same.

Variation B. The doilies do not have to be the large, 12″ size. Select any size and design you prefer. Several have designs that are great for corners on placemats and napkins.

Variation C. Cut apart sections of doilies, and use them around cuffs, hems, and ribbing. Removable transparent tape can also be used to block areas of the doilies you do not want painted.

Variation D. After removing doilies, embellish the design with lace, beads, jewels, nailheads, studs or grommets (Fig. 5-31). Use dimensional paint to outline the edges of the design. Sprinkle glitter over wet paint.

Variation E. Frame the doilies with tape strips, or cut picture mat (see Blockers in Chapter 9). Tape on inner edges of mat should be at least 1″ beyond the edges of the doilies. Paint the doily design with an opaque paint. Remove doilies when paint has dried. Roll transparent or translucent paint from the edges of the tape or mat to the center of the design. Remove when paint has dried. The doily design will be framed in the transparent

Fig. 5-31

color. The opaque color used on the doily will be visible through the transparent paint.

Variation F. The design of doilies is a natural for quilt blocks. You can paint the blocks individually or in strips. Mark strips in block measurements. Cut after painting. One package of smaller doilies often contains 12 doilies. You can do four to six blocks at one time.

PAINTING WITH A HARD RUBBER ROLLER (BRAYER)

NOTE: Before beginning this technique, please read about Cleanup Tips, Reverse Blocks, and Rollers in the alphabetical listings in Chapter 9.

If you didn't get enough finger painting when you were a kid, this technique will fill the void. If you got too much, use tools other than your fingers. Please note: this technique is easy but time-consuming.

Supplies

- ◆ T-shirt, adult size large
- ◆ Strip of freezer paper, 8″ wide and long enough to fit from bottom of neck ribbing to hem of shirt
- ◆ Freezer paper or Totally Stable for shirt board layer
- ◆ 3 to 4 ounces paint, soft or very soft (see Roller Painting in Appendix A)
- ◆ Sponge roller (see Rollers in Appendix C)
- ◆ Hard roller—rubber brayer or plastic wallpaper seamer (see Rollers in Appendix C)
- ◆ Plastic food wrap or plastic sheeting
- ◆ Removable marker

Getting Ready

1 Measure length of shirt from below neck ribbing to bottom hem. Cut 8″-wide piece of freezer paper strip that length.
2 Cut freezer paper strip in half lengthwise. You'll have two pieces, each 4″ wide, in the length needed (Fig. 5-32).
3 Press the plastic side of one strip to the paper side of the second piece, bonding two pieces together (Fig. 5-33). You'll use this for painting.
4 Turn shirt wrong side out. Bond another piece of freezer paper or Totally Stable shirt board layer down the center front (Fig. 5-34). The piece should be at least 5″ wide and extend from the neck to the bottom hem. Turn shirt right side out when cool.

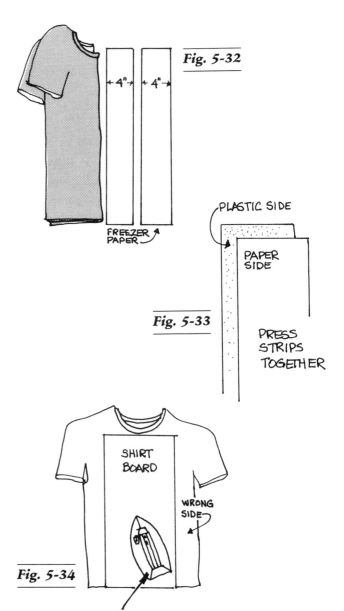

Fig. 5-32

FREEZER PAPER

PLASTIC SIDE
PAPER SIDE

Fig. 5-33   PRESS STRIPS TOGETHER

SHIRT BOARD

WRONG SIDE

Fig. 5-34

5 Determine center front of the shirt. Use a removable marker to mark a line 2″ on either side of center front (Fig. 5-35). The parallel lines will be 4″ apart and go from center neck to the bottom hem.

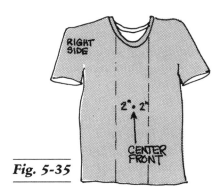

Fig. 5-35

6 Cover work surface with plastic wrap or sheeting.

7 Place shirt, front up, on plastic covering.

8 Mix paint, if water additives are used. Don't dilute too much. The paint should be reasonably stable.

Painting

1 Use sponge roller to roll a heavy layer of paint on cut freezer paper you made in steps 1–3 of Getting Ready. Do not paint out to the edges; leave at least ¼″ unpainted on each side. Keep the coating as even as possible.

2 Use your fingers, a sponge brush, the back of a plastic spoon or chenille to draw lines and curves in the paint (Fig. 5-36). The freezer paper should be visible in these drawn lines and curves.

Fig. 5-36

3 Pick up the painted strip by the unpainted side areas. Turn it over and place it, paint side down, on the shirt front between the markings.

4 Roll the hard roller over the length of the painted strip (Fig. 5-37). Roll over the width. You're transferring the paint from the painted strip to the shirt front. Don't miss any areas.

5 Pick up the painted strip. Set aside.

6 Dry shirt flat. Remove shirt board layer when paint is dry (Fig. 5-38).

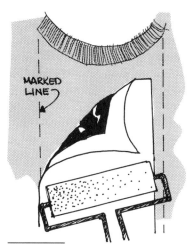

Fig. 5-37

Fig. 5-38

Cleanup

1 Immediately clean sponge roller and other tools used with paint.

2 Wipe the paint off the freezer paper strip with a damp sponge. You can use it for additional painting.

3 Wipe off work surface.

Laundering

1 Heat-set if required

2 Do not launder for 1 week.

3 Follow manufacturer's instructions.

PAINTING WITH A HARD RUBBER ROLLER—VARIATIONS

Variation A. Use this technique for all fabric weights and types (silk and denim; yardage or purchased clothing). Do not use hard/stiff dimensional type paints unless the design area is very small.

Always use a double layer of freezer paper for the painted strip. A single layer is too floppy and difficult to handle. Or use Totally Stable for the painted strip. Bond freezer paper to the back of it for stability. Apply paint to the paper side or the fusible side: the effects are different for each side.

The fabric can be laid on the painted strip, rather than vice-versa as in the basic instructions. This way you can use thinner paints.

You can also use thinner paints for "back prints." Place the wrong side of the fabric on the painted strip. The thin paint will bleed or seep through to the right side of the fabric. Pretest before using thinner paints.

Variation B. Cut narrow strips of freezer paper. Use a different color paint on each strip. Overlap placement on right side of fabric.

Variation C. This technique is not limited to straight-sided strips. Use curves, circles, angles, squares (quilt blocks)—whatever you want.

Variation D. Cut a pattern from freezer paper the size of the front and/or back of a shirt or jacket. Bond three layers of freezer paper together for stability. It's easier to place the painted paper on the clothing rather than vice-versa. Lining everything up when the painted design is that large can be difficult.

Using Purchased Stencils— Basic Instructions

NOTE: Please read about Stencils in Chapter 9 before beginning this technique.

Select either a quilting stencil or a fabric paint stencil. They require the same type of paint. One paint color will be used for the design on the pillow top.

Supplies

♦ Constructed or purchased 16″ × 16″ pillow cover
♦ Stencil
♦ Repositionable glue for back of stencil (see Stencils in Chapter 9)
♦ Paint (see Stencils in Appendix A)
♦ Brush, 1″ sponge or flat scrubber (see Brushes in Appendix C)
♦ Freezer paper
♦ 16″ × 16″ foam board or cardboard square (optional; but if used, board must be waxed as instructed in Shirt Boards, Chapter 9)
♦ Constructed or purchased 16″ × 16″ pillow cover (see Pillow Covers in Appendix D)
♦ Constructed or purchased 16″ × 16″ pillow form (see Pillow Covers in Appendix D)

Getting Ready

1 Apply glue to back of stencil.
2 Attach stencil to a piece of scrap fabric. Test paint to make sure it will not leak under stencil.
3 Remove stencil from test fabric. Wipe paint from stencil.
4 Bond freezer paper to wrong side of pillow cover front.
5 Fold pillow cover in half, then in half again. Crease fold lines. Center of pillow is where two lines cross (Fig. 5-39).

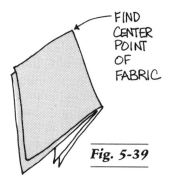

FIND CENTER POINT OF FABRIC

Fig. 5-39

6 Center stencil design on center of the pillow.
7 Use spoon or paper seam roller to push stencil down firmly. Check to make sure that the stencil and pillow are absolutely flat on the work surface. The fabric can be taped to the work surface to prevent it from moving when you are painting.
8 If the back or side seams of the pillow cover are heavy, the top may not be completely flat. In that case, insert a waxed piece of cardboard or foam board inside the cover. Stick push pins or straight pins through the fabric and into the board. This should flatten the cover.

Painting

1 Paint open areas of stencil design. Load brush with moderate amount of paint. Brush paint from edges toward center of design.
2 Lift stencil from fabric when paint does not stick to fingers (about 15 minutes).
3 Leave pillow cover flat until paint has dried thoroughly.
4 Remove freezer paper from wrong side of cover.

Cleanup

1 Wipe paint from stencil. Store stencil with flat, glued side on plastic side of freezer paper. To remove glue from stencil, use Goo-Gone (a spot remover) or cover glued side with duct tape. Press tape firmly on stencil; tear tape off quickly. Repeat if necessary.

2 Clean brush.

Laundering

1 Heat-set if required.

2 Do not launder for 1 week.

3 Launder according to manufacturer's instructions.

USING PURCHASED STENCILS—VARIATIONS

Variation A. The stenciled design can be painted with two or more colors. Decide which colors will be used for each section of the design. It's easier (and faster) if you use a different brush for each color.

Position stencil on pillow cover. Paint interior section of design first. A piece of ⅛″ basting tape (see Chapter 9) can be used as a blocker when colors are not separated by bridges. Don't remove paper from the tape.

After paint has dried, pick up tape and replace it on painted edge (Fig. 5-40). Now you can paint up to that painted edge without worrying about smearing the second color into the first. You can substitute lift-off cellophane tape for the basting tape, but the wider width is usually cumbersome and difficult to position.

If you decide not to use any type of tape, use a soft flat brush when painting adjoining colors. If the second color should smear over the first, wait until the second color has dried before repainting the line of the first color.

If the paint really smears (it happens!), add a line of opaque or dimensional on top of the two smeared colors. Usually you can incorporate it into the design. (That's called a creative experience—if anyone asks you why it's there, just tell them that's where you wanted it.)

Variation B. Purchased fabric paint and quilting stencils can be used in dozens of ways on clothing. The procedure is exactly the same for yardage and clothing.

Because fabrics (knits and fleece) used for T-shirts and sweats have more texture, you must pay particular attention to attaching the stencil firmly to the fabric. Make sure those tiny bridges are really secured.

Stenciled designs look great on denim. The most important rule to remember when stenciling denim is to prewash to remove all sizing before you apply paint. Use an opaque paint for complete coverage of the fabric. Some paints may require two coats.

Variation C. You can spray stencil designs with the Preval Power Unit. Remember to block adjoining areas with either tape or freezer paper (see Spray/Mist Bottles, Chapter 9). Manual spray or mist bottles may not give satisfactory results.

Variation D. One method I love uses a quilting stencil, glue, and glitter. A single design can be used at the neck, or repeat designs can be used around the neck ribbing or sleeve hem.

The best types of glitter to use for this technique are "Extra Fine," "Ultra Fine," or "Fine Polyester." When this technique is used on outerwear garments, brush a glazing solution (See Appendix D) over the glitter after the glue is thoroughly dry.

Attach the stencil to a shirt. Apply a line of glue in the channels (Fig. 5-41). (See Glues Used with Glitter in Appendix D.) Be sure you can see the glue. The line must be heavy enough to hold glitter.

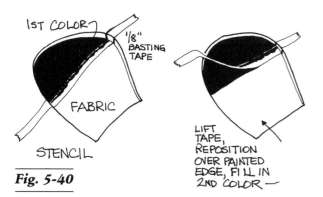

Fig. 5-40

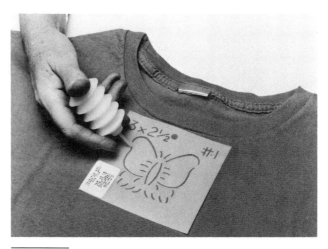

Fig. 5-41

Immediately pick up the stencil and sprinkle a heavy layer of glitter over the glue (Fig. 5-42). Dry flat for at least 4 hours.

Fold a piece of paper in half. Crease the fold line. Open the paper and sprinkle the excess glitter from the shirt onto the paper. Shake the glitter into the crease line and pour back into the bottle (Fig. 5-43).

Run the Lint Pick Up (see Glitter Drift, Chapter 9) over the shirt front (Fig. 5-44). You don't have to worry about wrecking the glued glitter. The only glitter that gets picked up was not glued to the shirt.

If you'd like to use more than one color glitter, apply glue for one color at a time. When that glue is dry, remove the excess glitter. Slide wax paper under the stencil covering the area that has been glittered. Apply glue in the lines that will be used for the next color glitter. Sprinkle glitter on glue. When glue has dried, pick up excess glitter.

Fig. 5-42

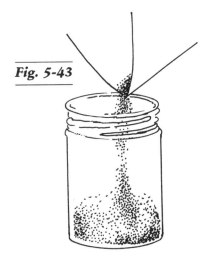

Fig. 5-43

Fig. 5-44

Wait 2 or 3 days before wearing the shirt. Do not launder for 2 weeks.

You can substitute paint for glue. Use any paint listed as "suitable as glue substitute" under Features in Appendix B. The color of the paint does not have to be the same as the glitter. Contrasting colors produce wonderful results.

Variation E. Stencils can be used to create beautiful beaded and sequined designs. Small designs can be attached to clothing. If the design is large, it's usually better to make it a "lift off" (repositionable) appliqué (see Chapter 7). Beads, sequins, and glitter can be used in any combination, or independently.

Do not use paints that require heat-setting if the beaded or sequined design is to be applied directly to clothing or any item that will be laundered. You won't be able to heat-set at the needed temperature. Sequins, especially, have a way of melting when pressed with a hot iron.

Select an open stencil (heart, fish, car, etc.). Cut the fabric used for lift-off designs at least 2″ larger than the stencil. Stabilize the wrong side of the fabric. Place stencil on right side.

Apply a thin bead of glue or of paint that is suitable as glue substitute (see Appendix B) along the outer edge of the design. Position the beads or sequins on the glue or paint (Fig. 5-45). Continue gluing or painting and attaching the trim around the entire edge. Add adjoining lines of trim until the stencil opening is filled.

You do not need to fill the opening completely with beads or sequins. Outline around outer edges of the stencil with two or three lines of trim. Paint the remaining area of the stencil. You can also use glue or paint to attach glitter in this opening.

When the glue or paint is almost dry, gently lift off the stencil. If glue or paint is holding the stencil

White shirt with heart flag: For the heart shape, a positive stencil was cut from freezer paper and pressed to the shirt front. Tape was used as a block for the line dividing the area between the stripes and the stars. Star shapes were cut from freezer paper and pressed to the shirt. The blue paint was rolled over the star area of the heart first. When the paint dried, tape was applied as a block along the edge of the blue paint. Tape was also applied as a block for the unpainted stripes. Red paint was rolled over the lower section of the heart. Tape and freezer paper were removed when all paint was dry. (Purchased shirt.)

Blue sweatshirt with flowers: Wire stems were cut from the flowers, then repositionable glue (liquid) was applied to the back of the flowers. Next, stems and leaves were painted on the shirt front. Flowers are removed when the shirt is laundered.

Red, white, and blue shoes: Tape was used as a block for the red and white shoe; stick-on stars (from an office supply store) were used as the block for the blue and white shoes. The laces are sewing trim. The soles were painted with textured paint containing strands of red, blue, and gold.

Polyester/cotton dress with ruffle: *Floral fabric was enhanced with paint, then an iron-on fusible was bonded to the wrong side of the fabric. The floral design was cut out and fused to the shirt. The painted fabric was covered with cooking parchment paper to protect it during fusing. (Purchased dress.)*

OPPOSITE PAGE TOP:

Pink T-shirt with glitter design: *The quilting stencil was attached to the shirt front, then glue was applied in the lines of the leaf. The stencil was removed, then green glitter was sprinkled over the glue. Excess glitter was picked up with a Lint Pic-Up after the glue had dried. The leaves were covered with cooking parchment paper, then the stencil was repositioned on the shirt. Next, glue was added to the flower portion of the stencil. Again, the stencil was removed, then gold glitter was sprinkled on the glue, and the excess glitter was picked up when the glue had dried. Finally, glue sprinkled with crystal glitter was added to the center area of the flower. (Quilt stencil by Quilting Creations by D.J., Inc.; purchased shirt.)*

Blue T-shirt with gold doily print and jewels. *The center area of the doily was cut out to fit the neckline of the shirt. Paint was applied with a sponge (foam) brush. Jewels were attached to the design after the doily print dried. (Doily from Wilton Enterprises; jewels from The Beadery.)*

OPPOSITE PAGE BOTTOM:

Blue butterfly shirt: *The shirt was stuffed with plastic bags and sprayed with paint. (Iron-on transfers by Rainbo, Glitterlooks by Dizzle.)*

Aqua and pink T-shirt: *The aqua shirt was dipped into slightly diluted paint, then tightly twisted. Nylon bands were used to hold it in position, then water was poured over the shirt. When the shirt was almost dry, the bands were released. Soft glitter tint was applied into the folds, then the shirt was twisted one more time before it dried.*

Black glitz sweatshirt: *Crystal paint was applied with a brush, bottle tip, and spreader. Cross-locked beads and sequins were applied on top of dimensional paint lines. Jewels were positioned on dimensional paint. (Cross-locked beads and sequins from EZ International; jewels from The Beadery.)*

OPPOSITE PAGE TOP:
Save Our Planet T-shirt: *Striped T-shirt has an iron-on transfer, partially painted. (Brite Ideas transfer by Tulip.)*

OPPOSITE PAGE BOTTOM:
Denim jacket: *Metallic gold and silver paint was applied between the seam lines. Jewels, stones, and mirrors were applied with permanent fabric glue. The paint and glue were heat-set after dry. An iron-on transfer was applied to the inside of the jacket. The lines of the transfer were colored with metallic marking pens. A light coat of extender was applied over the transfer area, then a small amount of glitter was sprinkled over the wet extender. (Transfer by Brite Ideas, Tulip; jewels, stones, and mirrors from The Beadery; extra jewels included for display.)*

NECKLINE: Cut outer lines from design. Press photocopy design under ribbing. Use paint or fabric marker.
DESIGN FROM DECORATIVE DOORWAYS STAINED GLASS PATTERN BOOK, DOVER PUBLICATIONS, page 13.

BUTTON-DOWN: Tie-painted using plastic rings. Two colors used.

FRONT: Negative stencil, outer edges blocked with tape. Paint is rolled over the stencil. Stencil is picked up when paint is dry. Diluted tint is brushed over area covered with stencil.
DESIGN FROM STAINED GLASS PATTERN BOOK, DOVER PUBLICATIONS, page 6.

FRONT: Sun-sensitive square is covered with design cut from freezer paper. Fabric is cut into a circle shape before exposure. Circle is fused or stitched to shirt front.

SUN-SENSITIVE FABRIC FROM BLUEPRINT-PRINTABLES.

SHIRTS

POCKET: Fusible is applied to wrong side of floral design cut from yardage. The design is applied to the shirt. Floral shapes are enhanced with fabric paint.

SLEEVE: Positive stencil is used on sleeve and the bottom cuff.

POCKET: Lace is applied across top. Lace is also used around sleeve hem. Lace is stitched or applied with fabric paint.

VEST: Bag paint. If constructed, line with marbled fabric.

BELT: Use a prepasted wallpaper water tray for the marble size. (Mine is 32" long by 5" wide, is disposable and cost $2.00). Marble a 4-inch-wide strip of fabric. Piece to obtain desired length. Use EZ International Turn-It and Belt & Buckle Kit.

SCARVES: Purchase hemmed silk scarf blank.

① ②

PLACEMATS: Cut fabric to size desired for mats. 15" X 18" is a good size. (½ yard of 45" fabric makes six placemats.) Stitch ¼" from the cut edge and fringe to the stitched line. Use iron-on transfer along all edges next to the stitched line. Paint or color the design with fabric markers.

NAPKINS: Cut 10-inch squares of fabric. Fringe edges. Use a single transfer design in one corner of each napkin. Paint or color.
DESIGNS: TULIP BIG AND EASY IRON-ON TRANSFERS.

OTHER GOODIES

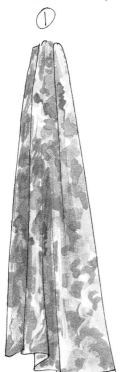

Place teeny plastic rings on scarf. Dip tied ends into fluid paint. (Deka Silk or FabricArt). Remove rings. Twist to disperse paint. Place scarf on freezer paper. Use a small brush to apply second color.

Press hemmed scarf blank to freezer paper. Stamp with a bent file card dipped in paint.

JACKET: Spray yardage for jacket with two colors. Tint yardage for lining, wring and twist when wet for a mottled effect.

Wrapped packages: *Paint was applied to the plastic side of freezer paper. Glitter or spangles were sprinkled on wet paint. After the paint dried, the shapes were picked up, placed on paper, and finger-pressed down.*

Hand towel (left): *Soft glitter paint was applied to the band on the towel.*
Dish towel (right): *A velour iron-on transfer was applied to the cloth strip of the towel, which is the type sold for cross-stitch embellishment. (Transfer by Seitec.)*

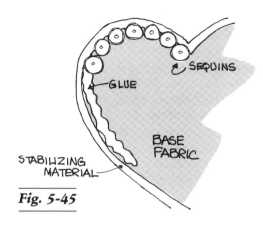

Fig. 5-45

against the fabric, slide the point of a pin under those spots to lift the stencil.

Dry flat at least eight hours. Check to make sure all trim is stable and firmly attached to fabric. Use a fine-line brush to apply paint into areas that need reattaching. Remove stabilizing layer.

Apply glue or tape to the backing of large designs after paint is completely dry (see Chapter 7). Store design flat on freezer or parchment paper when not in use.

You can stitch or glue the design to fabric for permanent placement. Do not launder for 2 weeks. Line-dry.

Variation F. You can use an open-shape fabric paint stencil (hearts, cars, floral designs, etc.) for outlining. Secure stencil on fabric. Place tip of bottle next to cut edge of design. Run paint line around edge. If you like, you can apply transparent paint within the outline after the dimensional paint has dried.

Making Your Own Stencils— Basic Instructions

You can use Totally Stable, freezer paper, stencil plastic, or plastic sheeting to make stencils. The design can be an original drawing or one that you copy. Read Chapter 2 for tracing, copying, and cutting methods.

Use Totally Stable and freezer paper stencils for the project described in these basic instructions. Instructions for tracing a design on stencil plastic are given in Variations. Select a not-too-intricate design from a needlework or design book for your first project. The design I selected is from Mary Mulari's book, *Adventure in Appliqué*. The design is centered on the shoulder seam of a T-shirt an extends to front and back of the shirt.

Paint and methods of application are the same as with purchased stencils. The variations described in the preceding technique, Using Pur-

chased Stencils, can also be used with stencils you make.

Supplies

- ◆ T-shirt, adult size large
- ◆ Design of your choice
- ◆ Two 8½″ × 11″ pieces of freezer paper or Totally Stable
- ◆ One 8½″ piece fine-woven fabric, cotton or poly/cotton blend (organdy, batiste, etc.)
- ◆ Support or dressmaker's ham
- ◆ Lift-off tape
- ◆ Scissors
- ◆ Craft knife (optional)
- ◆ Iron and board
- ◆ Paint (see Stencils in Appendix A)
- ◆ Disposable sponge-type brush or stencil brush (see Brushes, Appendix C)

Getting Ready

1 Copy stencil design (photocopy or trace) as directed in Chapter 2.
2 Cut stencil.
3 Place stencil on scrap fabric (or tester shirt) and test-paint. Wipe paint off stencil after testing.
4 Mark center width and length of stencil.
5 Turn shirt inside out and place shoulder area over end of ironing board. Press stabilizing layer in place (Fig. 5-46).
6 Turn shirt right side out and place shoulder area over end of ironing board. Position stencil on center of shoulder seam. Attach in place.
7 Shoulder area must be supported for painting. If ham is not used, roll towels into a fat tube shape that is wider and longer than the stencil. Place dressmaker's ham or towels in plastic bag and tape securely.

Fig. 5-46 STABILIZE

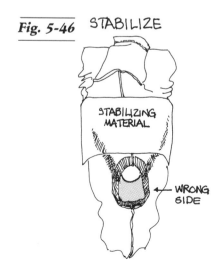

8 Slide bagged towels or ham under shoulder seam area. Stencil area of shirt must be smooth. Secure shirt to support with pins (Fig. 5-47).

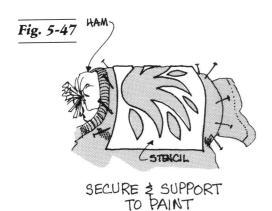

Fig. 5-47

SECURE & SUPPORT
TO PAINT

Painting

1 Follow painting procedures given in Using Purchased Stencil—Basic Instructions.

2 Allow paint to dry to touch before removing stencil.

3 Leave shirt on support, and stabilizing layer in place, until paint has dried.

Cleanup

1 Wipe paint from stencil.

2 Clean brushes.

3 Remove towels or ham from plastic bag.

Laundering

1 Heat-set, if required.

2 Do not launder for 1 week.

3 Follow manufacturer's instructions.

MAKING YOUR OWN STENCILS— VARIATIONS

Variation A. You can use crayons, china markers, or template markers (see Supply Sources) to mark stencil plastic. Crayons and china markers rub off the plastic easily, so be careful when handling the stencil when cutting. Apply glue to the back of the stencil as directed for purchased stencils. You can use regular scissors to cut stencil plastic. This is a good time to use scissors no longer sharp enough to cut fabric.

Variation B. It won't surprise you that a negative stencil is the opposite of a positive stencil. The results obtained with this type of stencil are the reverse of the previous methods.

It's hard finding negative stencils in the stores. So unless you've got lots of time to hunt them out, it usually takes less time to make them.

When looking at designs for a negative stencil, remember that the exterior of the design is cut away. The design itself is not painted.

Bridges are seldom used in a negative stencil. The shape of the design is attached to the fabric. The area surrounding the stencil can be blocked. Paint is applied within that blocked area, over the stencil. When the stencil is lifted, the unpainted design is surrounded by a painted area.

Variation C. One easy method of using a negative stencil is to surround a cut shape with a precut mat used for framing needlework or pictures (see Blockers in Chapter 9).

Coat back of mat with repositionable glue. Attach mat to fabric. The stencil can be offset or centered in the framed area. Attach the stencil to the fabric, within the framed area.

Paint from the inner edge of the framing, just to the edge of the stencil. Paint from the edge of the stencil into the painted area. Remove the framing and stencil when the paint is dry to the touch. There are several painting options that can be used with a negative stencil. Using one color of paint is the most obvious.

Or use opaque paint for the first coat. Remove the stencil and mat when the paint is dry. Paint unpainted area (the area that was under the stencil) with transparent paint.

A row of sequins, beads, or lace can be applied (stitched or glued) around painted edges.

6

More Painting Fun

This chapter is slightly different from Chapters 4 and 5. Rather than give Basic Instructions with Variations, I suggest projects that combine several techniques described in Chapters 4 and 5, often using specific products.

Several of these projects are non-wearable—for example, place mats and throw rugs. But you don't have to limit a technique to wearable or non-wearable. Usually what works for one works for the other.

Refer to Supply Sources when a brand name is given.

Dimensional Velour Designs

Seitec Dimensional Velour Designs are iron-on transfers with many uses. After transferring the velour design to fabric (as directed on the package), you'll notice that a design is still left on the backing paper. These paper designs can be cut out and applied with glue to surfaces that will not be laundered. For an item that must be laundered, or for plastic surfaces, use repositionable glue or indoor-outdoor (fiberglass) tape on the paper backing so that you can remove the paper design before laundering.

I used the turtle designs on a T-shirt for my grandson. After transferring the designs to the shirt, I lifted the paper from the shirt and applied fiberglass carpet tape to the back of the paper (not on the velour side). Then I cut out the designs and stuck them on his plastic lunch box.

The shirt has been laundered repeatedly and still looks great. The designs are still on the lunch box, each turtle grinning. Since this kid needs a lunch box that is guaranteed to float in a mud puddle, it says a lot for both the tape and the velour.

The designs can be stuck on tennis shoes, visors, backpacks, or just about any surface you want. Do use care when sticking them to painted surfaces, leather, or plastic. The tape may damage those surfaces.

The cut-out designs also make great gift tags (Fig. 6-1), especially if you decorated an item with a velour design. Just write on the paper backing.

Fig. 6-1

Sun-Sensitive Fabrics

Blueprints Printables has wonderful sun-sensitive fabrics available in constructed clothing, cut blocks, or yardage. These products offer so many creative options you hardly know where to begin.

Place items on the fabric, and stick it in the sun for 10 minutes. Remove items. Rinse fabric in warm water. A darkened image of the items remains on the fabric. (The directions that come with the fabric are slightly more explicit than that! Please follow them.)

After rinsing and drying, constructed clothing is ready to wear; blocks and yardage are ready to be stitched. It can all be fused, glued, glittered, or painted.

Freezer paper cutouts, stencils, feathers, lace, leaves, and photographs are some of the items that can be placed on the fabric for "sun prints." Sax Arts and Crafts sells transparencies in several designs that are intended for this fabric.

Clothing, jewelry, covered buttons, and quilt blocks are just a few of the projects you can make.

Painting Patterned Clothing

Sometimes we overlook patterned clothing as a painting surface. Purchase items with patterns and designs you can jazz up. Don't forget button-down-the-front shirts.

Check your closet. I'll guarantee one or two items would be ideal for decorating. (The one with the big mustard spot on the front could be the first one on the list.)

I found a great long-sleeved T-shirt in a large floral print on the sale rack. All it needed was brushed translucent crystal paint on the flowers. Ordinary became special.

Overpaint shirts. Tint or dye patterned fabrics. Roll constrasting colors of paint over polka dots or stripes (Fig. 6-2). Polka dots look great misted or sprayed.

Fig. 6-2

BASIC STRIPED SHIRT BRUSHED WITH TRANSLUSCENT PAINT THEN ACCENTED WITH GLITTER PAINT IN A RANDOM LINEAR PATTERN

Use the hard rubber roller method (Chapter 5) for a subdued pattern. Use different colors, beginning with the lightest first.

The "On-Again, Off-Again" Shirt

Thanks to repositionable glue and double-faced carpet tape, one shirt becomes the shirt of many moods, seasons, or holidays (Fig. 6-3). I call it the on-again, off-again shirt.

Probably the best part of an on-again, off-again design is laundering. You won't have to hand-wash—just remove the decoration.

Please read about lift-off Appliqués in Chapter 7. Apply repositionable glue or double-faced tape (fiberglass carpet tape for large or heavy items) to the back of your appliqué.

Carpet Tape Magic

This method requires indoor-outdoor, water-resistant, double-faced carpet tape (fiberglass type). Do not substitute regular-weight carpet tape or repositionable glue. Don't use this tape on painted surfaces, leather or plastic shoes, or purses unless you intend to always use a stickable in that spot.

Projects made with double-faced carpet tape must be limited to designs that are not used frequently (holidays designs, for example). Although this type of tape has incredible holding power, the "stick" starts to go after about three lift-offs. Add another layer of tape on top of the old, as necessary.

Trace a design (nothing over 3″ square) with a fine-line permanent marker on cooking parchment paper. Turn paper over. (Leave traced side up for a reverse of the design.)

Place tape over tracing (Fig. 6-4). Don't overlap the edges of the tape; they should butt together. Don't remove the paper backing from the tape until all strips are in place.

Make a slight cut on the tape's paper backing with either the point of a pin or a seam ripper. Slide the pin under the cut, raising a piece of the paper. Remove paper.

Cover those strips with strips running in the opposite direction (Fig. 6-5). Don't remove the paper backing from the second tape layer.

Turn over, and cut the tape and parchment paper along the traced line.

Use a straight pin or the point of a seam ripper to make a slight cut in the cooking parchment pa-

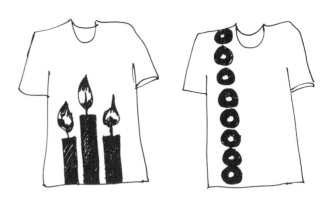

Fig. 6-3

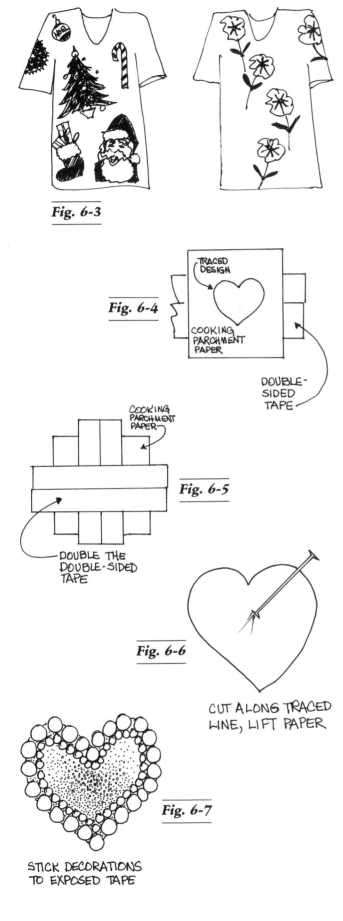

Fig. 6-4

TRACED DESIGN

COOKING PARCHMENT PAPER

DOUBLE-SIDED TAPE

COOKING PARCHMENT PAPER

Fig. 6-5

DOUBLE THE DOUBLE-SIDED TAPE

Fig. 6-6

CUT ALONG TRACED LINE, LIFT PAPER

Fig. 6-7

STICK DECORATIONS TO EXPOSED TAPE

per. Slide the pin under the cut and remove the cooking parchment paper from the tape (Fig. 6-6).

Position sequins, beads, jewels, trim, whatever, on the tape (Fig. 6-7). When the design area is filled, turn over. Rub the back of a plastic spoon over the paper backing. Be sure all items are attached securely to the tape. Check threads of cross-locked beads and sequins; squash them into the tape.

Remove the paper backing with the tip of a pin or seam ripper, and you've got a repositionable sticker!

Small designs and lighter-weight items (lace, yarns, threads, glitter, etc.) can be made with just one layer of tape.

Cover backs of jewels and ceramic buttons with fiberglass tape. Attach to button covers (Fig. 6-8).

Glittered strips, squares, circles, triangles, or shapes are made in a flash with this tape. Sprinkle a generous coat of glitter on a single layer of tape. Roll it in well with a bottle, hard rubber roller, or wallpaper seamer. Trim excess tape. Remove back-

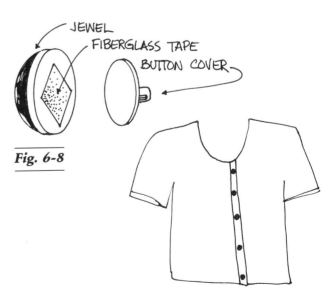

JEWEL
FIBERGLASS TAPE
BUTTON COVER

Fig. 6-8

ing paper. This is a great way to jazz up canvas shoes (Fig. 6-9). In fact, double-faced fiberglass tape and any trim you want to add will turn an inexpensive pair of canvas tennis shoes into shoes Cinderella would die for. (Don't substitute any other type of tape.) Cover the areas of the shoes you want decorated with one layer of tape. Remove the paper backing and start sticking away. Cross-locked beads and sequins, buttons, laces, and trims all work beautifully.

I stuck every kind of doodad possible on my shoes and wore them for a good month. Although the shoes looked a little bizzare, nothing budged. I finally had to take the stuff off because my 10-year-old granddaughter wouldn't go to the store with me anymore. She said she got tired of people staring at my funny-looking shoes.

You can also use permanent fabric glue to attach items to canvas shoes. Gluing takes longer than taping—it's also permanent.

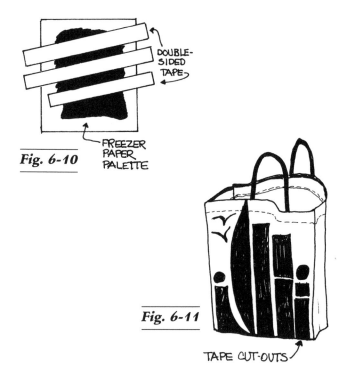

Fig. 6-10

Fig. 6-11

TAPE CUT-OUTS

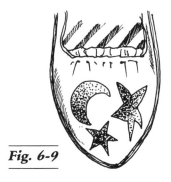

Fig. 6-9

Recycled Paint Creations

You can recycle fabric paint. Save the freezer paper you used as the surface for hard rubber roller painting (see Chapter 5).

Press double-faced tape into the dried layer of paint left on freezer paper (Fig. 6-10). Generally the best tape for this recycling is indoor-outdoor (fiberglass), double-faced carpet tape. The lighter-weight carpet tape does not hold as well. Roll tape flat with a bottle, hard rubber roller, or wallpaper seamer. Lift tape carefully. The paint will be stuck on the tape. Trim excess tape and paint.

Draw your designs or shapes on paper backing after lifting the paint. Cut them out, then remove the paper backing from the tape, and stick it on your project (Fig. 6-11).

This is an easy way to make removable fluorescent strips for clothing (great for kids' clothes on Halloween). Roll a heavy layer of fluorescent or neon paint on freezer paper. Pick up with regular-weight carpet tape when paint is dry.

If you prefer a heavier coat of paint, apply paint with a spreader, brush, or bottle tip directly on the fiberglass tape. Use a heavy layer of dimensional paints to attach jewels, beads, and sequins. Dry flat. Trim excess tape before removing paper backing.

The type of double-faced tape you use depends on how you will use it. Indoor-outdoor fiberglass carpet tape is not necessary if the glitter or paint strips you make are not used on clothing.

Remember, stickers with either a glue or tape backing should not be left on clothing for more than 12 hours at one time. (And don't forget to remove them from a garment before you launder it.) If stickers stay on too long, remove glue or tape residue with hair spray. When they are not in use, store your stickers on cooking parchment paper in a cool place.

Ready-Made Sequin Designs

For a time-saver, purchase a ready-made sequin design (these are attached to net backing). Unless the design is larger than 4″ square, one layer of double-faced fiberglass tape is all you need to hold it. Apply tape to the back of the design as directed under Carpet Tape Magic, above.

Silk Flowers

Silk flowers are always an interesting addition to clothing. With repositionable glue or double-faced tape, you can attach them whenever you want.

I prefer the non-stem type of flower. Stemmed

flowers have a wad of wire in the back, behind the center of the flower. To get them to lie flat on a shirt, you have to take them apart and reglue them (or take them apart and fuse them to the shirt). I don't mind gluing, but don't see much sense in doing it if there's a product available that doesn't need it.

Most EZ International flowers don't have that wire wad (some teeny ones do). Look for them in the bridal department of craft and fabric stores. They have a nice flat surface that's almost 1″ square. It's just the right size and in just the the right spot.

Snip the thin wire on the back about ⅛″ from the flower (Fig. 6-12). Bend it over to hold the petals in place. Snipping the wire releases the leaves. Peel the thin wire away from the back of the leaves.

Apply either repositionable glue or double-faced tape to the center back of both leaves and flower. You can embellish them before applying glue or tape to the back. Apply a thin line of glitter paint to the edges of the leaves and petals; you can add sequins or pearl-tone paint for dew drops.

Here are a few more suggestions for using flowers and leaves.

◆ Combine flowers with sequined leaves (Fig. 6-13).
◆ Use leaves and/or petals as negative stencils; press flat under parchment paper before painting.
◆ Use leaves for sun-printing fabric as described under Sun-Sensitive Fabric, above.
◆ Stick bunches of flowers around the brim of your sun hat or visor.

◆ Go all out—buy an inexpensive liner instead of an expensive shower curtain. The liner is no longer plain when you stick flowers on it (Fig. 6-14). (Use only fiberglass tape for this.)
◆ Stick flowers across the top of your mirror. Neither liner nor mirror needs a lot; just a few will do the job.

Fig. 6-14

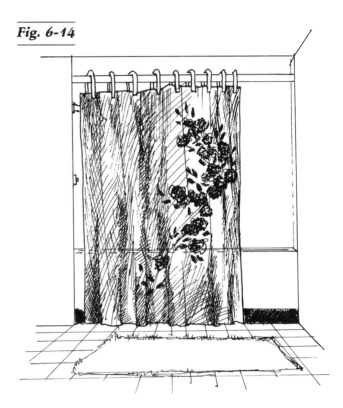

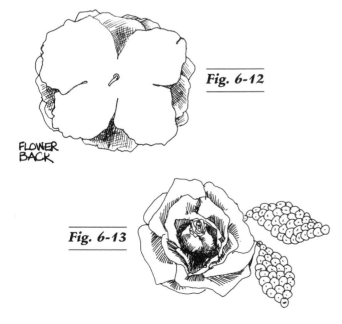

Fig. 6-12

FLOWER BACK

Fig. 6-13

Permanent Appliqués

Instead of using repositionable glue or double-faced tape, you can fuse, glue, or stitch your design to a garment for permanent placement.

Heat'n Bond Original (a paper-backed fusible) does not require high heat, so you can use it to fuse items that normally do not tolerate heat—sequins in particular (Fig. 6-15).

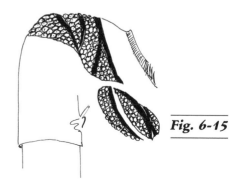

Fig. 6-15

Place a double thickness of towel or a layer of batting on your ironing board. Put a beaded or sequined design right side down, on this extra padding. Fuse Heat 'n Bond to the back of the sequin design (Fig. 6-16). Press at synthetic setting for 1 or 2 seconds. When cool, cut Heat 'n Bond paper and fusible to the shape of your design. Remove paper backing. Place the fused design padding, fusible side up. Place right side of shirt over design (Fig. 6-17). (Be sure it's positioned where you want it.) Press at silk setting, 5 to 7 seconds. Allow to cool before removing from ironing board.

If the fusible should release slightly after laundering, press on wrong side of garment for 5 to 7 seconds.

You can also glue decorations to your projects. When gluing, use only enough to secure the design to the fabric. Select a glue that dries soft.

Or you can stitch your design, by hand or machine.

The method you select (fusing, gluing, or stitching) to attach this type of appliqué to fabric is your choice. A decorative machine stitch, with decorative thread, is always an excellent choice. If you don't own a sewing machine, and hand-stitching is low on your list of fun things to do, you will obviously select fusing or gluing. Follow manufacturer's directions exactly when using either of these methods.

Clothing with beaded and sequined designs, whether fused, glued, or stitched, should be hand-washed and line-dried.

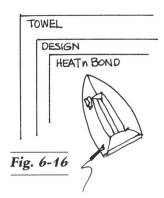

Fig. 6-16

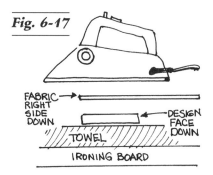

Fig. 6-17

Beaded Designs

I don't think it's possible to look at a copy of any craft magazine without seeing an ad for The Beadery. Beadery Crafts produces a wide range of acrylic jewels, stones, and beads. Several designs pictured in their ads are available in iron-on transfers.

After transferring the design to clothing, apply glue or paint to the markings. Push bead (jewel, etc.) into glue or paint (Fig. 6-18). Remember, glue or paint should squish up around the edges of the beads or jewels.

If you prefer not to use paint or glue, attach studs, nail heads, or pronged jewel settings with the appropriate tool on markings.

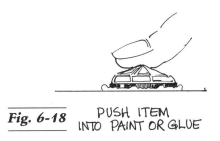

Fig. 6-18 PUSH ITEM INTO PAINT OR GLUE

Overpainting an Appliqué

Any brand of soft transparent or translucent paint (with or without crystals) that can be heat-set gives a distinct look to fused fabric appliqués.

Apply fusible to the back of a fabric appliqué. If your fusible has a paper backing, leave the backing in place. If your fusible does not have a paper backing, cover the fusible (which is placed on the wrong side of the appliqué) with cooking parchment paper before fusing. The cooking parchment paper will protect your iron from melted fusible. (See Fusibles in Chapter 9.) If you are using liquid fusible, cover the wrong side of the appliqué with cooking parchment paper before pressing, after fusible is dry.

Paint the right side of the appliqué with transparent or translucent paint (Fig. 6-19). The paint must be dry before you can fuse the appliqué to the background fabric.

Cover the ironing board with cooking parchment paper. Place painted appliqué right side down on board. Position the right side of the garment on the fusible. Cover the wrong side of the garment with cooking parchment paper or a pressing sheet. Press, on wrong side of garment, according to the directions for your fusible. Cool. Remove parchment paper.

You can, of course, add embellishments (beads,

Fig. 6-19

Fig. 6-20

sequins, cording, laces, etc.), or outline with paint after fusing the appliqué to the garment.

When you're using a piece of yardage containing several designs that will be cut out, leave it in one piece. Apply fusible to the wrong side of the yardage. Turn over; paint; dry flat. It's much faster brushing or rolling paint over one large piece than over several small pieces. Unless the designs are widely spaced, you really won't waste that much fusible or paint.

When the paint is good and dry (if in doubt, wait), cut the excess fabric and fusible from the edges of the design. Grade as directed in Chapter 7. Remove paper backing or cooking parchment paper from the back of the appliqués.

Decorating a Denim Jacket

Jean jackets are among the best outerwear garments to decorate. The only requirement for painting is a "cover-all" (opaque) paint. Transparent or translucent colors are swallowed whole by denim.

If you'd like to use a transparent or translucent paint, paint the design area with a neutral opaque color first, let it dry, then overpaint with transparent or translucent paint.

Several iron-on transfers are designed specially for dark fabrics, including denim. They're available in preshaded, painted, and velour designs. Remember, you can also make you own opaque transfer. (See Chapter 2.)

Denim and Lace

Denim and lace are a great combination (Fig. 6-20). And Battenberg lace is the ultimate. Stitch your own designs. Or buy ready-made inserts and collars for blouses (see Supply Sources).

Launder the jacket twice (warm water, low-heat dryer). Then launder it a third time with a piece of white scrap fabric (preferably 100% cotton). If the denim runs onto the white fabric, don't use the lace—unless you plan to dry-clean the jacket. If the denim doesn't run, hand-wash the lace, then dry it at low heat in a pillow case. Cover with cooking parchment paper and press. Check all stitching on the lace. Repair or replace any that is not secure.

Ready-made blouse inserts (lace and embroidery) will fit below the back collar of most jackets that don't have a yoke. Cut strips of yardage for cuffs and pocket flaps. Lace can be attached with glue or stitches. To prevent raveling, treat raw edges with seam sealant, such as Stop Fraying or Fray Check.

Don't get too heavy-handed with the glue. Use a glue that dries soft. Battenberg lace looks best when it appears to be floating over the fabric (as opposed to nailed down).

Before applying glue on marked design lines, place a piece of foam core or cardboard under the area of the design. After the lace has been positioned on the glue line, insert pins into the edges of the lace through the foam. Pins should be perpendicular to the lace edges. Leave pins in place until glue is completely dry.

If you are stitching instead of gluing, hold lace in place with water-soluble basting tape when stitching. Spray water on tape when stitching is complete. (See Basting Tape, Chapter 9.)

Use a fine machine embroidery, or use invisible thread when machine stitching. Test-stitch to determine the best needle size. Select a stitch that does not interfere with the design of the lace. The blind hem stitch works well for me.

I wouldn't recommend that you wear the jacket when you're cleaning the garage. It isn't as fragile as it looks, though. Reasonable use and care is all that's required.

Iron-on rhinestones are available from Seitec. They're a beautiful decorative addition to laced jackets.

If you'd prefer to remove jewels before laundering, use Snap-On Beads from Shafaii. Shafaii has both jewels and pearls that are easily removed and replaced when, or where, desired.

Wash your jacket inside-out on gentle-action cycle in warm water. Line-dry.

Lace on T-Shirts and Sweats

Lace inserts and yardage (Battenberg and others) can go just about anywhere on T-shirts and sweats. Traditionally the fabric is cut away from behind these types of needlework. But leaving the fabric in place provides stability and gives you more options for placement.

A band of lace across the front of a sweatshirt (Fig. 6-21) combined with a band around the lower sleeve is a fast way to add your touch to a shirt. You can stitch or glue it.

Prewash lace as directed under Denim and Lace, above.

Measure width of lace. Mark lines across shirt front for top and bottom edges of lace (Fig. 6-22).

If lace will be stitched, put water-soluble basting tape (see Chapter 9) on all marked lines. Tear off paper, position lace on tape, and push lace into tape. If you don't like the way it looks, now's the time to change it: Pick up the lace (the tape will be attached to the back), and reposition lace. Now stitch away! Launder to remove basting tape.

If you are gluing the lace, begin on shirt front. Bead a fine line of glue on line marking top edge of lace (Fig. 6-23). Finger-press lace into glue. Use a cotton swab to pick up any excess glue that oozes out from under the lace.

You can use a strip of masking tape just above the line at the top edge of the lace, and just below the line at the bottom edge of the lace. This will keep the glue off the shirt. When this glue has partially dried so that the lace is stable, glue the bot-

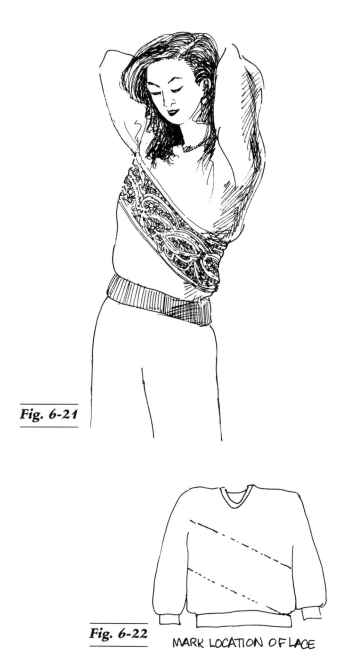

Fig. 6-21

Fig. 6-22   MARK LOCATION OF LACE

tom edge of the lace. Don't glue or stitch the bottom edge of ruffled lace.

Put a layer of foam board or cardboard inside shirt, then pin through lace into board until glue has dried. Wait for glue to dry before attaching lace to sleeves.

Slide a plastic bottle (usually a 2-liter soda bottle is just right) inside one sleeve. Stick pins through sleeve into bottle to hold fabric stable.

For sleeves, use the same gluing procedure as you used for shirt front band. Let the glue on the first sleeve dry before beginning second sleeve. Leave sleeves pinned to bottles until glue has dried.

Do not launder glued garment for 2 weeks. Turn inside out before washing.

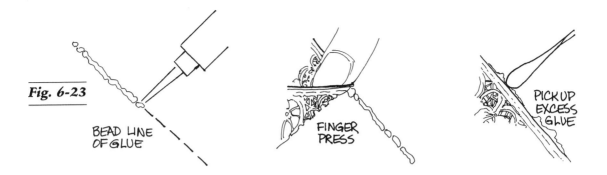

Fig. 6-23   BEAD LINE OF GLUE   FINGER PRESS   PICKUP EXCESS GLUE

Ruffled Eyelet Yoke

Ruffled eyelet (ruffled anything) is another quickie embellishment. Get the type with the bias tape stitched over the top edge. The bias edge curves nicely around a neckline (Fig. 6-24).

It is usually a little easier to stitch ruffled eyelet to the neckline of a shirt with inset sleeves, but you can use a shirt with raglan sleeves, too.

Using your shirt as a guide, make a freezer paper pattern of the yoke shape. The eyelet can be used just on the front or on both front and back. Press pattern on shirt. Put the shirt on to check the shape.

Prewash, dry, and press eyelet.

Using pattern as a guide, mark the outline of the yoke on the shirt with removable marker. Mark lines for each row of eyelet. Bias edge should be

covered by the next row of eyelet. Arrange rows so bias edge of last row is just below neck ribbing.

Begin gluing or stitching on bottom row. Work up to neck edge. The technique for gluing or stitching is the same as under Denim and Lace, above.

Do not launder glued garments for 2 weeks. Launder inside-out, gentle cycle. Line-dry.

Making a Tie

Fasturn has a sewing pattern for constructing neckties that eliminates the usual hassle of making a tie. The finished tie is easily made and perfect for fabric painting. Marble the fabric (see Marbling, Chapter 4 and in Chapter 9) before marking and cutting your pattern pieces. It's a lot less hassle marbling a piece of fabric than a completed tie.

If you want to stamp or print designs on the tie, you can do so before or after you stitch it.

Christmas Tree Shirt

This is a fun shirt to make and wear. You'll be the show stopper at every party you go to during the holidays. A sweat shirt is the perfect "canvas" for this creation. If you want the tree good and fluffy, machine wash and dry the shirt a couple of times after attaching ruffles and *before* adding paint, glitter, and jewels. After all the decorations go on, launder by hand and line-dry. Don't forget to remove the lights and music box before laundering.

Note: This shirt is not suitable to make for children under the age of 10. There are too many items (lights, buttons, etc.) that can be pulled off and swallowed.

To begin, make a paper pattern. I make my tree about 11″ tall and 8″ wide across the bottom. The rectangle (trunk) is about 3″ tall and 2″ wide.

Grab an 8½″ × 11″ piece of notebook or typing paper, and fold it in half the long way. Place a ruler ¼″ beyond the fold line, at the top of the paper. Angle the ruler to the bottom outside corner of the paper. Draw that line. Leave paper folded and cut on the marked line. Open paper—one Christmas

Fig. 6-24

tree! The top of the tree will be ½" wide. The bottom of the tree will be 8" wide. Now make a trunk pattern out of a small piece of paper.

Don't worry about making it look like a real tree—this thing is made out of fabric and covered with glitter, jewels and paint. Looking real is not the goal.

A full, fluffy tree will require 3 yards of ruffles. You can reduce the yardage if you wish. Prewash and dry your ruffles. I stick the 3 yards in a pillowcase with the top tied to wash and dry.

The best way to tell if this shape fits your shirt is to put the shirt on and stick the tree pattern on the front, using removable cellophane tape. If it's too long, cut it down to size. If it's too short, add width and length at the bottom. When the size and shape suit you, it's time to add guidelines for glue or stitching to the pattern.

Mark center of tree from top to bottom. Measure that line. Multiply the inches by 2. That's how many lines you'll have (twenty-two for my 11" tree) if you use Wright's Ruffles in a 3" width.

Draw lines every ½" across the tree, beginning at the bottom. If you use a narrower ruffle, reduce the distance between lines.

Fold shirt in half lengthwise. Press fold line to mark center front.

Position pattern on shirt so center line of tree is on center front of shirt. Tape pattern to shirt across entire bottom edge of pattern.

Slide a piece of chalk transfer paper under pattern. Transfer all lines, including outer edges, to shirt front (see Tracing and Transfer Hints and Supplies at the beginning of Chapter 2).

Before removing pattern, flip it back. Remove transfer paper. Check to make sure all lines are transferred and can be read. Re-mark if necessary.

You can stitch or glue the lace onto the shirt. If you stitch, first position basting tape on the marked lines. Begin at the bottom row on the shirt, and work your way up (Fig. 6-25). If you are using purchased ruffles, stitch between the two rows of stitching across the top. Don't worry about raw ends, since we're making rag strips and everything is raw edges.

If gluing, insert foam board or cardboard inside shirt. Apply glue to bottom marked line. Glue ruffle on bottom row. Glue next row. Work in this manner to top of tree. After you have glued on all rows, push pins through lace into foam board or cardboard to hold lace until it is completely dry.

When glue is absolutely dry (or all stitching is completed) slide scissors inside ruffle, along bottom fold. Cut along fold line of each ruffle, creating a double layer of fabric (Fig. 6-26).

Slide scissors under both layers of the ruffle and cut to the bottom of the stitching across the top. Cut every ¼" across the length (Fig. 6-27). Begin at the bottom row and work to the top. Be careful not to cut the shirt. Don't make little snips. Snips take more time, and have a way of clipping shirts.

Cut a piece of brown fabric for the trunk (corduroy looks kind of barky). Glue, fuse, or stitch so the trunk just shows under the bottom row of cut ruffles.

Now it's time to decorate the tree (Fig. 6-28)! You can go kind of hog-wild on this if you want— use jewels, nail heads, glitter, sequins, beads, crys-

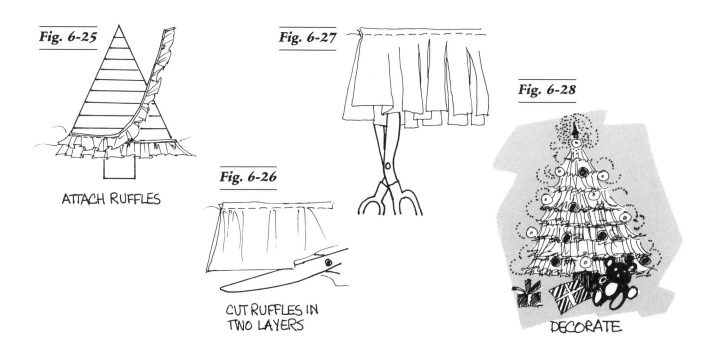

Fig. 6-25

ATTACH RUFFLES

Fig. 6-26

CUT RUFFLES IN TWO LAYERS

Fig. 6-27

Fig. 6-28

DECORATE

tal paint (perfect snow), laces, and who-knows-what-else.

Slide a music box insert under the tree trunk. You can get those little ones that need only a touch to start the music. Teeny lights, with a small battery pack, are available as well (see Christmas Shirt in Appendix D). Cut holes in the shirt behind the tree to stick them through. The battery goes on your waist.

Surround the tree with star sprinkles, sprayed glitter, or falling snow. (Sparkling tint or glitter paint looks kind of snowy.)

Any decent tree has presents. A Homespun Heart (see Supply Sources) has several buttons and blanks (buttons without the holes) that are perfect. You can stitch the buttons and use fiberglass tape for the blanks. Get an extra set and make earrings.

You can, of course, cut your own strips for this raggedy tree. A rotary cutter and ruler make fast work of strip cutting.

Place Mats and Napkins

Place mats and matching napkins can be marbled, stenciled, sprayed, stamped, or block-printed (Fig. 6-29). The painting is always the easy part. You can hem the edges in several ways. Read Edge Finishes in Chapter 9 for suggestions. If you want fringing, select fabrics that fringe quickly. Machine-stitch ½" from the edge; fringe to stiched line. Even faster is serging the edge if you have a serger.

For napkins, choose a poly/cotton in a color that matches one of the paints you used.

One fabric often overlooked for place mats is denim. It's heavy, doesn't show every little spot, washes easily, and fringes in the washing machine. I don't even bother to stitch around the edges. The heavier fabric I've used ravels only so far, then stops. I cut the long strings off after the first washing, and that's it!

Fig. 6-29

Throw Rugs

And don't forget throw rugs! Denim, canvas, and heavy duck are all excellent fabric selections. Block-print or stencil them for a fast project. Tape (heavy-duty types) can be used as blockers for large designs. Coordinate rugs with place mats and napkins or with bedroom and bathroom fabrics.

Throw rugs can be coated on the back with nonskid paint, which is found in craft and hardware stores. These stores also sell hardware that can be used to hang rugs as wall decorations.

Dye Ties

One fast painting method for place mats or throw rugs is not really painting. Dye Ties (Distlefink) are ties containing dried dye. (Now that's a tongue twister!)

After ties are in place, fabric is put into a pot of boiling water for 30 minutes. (Follow manufacturer's instructions.) The ties can be used for clothing or yardage.

Tube Projects

Fabric tubes are quickly stitched with the Fastube (see Golden Touch, Inc., in the Supply Sources). This specialty foot for your machine allows you to stitch tubes quickly and accurately in a variety of widths. The Fasturn is one of those gadgets that save time and frustration. With it, you can turn teeny tubes right side out in a snap.

Belts, baskets, quilts, and placemats are just a few of the items you can make from the tubes. Paint fabric before making tubes, or after you have finished stitching. For special baskets, stamp designs on the fabric strips before making tubes.

Gift Wrap and Tags

Use leftover paints to decorate gift wrap and tags. Those little bits left in the bottom of jars and tubes make stunning papers.

Squirt paint on the plastic side of freezer paper (Fig. 6-30). Go every which way—it's doodle time. Sprinkle with leftover glitter and spangles.

When it's good and dry, peel it off the plastic

Fig. 6-30

LEFT-OVER PAINT ON FREEZER PAPER

and stick the pieces on tissue paper. Stick it down before or after you wrap the box. It certainly takes care of any bow problems.

Use this method whenever you get three or four almost empty tubes and jars. When the paint is dry, roll the freezer paper up and stick it inside an empty tube from paper towels (Fig. 6-31). It'll keep for months and months. When you need it, it's ready to go.

When you want specific shapes or designs, trace them on the plastic. Fill outline with paint (Figs. 6-32 through 6-34).

Fig. 6-34

LET DRY, ROLL AND STORE UNTIL NEEDED

Fig. 6-31

Making Your Own Stickers

If your children are sticker collectors, they'll have a great time making their own stickers. Dizzle Paints has kits with all the needed supplies.

This is a great way to use leftover paint and just a fun rainy day activity.

Mobiles

Mobiles made from small wooden figures (bears, hearts, flowers) take just a few minutes to make (Fig. 6-35). Purchase those with holes drilled in the top. Look for them in crafts stores.

Fig. 6-32

Fig. 6-35

Fig. 6-33

Color figures with permanent markers. Drying time is immediate. Use either fine wire or invisible thread to attach figures for hanging.

Wooden Figures

You can also use wooden figures as gift tags. After coloring them with permanent markers, use a very fine-line marker to write the recipient's name on the back. Include the date and your name or initials, too. The tags can be used as tree ornaments.

And now the most important instruction of all. Sign and date each of your creations. You can add teeny initials on the back of a place mat, your full name in script across the back of a jacket, or something in between. Use anything from a fine-line marker to glitter paint to a stamp with your name. Or, you can hand- or machine-stitch your signature.

7

Appliqués and Outlining with Paint

Fabric appliqués can be used in a variety of ways on clothing. Appliqués can be fused, glued, stitched in place, or attached in a non-permanent way (lift-off). Fused appliqués often require the application of fabric paint around the edges. I think you'll find that the tips included in this chapter will solve some of the problems you may have encountered when outlining with paint. The "No Pain Satin Stitch" is exactly that!

Fused Appliqués

Please read about Fusibles and about Cooking Parchment Paper in the alphabetical listing in Chapter 9: see also Appendix D.

Fusible web or liquid fusible bonds just about any fabric to another fabric. The only restriction is that you cannot use treated or coated fabric for either the appliqué fabric or the background (base) fabric. Fusibles simply do not adhere to treated or coated fabrics. It's a case of guaranteed fall-off.

Many decorator fabrics (chintzes, polished cottons, etc.) are treated. Check the label at the end of the bolt before purchasing those fabrics. If you have your heart set on one of those fabrics, you'll have to stitch down the appliqué.

Because the permanent press treatment seals fibers, fabrics labeled "permanent press" won't accept fusibles, glues, or paints. Results will not be satisfactory with this type of fabric.

In order for liquid fusible or fusible web to work, you must follow manufacturer's directions. Iron temperature and pressing time are determined by the type of fusible. Too hot, too cool, too short, and too long will affect results.

The heat of the iron melts the glue, so that it becomes fluid. It's not set until the fabric is cool to the touch. If you pick it up too soon, the bond will not be secure.

Sliding the iron around all over the place also disturbs the bonding process. You must *press*—that is, lift the iron up when changing placement. Use steady pressure.

For fusibles requiring steam, be sure the iron is placed (and replaced) on the appliqué so the steam vents are over the edges of the appliqué. When a fusible requires a dry iron, place and re-place the iron so the steam vents are *not* over the edges. Steam vents prevent the iron from making good contact over areas of the appliqué. No heat—no stick.

Be sure to use the correct weight of fusible. The weight and types of the appliqué and base fabrics and the intended use of the finished project determine what weight fusible to use. You will find recommended uses printed on the manufacturer's information sheet included with the fusible.

Types of Fusibles

Fusibles are available in three forms: paper-backed, with no paper backing, and liquid.

Paper-backed fusibles. The paper layer on fusible web protects the iron. To fuse, place the non-paper side of the fusible against the wrong side of the appliqué and press (Fig. 7-1). You remove the paper after cutting out the appliqué. The fusible layer will be barely visible on the wrong side of the appliqué.

Several weights of paper-backed fusibles are available by the yard, in precut pieces, and in rolls of cut strips.

Fusibles with no paper backing. Think of fusible web without paper backing as stable glue

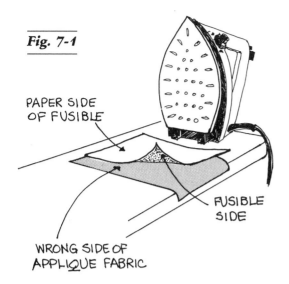

Fig. 7-1

PAPER SIDE
OF FUSIBLE

FUSIBLE
SIDE

WRONG SIDE OF
APPLIQUE FABRIC

(more stable than liquid, that is). You place pieces or strips exactly where fusible is needed.

To protect your iron, cover your project with cooking parchment paper (see Chapter 9) while you are fusing. Any fusible residue on the cooking parchment paper can be lifted off when the paper is cool to the touch. In fact, you can use cooking parchment paper in this way to turn your fusible with no paper backing into "paper-backed fusible."

Fusibles without paper backing are also available in several weights by the yard, in precut pieces, and in rolls of cut strips.

Liquid fusible. An appliqué coated with liquid fusible can be used in exactly the same way as one with an application of web.

Liquid fusible is similar to permanent fabric glue and can be used as a glue substitute. It is water-soluble until dry (goofs can be rinsed out).

Cover your project with cooking parchment paper to protect your iron when fusing. Remove paper when fusible is cool to the touch.

Liquid fusible is available in 4-ounce plastic bottles.

Applying Fusible to the Appliqué

Cut out the appliqué design, leaving at least ½″ extra fabric around the outer edges of the design.

Place a piece of cooking parchment paper (see Chapter 9) on the ironing board to keep fusible bits off the board. Then set the iron at the correct temperature (follow manufacturer's instructions). Lay the appliqué wrong side up on the cooking parchment paper.

If you are using fusible web, cover the appliqué with the fusible web. If the fusible web is paper-backed, the paper side will be up. If there is no paper backing, cover with cooking parchment paper. Press web as directed by the manufacturer.

When cool, remove the appliqué from the ironing board.

If you are using liquid appliqué, apply it to fabric, and let it dry slightly before removing from the ironing board.

Cutting Out the Appliqué (Grading)

The way you cut the edges of the appliqué before fusing to the base fabric is a factor in satisfactory results (Fig. 7-2).

The fusible not only bonds the appliqué to the base fabric, but also seals the edges of the appliqué to prevent raveling. Roll the outer blade of the scissors over the fabric when cutting out the appliqué. The edge will be cut on an angle. (The right, or outer, blade of the scissors is over the fabric for right-hand cutting.)

The top layer (fabric appliqué) will be slightly shorter than the bottom layer (fusible). The more you roll the scissors over the appliqué when cutting, the greater the angle. The difference between top and bottom layers is very obvious on heavy material.

This grading (that's what it's called) allows the fusible layer to extend beyond the appliqué. It helps secure the edge to the base fabric. Most important, it eliminates raveling problems. If the appliqué is a ravelly fabric (rayon, polyester blend, etc.), lay the right blade of scissors almost flat over fabric when cutting (see also Machine-Stitched Appliqués, below).

Applying the Appliqué to the Base Fabric

Position the appliqué right side up on the base fabric. When pressed (at the correct temperature, for the correct amount of time), the glue of the fusible

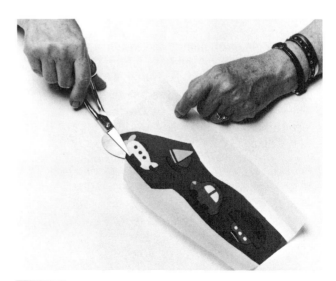

Fig. 7-2

bonds the appliqué to the fabric. Leave your project on the ironing board until the fabric is cool to the touch.

Glued Appliqués

See also Glues/Adhesives in Appendix D.

The following directions are generic. These are standard procedures for most glues. Before beginning, read manufacturer's instructions for the specific glue you are using. Some glues require heat-setting after they dry.

Liqui-Fuse, a liquid fusible, can be substituted for fabric glue. Follow the directions on the bottle.

Gluing appliqués can be tricky. Too much glue and you've got a sticky, gloppy mess. Too little means instant fall-off. I recommend pretesting. Simply cut an extra appliqué and glue it to a sample (old) shirt or piece of fabric. Include laundering in your pretest, too.

Gluing a large fabric appliqué is not recommended—use a fusible instead. Gluing is great for embellishments (see Embellishments in Chapter 9).

Before you apply glue, cut out your appliqué along edges. (Cutting fabric covered with wet glue is a mess.) Press freezer paper to the right side of the appliqué. Leave at least 2″ of paper beyond the edges of the appliqué.

Spread a thin, even coating of glue on the wrong side of the appliqué. It's usually easier to use a plastic charge card or paint spreader rather than a brush to pull the glue across the surface.

The ideal glue layer is thick enough to coat and fill the fibers of the fabric, and thin enough not to soak completely through to the right side.

Cut two slashes in the freezer paper outside the appliqué to use as handles when you pick up the appliqué and when you place it on the base fabric (Fig. 7-3).

Let the glue get slightly tacky before you place the appliqué down on the base fabric. (You did, of course, mark exactly where the appliqué was going to be placed before you started all of this.)

Press the appliqué down with your fingers, starting from the outer edges and working toward the center. This prevents the mess from oozing out and the edges from sticking to everything in sight. If the glue starts oozing up in the center of the ap-

pliqué fabric, dab it with a paper towel. Don't use water, which will dilute the glue. If there's a lot of glue squirting out the edges, use a cotton swab to pick up the excess. Before the glue is completely set, roll a pencil across the appliqué to remove any air bubbles.

Cover the appliqué with cooking parchment paper or plastic wrap. Place a *cold* iron or book on top of it. You want weight and even pressure. Remove the "weight" after the glue is completely dry. Don't even think of laundering the item for 2 weeks, even if the glue was heat-set.

If you end up with a gooey mess, don't put a weight on top of it. Remove the appliqué, and get everything into the washing machine or warm water immediately. The glue is water-soluble until it's dry.

Lift-Off Appliqués

See also Glues/Adhesives (Lift-Off or Pressure-Sensitive) in Appendix D; Tapes in Chapter 9.

Thanks to repositionable glue and double-faced carpet tape, nothing has to stay in one place or be used on only one thing. Chapter 6 features several ideas for lift-off appliqués.

Repositionable glue comes in two forms, liquid and spray. Liquids provide a stronger hold and are better for fabric. Sprays provide a light tack and are better for the backs of stencils and doilies. Glue sticks are not suitable for lift-off appliqués because the glue doesn't provide enough holding power.

Double-faced carpet tape is repositionable and is available in both regular (plastic) and heavy strength (fiberglass).

The type of product you use on the back of a lift-off depends on its weight and size, intended use, and surface of the base fabric. For example, fiberglass carpet tape is not required for a small silk flower. Liquid glue would not support the weight of a beaded appliqué.

Any repositionable-type product may cause damage to porous and painted surfaces. *Don't leave appliqués or embellishments on fabric for more than 12 hours.* Use caution when applying appliqués to leather or plastic.

Store lift-off appliqués made with liquid repositionable glue on freezer paper. Store those made with carpet tape on cooking parchment paper. Don't use wax paper as a storing surface.

Machine-Stitched Appliqués (The No-Pain Satin Stitch)

See also Stabilizers in Appendix D; Cooking Parchment Paper, Sewing Machine, and Stabilizing Fabric in Chapter 9.

Fig. 7-3

PICK UP TAB

FREEZER PAPER

Three methods work well for a smooth and even zigzag stitch around the edge of a fabric appliqué. (This tight zigzag stitch around an appliqué is called a satin stitch.) Read all three methods, then select the one you prefer.

Although instructions are for a traced design, you can also use any of these methods for appliqués cut from patterned fabric.

Before stitching, bond a layer of freezer paper (Fig. 7-4) or Totally Stable to the wrong side of the base fabric, or apply Perfect Sew, a liquid stabilizer. The stabilizer is under the area where the appliqué will be stitched. Don't skimp; the entire area should be stabilized.

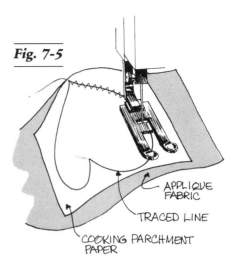

Fig. 7-5

APPLIQUE FABRIC

TRACED LINE

COOKING PARCHMENT PAPER

Fig. 7-4

METHOD 1

Supplies

♦ Appliqué fabric
♦ Cooking parchment paper
♦ Marker
♦ Glue stick or a repositionable spray glue
♦ Fusible thread (optional)
♦ Thread

Trace the design for the appliqué on cooking parchment paper. The cooking parchment paper should be at least 2″ wider and longer than the design. Make the tracing line as narrow and light in color as possible; a wide, dark line will show under the stitches.

Apply a light coating of glue stick or repositionable glue on the back of the tracing (a light coating will not stain the fabric). Position the tracing on the right side of appliqué fabric. Smooth paper flat.

Center your machine needle on the traced line and stitch a narrow zigzag stitch around the design (Fig. 7-5). The stitch should not be a tight satin

stitch. This stitching has two purposes: it stabilizes the edge of appliqué to prevent raveling, and you get to practice the ins and outs of the design.

Grading

Cut the excess fabric and cooking parchment paper away, next to the stitching (Fig. 7-6). Roll the outer blade of the scissors away from the edge of the appliqué. The left blade of the scissors is against the wrong side of the fabric (reverse if you are left-handed).

The paper over the appliqué (inside the traced lines) can be removed or left in place after you cut away the excess fabric. Usually it just falls off when the paper is cut away from the outer edges.

This grading procedure is the opposite of that explained under Fused Appliqués, at the beginning of this chapter. The position of the scissors allows you to cut under the stitches. Don't worry if you nip a stitch or two. You will stitch over these stitches later.

Apply a light coating of glue (spray or stick) to

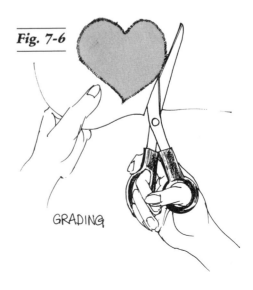

Fig. 7-6

GRADING

the wrong side of the appliqué. Position the appliqué on the base fabric. Press it down securely with your fingers. Remove the paper covering from the inner area of the appliqué, if you left it in place after the first zigzag stitching.

Center your machine needle over the first stitching. Stitch with a slightly wider and tighter zigzag stitch on top of the first stitches on the appliqué (Fig. 7-7).

The second zigzag stitches attach the appliqué to the base fabric. They also fill in areas on the appliqué edge not covered by the first stitches. The two lines of stitches combine to give the appearance of a tight satin stitch, without the hassle.

If you prefer not using glue to hold the appliqué to the base fabric for the second stitching, use Stitch 'n Fuse in the bobbin when doing the first stitching. Stitch 'n Fuse is a fusible thread product that bonds the appliqué to the base fabric. Press appliqué in place, using a hot iron and steam.

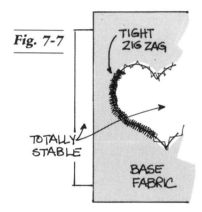

Fig. 7-7

METHOD 2
Supplies

♦ Appliqué fabric
♦ Freezer paper or Totally Stable
♦ Marker
♦ Glue stick or repositionable spray glue
♦ Fusible thread (optional)
♦ Thread

The second method is almost exactly the same as the first, but you don't glue the tracing to the appliqué.

Trace your design on Totally Stable or freezer paper. Trace on the dull side of Totally Stable or the paper side of freezer paper.

Press the shiny side of Totally Stable or freezer paper to the right side of appliqué fabric.

Stitch your first zigzag stitch (see Method 1) on traced line. Cut excess fabric and Totally Stable or freezer paper away, next to stitches. Follow grading procedure used in Method 1.

Use glue on the back of the appliqué to position it on the base fabric. Finger-press the appliqué in place. Remove Totally Stable or freezer paper from the design.

You can use fusible Stitch 'n Fuse thread in the bobbin in your first stitching instead of using glue to hold the appliqué in position on the background fabric for the second stitching. After cutting excess fabric from the edge of the appliqué (grading), press the appliqué on the background fabric. The thread will melt, forming a temporary bond.

Stitch your second zigzag stitches over the first stitches on appliqué. This stitching attaches the appliqué to the base fabric. The second zigzag stitch should be slightly wider and tighter than the first (see Method 1).

METHOD 3
Supplies

♦ Appliqué fabric
♦ Cooking parchment paper
♦ Fusible (web or liquid)
♦ Thread
♦ Freezer paper or Totally Stable (optional)

You can, of course, use a fusible to bond the appliqué to the base fabric, then stitch. Trace your design on cooking parchment paper. Apply a very light coating of glue to the back of the traced design, then place it on the right side of the appliqué fabric.

Stitch the first zigzag stitches on the traced line. Tear the parchment paper away from the outer edges, but don't cut the fabric yet.

Apply fusible (liquid or web) to the back of the appliqué. Cut excess fabric and fusible away, next to the stitched line. Follow the grading procedure explained under Fused Appliqués.

If you used paper-backed fusible web, remove the paper backing. Fuse the appliqué to the base fabric. When cool, complete the second zigzag stitching as directed in Methods 1 and 2.

You can substitute Totally Stable or freezer paper for cooking parchment paper when you use a fusible to attach the appliqué to the fabric. These supplies can be left in place, or removed, before you bond the fusible to the back of the appliqué. Remove the Totally Stable or freezer paper before you stitch the second zigzag stitches.

Outlining

Now that you have attached your appliqué, you may want to paint an outline around it as an accent. This kind of outlining requires lots of practice.

Paints suitable for outlining are usually (although not always) labeled "dimensional." The consistency of dimensional paint doesn't make outlining easier. To be dimensional, the paint has to be reasonably thick—otherwise, it would just collapse like an old balloon.

A simple test tells you if a paint is dimensional. Run a 4″ long, ¼″ wide line of paint on a piece of fabric. One quick look after it's dry tells you whether it's dimensional. Non-dimensional paint spreads or flattens as it dries; dimensional paint doesn't.

A description of dimensional paint is given in Chapter 3, under Types of Fabric Paint. Refer to Appendix B for information concerning specific brands and Appendix C for descriptions of tools used for fine-line application of paint.

Paint manufacturers are very aware of the difficulties of fine-line outlining. They are constantly improving bottle shapes, tips, and paint formulas.

Practice, Practice, Practice

One element manufacturers cannot provide, though, is practice! The more you do, the easier it is. Practicing on new items can get pretty expensive. An inexpensive option is to cover the pages of a children's coloring book with plastic food wrap and "trace" designs or shapes with dimensional paint.

If you have fused a design (birds, flowers, trees, etc.) cut from yardage, you probably have leftover designs or portions thereof in the scraps along selvage edges. Use them for practicing. Bond freezer paper to the wrong side of the fabric to stabilize it. Use paint left over from other projects, or purchase paint at sale prices to keep costs down.

Paint Applicators

Try cutting the tip of the bottle at a *slight* angle. If you cut off too much, or at too deep an angle, you will get more paint flow than you want. Put some paint into an empty bottle. Cut the tip and practice to see if that is easier for you. Remember to drag the point of the angle on the fabric.

Refillable bottles made of soft plastic are available in different sizes. These are referred to as "resist bottles" or "fine line applicators." (See Appendix C.) Metal tips for those bottles are available in three sizes of openings (Fig. 7-8). The tips can be used on other paint and glue bottles as well.

Refillable bottles sold with metal tips are easy to use because they are so soft. The tips are metal because the bottles are intended for Resist, which must be pushed into the fabric (see Chapter 9). The same principle holds true for fabric paint.

Because the metal tip fits bottles of several paint brands, it isn't always necessary to transfer your paint to the smaller refillable bottle. If the tip fits the bottle you are using, push the tip down firmly. It has little grooves on the inside that hold it on the

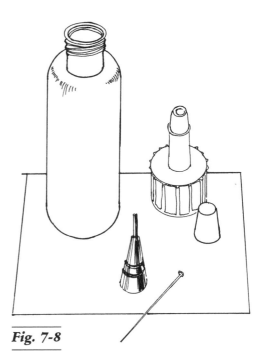

Fig. 7-8

bottle top. Just make sure it's a tight fit. The tip is a life saver if the teeny snip you made when you cut the top off a bottle ended up being a big chunk.

Rupert, Gibbon & Spider sells a 16-ounce applicator bottle made from a very soft plastic. Three sizes of tips are made specifically for the bottle. I like the larger size, which is particularly nice for applying glue lines.

Remember to shake the bottle toward the tip (with your finger over the tip). Paint (or glue) must be forced into the tip area to reduce the possibility of air bubbles.

A large plastic syringe (see Syringes in Appendix C) can be filled with paint or glue (Fig. 7-9). The plunger pushes the paint out the tip. Some

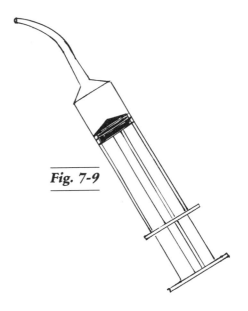

Fig. 7-9

people find this tool easier to use than a bottle. The tip is long; some tips are slightly curved, which enables you to see where the paint is going. The tip can be cut on an angle, if you prefer (more things to practice!).

To fill, remove the plunger from the syringe. Fill the cylinder with paint, leaving about ¼″ space at top. Hold your finger over the tip and stir the paint to eliminate air spaces. I use a wooden or bamboo skewer, but you can also use wire. Replace the plunger. Hold the syringe tip up and push the plunger until paint begins to flow from the tip. You'll know instantly if any air locks remain because if so, paint won't come out of the tip. Add more paint as necessary, but repeat the beginning process each time.

If you want to store paint or glue in a syringe for short periods (up to 2 days), you need to plug up the tip so the paint won't dry up. One of the reasons I like the syringe from Rupert, Gibbon & Spider is that it comes with a snap-on cover for the tip (see Jacquard, Appendix B).

If you use a different brand of syringe, push a pin (carefully!) down the tip. The plastic head of the pin will keep the paint from drying out.

When paint is removed from syringe, clean the syringe immediately. Remove the plunger. Rinse the plunger and barrel in soapy water. Use your stirring wire or a piece of covered floral wire to clean any paint particles from the tip. Rinse the plunger and barrel in clear water.

If you don't have time to clean it right then, stick it in water so that the paint won't dry up in the syringe.

Testor's Gluing Tips (see Supply Sources) can be used on the tip of most syringes and some paint bottles. These plastic tips, which have a very small opening, are excellent when you want a very fine line of paint. The end of the tip can be cut on the angle. Be sure to push the tip securely on the bottle or syringe. The last thing you want is the tip falling off in the middle of a line and the paint flying all over the place. (Test, then retest.)

The disposable bags and metal tips used for cake frosting may be the answer to your problems (Fig. 7-10). (See Wilton Enterprises in the Supply Sources.) The consistency of frosting and of thicker types of fabric paint (glitter, stretch, puff) is similar. Just don't let the kids think that's frosting in the bag. (Of course you should label all your painting supplies and keep them out of the reach of children.)

Disposable plastic frosting bags are easily cleaned for reuse. I cut about 4″ off the wide end of the bag to make it easier to handle. Use a connector (screw-on collar) on the bag when you want to

Fig. 7-10

use more than one decorator tip with the same paint. The connector also holds the tip securely on the bag.

Getting Ready

Before you even think about painting, shake the bottle. The tip should be pointed downward (make sure it's closed). The shaking motion is the same as used for hammering a nail (a big nail with a little hammer!).

Remove the cap and squeeze the bottle until the paint starts to come out of the tip. If nothing comes out, there's either dried paint in the tip or an air lock in the bottle. If the paint has not been opened and used, it is highly unlikely that dried paint is in the tip. If the paint has been opened and previously used, remove the tip. If the tip is not screwed into the bottle, use pliers to pull it out of the bottle. Clean out the dried paint by pushing a straight pin or piece of wire through the tip. Rinse the tip with clean water before putting it back on the bottle.

The size of the tip determines how fat the wire can be. Most tips are large enough to accept 20-gauge wire (the larger the number, the thinner the wire). Wipe paint off the wire and keep track of it because you'll use it again and again. That little piece of wire is a real time saver. Twenty-gauge wire is available in craft, grocery, hardware, and variety/discount stores.

If there was no dried paint in the tip, then there's a big air-bubble in the bottle (this is called air lock). Your first tendency will be to squeeze the bottle with as much force as possible. Either nothing comes out the tip, or a big glob comes flying out (usually when you're looking down the tip).

When air lock develops, run wire down the tip into the bottle (you do not have to remove the tip from the bottle). Stir the paint with the wire. Really crank it around inside the bottle, and pull the wire up and down in the bottle. You want to break up those bubbles of trapped air.

When the paint is flowing freely from the tip, draw a painted line about 4 inches long on a paper towel. If the paint is not flowing freely, the bottle still has air bubbles. Stir again with the wire.

Stirring glitter paint with the wire eliminates the all-glue, no-glitter, globs. How many times have you had to run several test lines before you finally hit glitter? Glitter paints require a lot of shaking before the glitter is completely mixed in the bottle. If you stir with wire, you'll still have to shake the bottle, but the shaking time is greatly reduced.

If the paint bottle is really stiff, and it's hard to squeeze the bottle with enough force to produce an even flow from the tip, warm water will soften the plastic bottle. Tighten the cap and drop the bottle into a cup of warm (not hot) water. Usually 1 or 2 minutes will soften the bottle.

But remember, no painting until the paint flows easily, and evenly, out of the bottle or container. That test line on the paper towel has to be perfect.

How to Paint

Don't begin painting unless you have enough time to complete the job. Hurrying has a way of creating problems. Select a work area that is well lit. Most important, choose a comfortable spot in which to do this type of detail painting. If you're leaning over a table that is too low, you'll increase the chances for mistakes.

Any activity that requires a steady hand requires that your lower arm, and hand, rest on a table. Sit down to do this type of painting. Keep your lower arm on the table as much as possible. If it makes things easier, steady the bottle with the index finger of your non-writing hand (Fig. 7-11).

Be sure the appliqué is positioned so you can see where you will be painting. (You already know where you have painted.) Stop often and rearrange things.

Always keep your hand and arm below, or to

the side of, wet paint. That position eliminates the possibility of "arm smudge." Begin large designs in the center and work to the edges.

The tip of the bottle should be to the side, or in back of, the paint flow. Don't drag the tip through the paint.

The tip of the bottle must be in contact with the fabric for paint to form a good bond. Don't hold the bottle above the fabric, so paint drops from the bottle. Not only will the line be uneven, but the paint will probably fall off in the first few launderings. (*Note:* A couple of paints *do* require that you hold the tip off the fabric—another reason to read instructions on containers carefully before beginning painting.)

Fabric paint is not absorbed by the fibers; it coats the fibers. Pushing the tip into the fabric ensures a better coating. The tip of the bottle should dent the fabric when you are outlining.

You want the paint to bond to the fabric, and you also want the paint to seal the edge of the appliqué to the fabric. Fabric paint not only adds a special touch to an appliqué, it reinforces the glue or fusible used to secure the appliqué to the base fabric. Position the tip so the paint overlaps the edge of the appliqué. Figure 7-12 shows paint being applied to a fused appliqué.

Don't try to outline the entire appliqué in one squeeze. Maintaining consistent pressure (the big squeeze) on the bottle for an extended period is difficult and causes the paint line to become uneven.

Short lines are not only easier to do; they provide a break in the paint. Painting in long, continuous lines can cause those little cracks across a line that start showing up after you've worn a shirt a few times. (The other culprit is incorrect laundering.) The wider the line of paint, the greater the

Fig. 7-11

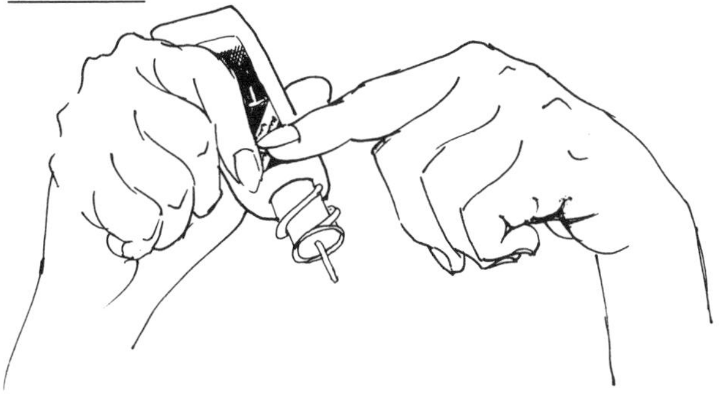

Fig. 7-12

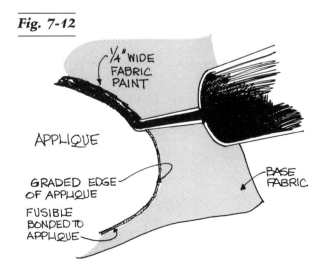

¼" WIDE FABRIC PAINT

APPLIQUE

GRADED EDGE OF APPLIQUE

FUSIBLE BONDED TO APPLIQUE

BASE FABRIC

opportunity for cracks. The breaks are really expansion joints.

As your hand or fingers become tired, you release pressure on the bottle. That's when air enters the bottle—another chance for air lock and the big splotch. Before you start painting again, shake the bottle toward the tip vigorously, and do a short test line on paper towel. If paint does not flow freely, use the wire to break up the air bubbles.

When you start again, place the tip just up to the end of the previous line. Squeeze the bottle gently so the new line connects to the previous line. If you do happen to squeeze a little too hard, the connection can be smoothed with the point of a pin the next time you stop (Fig. 7-13).

When you have finished, use the point of a pin to pop any small air bubbles in the painted line.

Problems occur if the fabric ruffles as you drag the tip along the shirt. That's why you bond freezer paper to the wrong side of the fabric before painting. It holds the fabric steady and also serves as a shirt board (See Shirt Boards in Chapter 9). Leave the paper in place until the paint has dried.

I found out quite by accident that having a padded surface under the fabric was a double plus. It was much easier to push the paint into the fabric, and it was also easier outlining in a very fine line. I use the same old padded surface I always use—my ironing board.

If you don't want to use your ironing board for painting, use two or three layers of quilt batting for

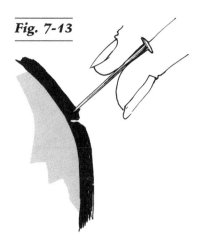

Fig. 7-13

a padded surface. Don't use towels; terry cloth has too many bumps.

To get the best benefit from the padded surface, use plastic food wrap inside the shirt as a shirt board. If the fabric is ruffling a great deal, you'll have to bond freezer paper to the wrong side of the shirt.

Unfortunately, there is no single applicator (or paint) that guarantees a perfect fine line. I do know results improve with practice. Try out different paints and applicators, and use those that work for you. Begin outlining basic shapes and advance to more intricate designs. And don't get discouraged when you see someone demonstrating the technique in a store or on TV. Remember, they were hired because they are good.

8

Oops!

I think I have enjoyed (endured) every conceivable type of painting disaster. You name it, I've pulled it off.

Every goof happened because I was either in too big a hurry, tried to do too many things at the same time, didn't read instructions (now there's a confession for you!), or tried to get to the phone before it stopped ringing.

Goofs happen. Expect them. The goal is to hold the numbers down as much as possible. The hope is to be able to turn them into a non-disaster. I think "creative experience" is a rather pleasant way of describing the events following a goof (Fig. 8-1).

Because most problems happen with paint, it seemed the logical place to begin. Remedies for other supply goofs follow.

Paint

Regardless of the size or type of mishap, don't let paint dry before you fix it. Changing a tire (without a jack) is easier than trying to get dried paint out of fabric.

Outlining Goofs

When a nice fine line suddenly turns into a big splotch, use the side of an expired plastic charge card or plastic spoon to scrape the paint off the fabric (Fig. 8-2). Get off as much as possible. Use a soft, dry toothbrush to scrub and lift the paint from the fibers (Fig. 8-3).

If the remaining paint did not penetrate the fibers, rub the spot with either cold water or a premoistened towel product for infants or adults. (Ingredients listed on the container must include alcohol.)

Fig. 8-1

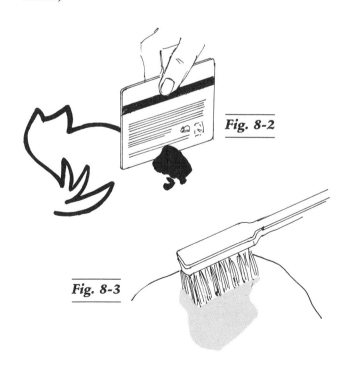

Fig. 8-2

Fig. 8-3

If cold water or the premoistened towel doesn't remove the paint, rub a brush cleaner or spot remover heavily into the area. Follow manufacturer's directions. Sometimes this procedure must be repeated. If so, leave the cleaner or remover on for a longer period before rubbing.

NOTE: Never mix one cleaning product with another. Rinse one product out thoroughly before trying another.

You can't paint over alcohol, cleaners, or removers. Launder the fabric after using these items.

If the fabric has other painted areas, let them dry after you remove the spot and before you launder. Heat-set the paint, if required. Launder fabric as directed on paint container. Line-dry. Finish painting.

If the paint penetrated through the fabric, you'll have to use hair spray (the hair spray must include alcohol as an ingredient), rubbing alcohol, or fingernail polish remover (*not* acetone-based) and a lot of rubbing. Launder as soon as possible. Line-dry.

Hair spray, alcohol, or nail polish remover may cause fabric to fade. Pretest as follows: Keep the spot area wet with paper towels. Rub the selected remover into an inconspicuous area of the fabric; check for colorfastness.

If the fabric does fade, try a brush cleaner or spot remover. Test first, following the directions on the container. Launder as soon as possible. Use both washing soda and laundry detergent in the wash water. Line-dry. Other painted areas may be damaged from this laundry method, so you should use it only as a last resort.

You can see that these treatments can cause more grief than the original problem. Sometimes it's better to try other methods. The first option you have is to scrape off as much paint as possible. Rub spot with cold water. And do nothing else.

If the spot isn't too large or glaring, you'll probably have good results. Complete painting the dry areas. When the fabric is dry, paint the area with the spot.

The second option is to turn the splotch into part of the design (Fig. 8-4). Scrape off as much paint as possible before beginning the Creative Experience.

Here are a few suggestions; I'm sure you'll have more. Use a soft, flat brush or fine-line brush to feather the outline paint away from all edges. Brush a slightly darker color paint around the edges. You can sprinkle glitter on that darker paint. Sometimes it's possible to place a small appliqué or embellishment on top of the splotch. Run a squiggle line of another color parallel to the first outline.

Each situation is different. If the splotch happened at the beginning of the project, removing all

SPLOT

BEE APPLIQUE
WITH GLITTER

Fig. 8-4

paint, laundering, and starting over is often the best way. But if you've completed most of the project, turning the splotch into part of the design is usually the best solution.

Smudges

Your arm or hand is the main culprit here. Dangling bracelets do a pretty good job, too. Any solution suggested in the preceding section of this chapter can be used on small smudges. The big ones are another story.

I had the happy experience of flipping a newly painted shirt all over the front of me (Fig. 8-5). The painted shirt was a disaster. My shirt was a mess. I call it my Super Smudge! The paint was a shiny bright yellow. My shirt was navy and brand new.

Getting the shirt off was the first task. A lot of paint ended up in my hair. (I did not think any of this was necessary research.)

Fig. 8-5

I threw the shirts into a bucket of cold water, and I ran (literally) to the shower. After my hair was back to normal, I started scrapping paint off both shirts.

They were colorfast, so I used rubbing alcohol liberally. I even brushed it in with a toothbrush. The first cold-water wash (detergent and washing soda) did a pretty good job.

I used more alcohol and washed the shirts again in cold water. Both shirts look almost as good as new. There are a few pin-dots of yellow here and there on the navy shirt. The painted shirt was aqua and is virtually spot free.

So it can be done. But to get it all out takes more than a minute or two.

Glue

Washable glue will wash out, although it may take two or three times before the glue is completely gone. Just keep washing.

Permanent glues and repositionable glues hang on to fabric with almost as much tenacity as paint. Don't let the glue dry if you want to remove it. Launder in hot water as soon as possible after the mishap.

One product that does dissolve repositionable glues, and fiberglass tape residue on scissors, is Goo Gone. As the name says, the goo is gone after you use the stuff. Do heed the warnings on the bottle, and follow all manufacturer's instructions when using this product.

Alcohol-based products and fingernail polish remover usually dissolve glues. Ammonia works sometimes. Start with a window cleaner containing ammonia. Use ammonia at half-strength as a last result. Never mix ammonia (or any cleaning product) with any other product. Rinse one product out thoroughly before trying another.

White vinegar can be used. The glued area must soak in the vinegar long enough for the glue to soften.

Dried glue can be lifted from some non-porous surfaces with duct tape. Place a strip of tape on the surface, press down securely, then pull off the tape. The tape strip can be used until it no longer picks up glue.

This is how I clean up the back of stencils when the buildup gets heavy. Usually one strip of tape takes care of the entire back.

One word of advice: many glues and paints have a plug inside the cap. It's there to keep the bottle from leaking during shipping. If the glue or paint isn't coming out of the tip of a new bottle, check to see if there's a plug inside the cap.

Once, I presumed the glue was very (very) slow in coming out of the bottle. If I squeezed harder, out it would come.

It came out all right. The side of the bottle split. This made the yellow paint business seem like child's play. You'd never believe how far and fast 4 ounces of repositionable glue flies through the air.

I sure didn't have time to ponder the situation, I was starting to stick to the kitchen floor (Fig. 8-6). This time I galloped to the shower—forget about running.

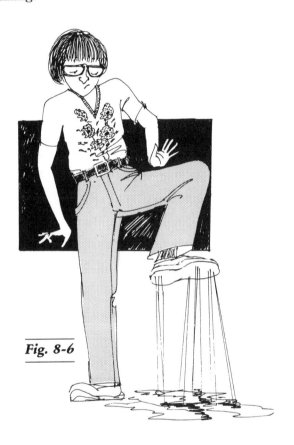

Fig. 8-6

To make a long story short, it all cleaned up. My clothing endured hot water, heavy detergent, and three trips through the washing machine. I'm not sticking to everything. (And things aren't sticking to me.) Fingernail polish remover finally did the job on the kitchen floor. My clothes still have a few spots here and there, but my clothes usually have a few spots here and there.

The good news was finding out I'm that strong. I never thought I could split a plastic bottle.

Fusibles

Fusibles rate a 10 for speed. They do demand a little respect, though. There's nothing quite as frustrating as fusibles on the bottom of a hot iron (see Iron Disasters, below, for advice on cleanup). Any fusible stuck where it doesn't belong has a way of wrecking your day.

Of course, prevention is best. If your iron doesn't have a non-stick surface, consider buying a Telfon plate that snaps on. It won't keep fusibles off the iron, but it does make cleanup easier.

Be sure your ironing board, the bottom of your iron, and your pressing cloth are fusible-free before you begin ironing. Those teeny pieces have a way of getting fused to the wrong place.

Use cooking parchment paper when fusing (see Cooking Parchment in the alphabetical listing in Chapter 9). Remember, when reusing the paper, pick off any fusibles remaining from the last use.

Rubbing alcohol and alcohol-based hair spray do a remarkable job of cleaning up fusibles mishaps. But do not use them on a hot iron. See the next section for advice on cleaning irons.

Apply alcohol with a cotton swab or use hair spray on fabric and the ironing board cover. Some hair sprays may leave a sticky film, so test before using. When the liquid has evaporated, the fusible can be rolled into a ball and removed. Launder fabric to remove alcohol or hair spray before fusing or adding paint. Wipe ironing board cover off with a damp cloth. Do not use board until cover is dry.

Iron Disasters

Use hair spray on the bottom of a *cold*, unplugged iron for minor cleanups. Wipe clean when dry.

I'll admit I was somewhat dubious when Heat 'n Bond told me that softener sheets (for clothes dryers) removed fusibles from the bottom of the iron. I couldn't believe the results when I tested it. The fusible is gone in a snap. No need to let the iron cool. The temperature used for the fusible is fine.

Protect the ironing board with cooking parchment paper or two layers of paper towels. Put the iron on the softener sheet for about 15 seconds.

Run the iron over a piece of scrap cotton to clean the residue from the bottom.

The first couple of times you do this will be a surprise. Clean as the bottom of your iron may look, the softener sheet seems to loosen up all kinds of stuff that were hiding on the bottom of the iron.

Unless you're into lingering scents, use unscented sheets. The ironing board really soaks up the perfume from those sheets, even though cooking parchment paper or paper towels were placed on the board.

If the bottom of the iron is one huge mess of paint, fusibles, glues, and glitter, rubbing alcohol will clean it up faster than a softener sheet. Line the bottom of a disposable pan with paper towels. Saturate the towels with rubbing alcohol. Sit *cold*, unplugged iron on towels. Remove iron in 30 minutes. After the alcohol has evaporated, the mess should wipe off. If the mess is layers thick, you may have to repeat this a couple of times (or buy a new iron). Wipe iron off with a damp cloth before using.

This method works if you happen to put a hot iron down on a piece of plastic, but you must let the iron cool completely before you clean it with alcohol. When I took the iron out of the pan, the whole hunk of plastic fell right off. Fortunately (for me and my iron) I had been given the rubbing alcohol tip from Aleene's the day before. I'll admit I had not planned to put it to such a severe test.

Keep in mind that accidents will happen. They're a part of any creative activity. Rarely are they irreversible.

The worst thing you can do is concentrate on things that have gone wrong. Instead, think of all the things that have gone right!

9

The Answer Box

This is the place to look when you need information, descriptions, and explanations for the many creative activities possible with fabric paint. Supplies and tools used for these activities are also explained. Topics are listed alphabetically and include cross-references.

ANTIFUSANT

See also Chapter 3, Appendix A, and Appendix B.

An antifusant prevents marker ink from spreading across the fibers of a fabric. With this product you won't have to worry about a little dot turning into a large circle when a marker tip is pushed into fabric. An antifusant also controls the spread of paint across a fabric. It is often applied to silk and other fine wovens before painting.

I prefer No Flow (available from Rupert, Gibbon & Spider, Inc.) because it rinses out of the fabric.

APPLIQUÉS

See Chapter 7.

BASE FABRIC

See also Fiber Content; Silk and Silk Painting; Stabilizing Fabric—all in this chapter. This term indicates the fabric that an appliqué or embellishment is attached to or the fabric that is painted on (shirt, jacket, pillow cover, yardage, etc.).

BASTING TAPE, WATER-SOLUBLE

This item is about as handy as a supply can be. It's a narrow, double-faced tape that dissolves in water. It hangs on like glue until immersed in water—

then it's gone. Best of all, it does not clog up the sewing-machine needle.

I prefer the basting tape manufactured by J. & P. Coats. The paper backing peels off easily, and the tape dissolves quickly. It's available in two widths—my favorite being ⅛" wide.

Position the tape on the fabric wherever you will be stitching any items (Fig. 9-1). (The sticky side is placed on the fabric.) Run your fingernail over the paper backing. This procedure pushes the tape into the fabric for a good seal.

After positioning the tape exactly where you want to stitch any items, remove the paper backing. Then push the items being stitched on top of the tape. (Basting tape even holds buttons in place for hand or machine stitching.)

To remove the paper backing, twist the tape until the paper breaks. Then slide the point of a pin under the break and lift up the backing from the tape (Fig. 9-2). Even with the backing removed, the tape can be repositioned one or two times. If the backing is not removed, the tape can be picked up and repositioned repeatedly.

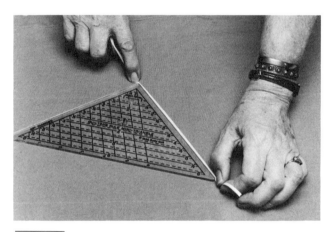

Fig. 9-1

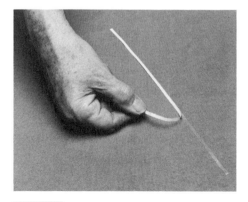

Fig. 9-2

Nothing else does a better job of holding cross-locked beads (Fig. 9-3) or sequins in place for machine or serger stitching. (See also Beads, Cross-Locked Glass, this chapter.) Use basting tape to hold cut strips when stitching "rag" designs. Not only does this tape hold the fabric strips in place, but it gives you a visual of the design before stitching. It's also great help when positioning fabric and adornments for crazy quilt designs.

If you live in a humid climate, keep the tape in a zipped plastic bag or closed container in the refrigerator. Humidity, heat, and sunlight soften basting tape.

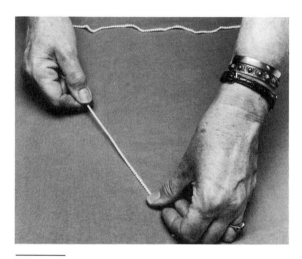

Fig. 9-3

BEADS

See also Embellishments, this chapter.

Acrylic. See Embellishments, this chapter.

Cross-Locked Glass. These little beauties end the hassle of the rolling bead. Each bead is attached; you'll notice threads running under and through each bead. Cut thread ends do have to be secured, but a teeny drop of glue, paint, or Fray Check handles this.

To embellish a painted design with a three-dimensional dingle-dangle, slide a pony bead on a 1½" length of cross-locked beads. Glue ends of the bead length next to each other on the fabric. Attach embellishment to fabric with glue, paint, or stitches. (See also Basting Tape, Water-Soluble, this chapter.) Now you've got a great dingle-dangle (Fig. 9-4), or a lot of dingle dangles!

Single (Crystal, Rhinestone, and Semiprecious). I'm a real bead lover. I love spending hours and hours hand-stitching teeny ones on fab-

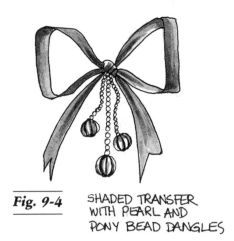

Fig. 9-4 SHADED TRANSFER WITH PEARL AND PONY BEAD DANGLES

ric. I've been told that some people think hand-beading is tedious, but I can't figure out why.

Bead shops and catalogs are loaded with the most glorious goodies you can imagine. Not every bead is teeny, and not every bead has to be hand-stitched.

Single beads can be glued or fused in place. Follow the same procedure used for acrylic stones and jewels (see Embellishments, this chapter). Medium- and large-sized beads are outstanding as buttons. They are also the perfect touch for artwear—just be sure you purchase those that are predrilled.

Prong settings hold beads and are attached to fabric in the same way a stud or nailhead is. They're fast and easy to use, and they come in a variety of sizes.

BLANK CLOTHING AND ACCESSORIES

See also Clothing Labels, this chapter.

Blank items are those considered printable or paintable. For a long time about the only blank items were silk. Now cotton and poly/cotton items are available in several fabric paint supply catalogs. Items are usually white or off-white, although there is a limited selection of black items. Some are labeled "Ready to Paint." This means that they're prewashed. Prewash those that do not have this label (see Prewashing, this chapter).

Don't feel that you are limited to using blank items for painting. Any fabric can be used—as long as it doesn't contain acrylic fibers.

BLOCKERS

See also Print Blocks; Reverse Blocks; Stamps; Stencils; Tapes—all in this chapter.

Blockers keep paint off fabric. They're different from a resist because they're not absorbed by the fabric. Technically they're a negative stencil. The most common blocker is tape.

Thanks to all the stickers on the market today, there is an endless array of shapes and designs that can be used as blockers.

An office supply store is loaded with removable labels (Fig. 9-5). The next time you have a chance, check out the array of basic shapes used for those labels. Don't overlook notary seals, stars, or those great reinforcements used on the holes of notebook paper.

Precut mats for pictures are also excellent blocks. Apply repositionable glue (spray or liquid) to the back of mat before securing on a fabric. Mats are available in numerous sizes and shapes. The best ones to use are those that have a beveled inner edge. Attach a negative stencil or blocker to the fabric. Center the mat over your design. Then paint from the inner mat edge to the center of your design. Lift the blocker when the paint is dry.

Blockers work best when paint is brushed or rolled over them, and when paint is thick enough so it does not seep under a blocker. Be sure not to push any paint under the edges of a blocker.

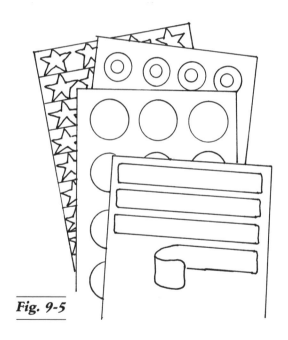

Fig. 9-5

CIRCLES

The "string tied to a pencil" system of drawing a circle used to drive me up the wall. I always ended up with a circle that looked like an egg. One day I noticed that nice little hole at the end of my tape measure. My circles have been round ever since.

You need a fiberglass tape measure (they don't stretch), a push pin, a pencil or marker, and a surface that you can stick the push pin into. The surface has to be larger than the circle you will be drawing. (A push pin looks like a thumbtack wearing a tall plastic hat.)

If the tape measure does not have a little hole in the metal end, make one by pounding a nail through the metal end. (Dritz Lifetime tapes do have a hole.)

If the only surface that is larger than the circle is your best table, cover it with cardboard or foam board. Otherwise the push pin will leave a hole in the tabletop.

Determine the measurement of the radius (the distance from the center of the circle to the outer edge). Then push the pin through the tape at that measurement. It should go through the center of the tape width.

Next put the fabric (paper or whatever you want the circle drawn on) on the soft surface. Push the pin/tape measure through the center of the fabric and into the surface, making sure it's secure and won't pull out.

Finally, flatten the tape and stick a pencil or marker into the hole in the end. Now all you have to do is swing the full arc of the circle (Fig. 9-6).

The tape should be taut when you're marking the circumference (the distance around the outer edge of the circle). If the pin is wobbly, hold it down with your nonwriting hand. Keep the pencil or marker perpendicular (straight up and down) to the surface. If a pencil doesn't leave a mark you can easily see, use any marker that fits into the hole. (A permanent marker is best since you don't have to worry about it bleeding.)

When the circumference must be an exact measurement, remember to take into account the distance from the end of the tape to the hole when placing the push pin. Most of the time, the hole is ¼″ from the end of the tape. If you need a circle with a radius of 10″ (or a diameter of 20″), place the pin at the 10¼″ mark. The pencil will then be 10″ from the center of the circle. If you put the pin in at the 10″ mark, it would be ¼″ shorter than 10″.

The tape will probably be 60″ long. That means

you can draw circles from ½″ to 10′ in diameter—and each one will be round.

CLEANUP TIPS

See also Dish Drainer; Stamp Pads; Stencils—all in this chapter.

I don't enjoy cleaning up messes. Since I'm an expert at slopping paint over everything, I had to find ways that took the mess out of cleanup.

Plastic food wrap sticks like glue to nonporous surfaces that have been wiped off with a damp sponge or cloth, making it a great drop cloth. Brand X works just as well as the more expensive food wrap. Use plastic food wrap to protect counters, sinks, tubs, walls, and faucet handles. Cover the counters surrounding your work area. Line the sink interior (both sides and bottom), cutting a hole over the drain. Also cover the faucets with plastic food wrap, and knot the ends of the wrap. (You'll see how important all this is if you don't do it!) Finally "splatter-proof" the wall adjoining the sink with either plastic food wrap or cardboard.

Wax paper is a "drop cloth" substitute, but it tears easily. The plastic side of freezer paper also sticks to damp surfaces, but freezer paper is more expensive and not as pliable as plastic food wrap.

You obviously can't cover the floor with plastic food wrap, but a couple of layers of newspaper in front of the sink does a good job. (Be sure to remove throw rugs.) If your work area is carpeted, cut open a large plastic garbage bag (or use an old shower curtain) for carpet protection. Plastic is slippery, so be careful not to take a header into the sink!

Dripping paint can cause big problems. So always use several layers of newspaper to cover the plastic (old shower curtain, plastic bag, etc.) under the drip area. *Never assume paint will not drip!* By the time I hear the splot-splot of dripping paint, the damage is done. Removing fabric paint from a concrete deck is an impossible chore—even for those who like to clean.

Misting and spraying paint also requires protection for surrounding areas (see Spraying and Misting, this chapter). Sometimes sprayers don't always spray where you thought they would. You can spray outside, provided the wind isn't blowing. If you spray inside, cardboard shields can be used as protectors for walls and floors. I use the bathtub as my "spray room."

Cut open a large garbage bag to make a flat sheet. use the less expensive brand; they're thinner and stick better. Wipe off the tub walls with a wet

Fig. 9-6

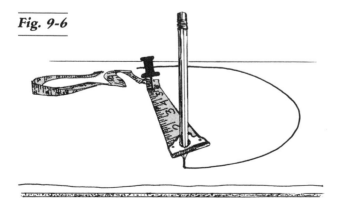

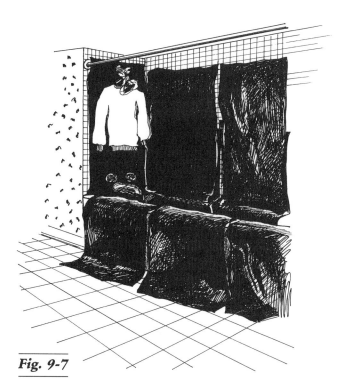

Fig. 9-7

sponge or cloth. Then "paper" the walls with the cut bags (Fig. 9-7).

The shower head is a handy "hook" for a hanger. Cover the shower head with plastic food wrap, and "paper" the shower head's wall with cut plastic bags. The bags are easily taken off when you're not using the tub for spraying (or when you don't feel like explaining to company why the tub looks like the Black Lagoon). I use the same old bags over and over.

Fill a container (pan, jar, etc.) with soapy water. As you finish with reusable tools (not brushes), drop them into the water to soak. Use paper towels for general cleanup. A wet sponge or premoistened towel (I use the "baby cleanup" kind) is handy for instant spot removal from your hands and work area.

Don't wear your Sunday best when painting. Instead wear a quickie artist smock made from a garbage bag. Simply cut out a "head hole" and two "arm holes."

If you do spill paint on anything porous, immediately put the item into water. The paint will not set if kept wet. If the paint dries, it's there to stay. Chapter 8 has remedies for removing paint spots.

If a spotted item can't be laundered (such as carpet), immediately wipe off the paint with a damp sponge. Then rub spot remover into the paint spot and cover with damp paper towels until cleaning can be completed. Remove the paint as soon as possible.

Despite your precautions, there will be some cleanup. Here are a few more helpful hints.

Use the scratchy side of a sponge to remove dried paint spots. A toothbrush gets paint out of grooves and niches. Fingernail polish remover wipes dried paint off ceramic tiles and fixtures. And premoistened towels (those for infants or for adults) that contain alcohol are good for small jobs.

I apply dishwashing detergent like hand lotion, let it sit for about 5 minutes, then wash my hands. I admit my hands usually look like those of a grubby three-year-old—the price I pay for not wearing gloves.

Items used for either food preparation or consumption (plates, cups, flat wear, pans, bowls, etc.) should not be used to mix or store paint.

I'm sure you're wondering if you have to do all this just to paint one T-shirt. The decision is yours; do as much or as little as you wish. What you can't do is mix paint in the cup you'll be drinking coffee from tomorrow.

CLOTHING LABELS

See also Blank Clothing and Accessories in this chapter.

Many directions tell you to remove clothing labels before painting. It's because those little tags have a way of soaking up paint. And that extra paint often leaves a darker color wherever there is a tag. Whenever paint is being applied in the area of a tag, remove the tag. I make it a point to remove all tags—*always*.

COOKING PARCHMENT PAPER

You may be wondering what in the world cooking parchment paper is. It's a treated paper used for baking and microwave recipes. It's also the handiest multi-use supply you can imagine. I think manufacturers should change the name to "craft paper."

It can be used in almost as many ways as freezer paper. It's an outstanding pressing cloth, iron and ironing board protector, and tracing paper. It can also be used for photocopying designs and patterns. It's completely nonstick and nonporous.

Buy it in the boxed roll (like wax paper) since the packaged cut sheets are expensive and not as handy. Don't throw bits and pieces away—it's usable until it disappears. I strongly recommend that you always have an extra roll in the house.

I have never used any type of pressing cloth that is as good as cooking parchment paper. When you need steam, mist the top of the paper with water before pressing. MEMORIZE THIS: over the board, under the iron (Fig. 9-8). That's the parchment paper rule to follow whenever you're using something that could stick to or stain either the ironing board or iron.

Use cooking parchment paper over fabric when heat-setting paint. You'll be able to use a much higher heat than the usual setting for any fabric.

If you have trouble finding cooking parchment paper in grocery stores, there are two mail-order sources listed in Supply Sources.

See also Shirt Boards; Tracing, Vellum, and Tracing Vellum Paper, this chapter.

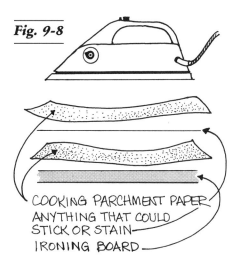

Fig. 9-8

COOKING PARCHMENT PAPER

ANYTHING THAT COULD STICK OR STAIN

IRONING BOARD

DESIGN PLACEMENT

There's nothing worse than finishing a shirt and discovering that ducks (or flowers or birds or whatever) are resting in a rather precarious spot. Placement that looks great when the shirt is flat changes drastically when the shirt is worn. The obvious areas of concern are the shirt front and sleeves. It's also very difficult to imagine design placement on a flat sleeve.

Fused and glued embellishments usually add bulk or stiffness. And there's nothing more uncomfortable than a shirt that is bulky or stiff in the underarm area. So the placement of fused silk flower appliqués requires special attention.

Before decorating a shirt with specific designs (painted, glued, or fused), put on the shirt. Stand in front of a mirror and use safety pins to mark the areas where you *do not* want designs. Leave the pins in place until after the embellishments (appliqués, beads, etc.) have been attached to the shirt.

If you use a shoulder strap purse, there's a lot of friction and wear on one shoulder. (How many wiggly shoulder pads needed restitching, thanks to that valise you're lugging around?) So one other

place that shouldn't be forgotten is your load-bearing shoulder. Don't "pack up" this shoulder with appliqués, glued embellishments, or heavy layers of paint. These items suffer more wear and tear than shoulder pads.

DISH DRAINER

See also Cleanup Tips, this chapter.

Excess paint can drip from an item for as long as 30 minutes. During this time leave the item in a dish drainer, and let the paint go down the drain. If you want to salvage the paint, put a flat pan under the drainer. An old colander, vegetable steamer, cake cooling rack, or oven rack can be substituted for a drainer. (You simply want something that keeps the item off the sink bottom.) Use plastic food wrap to keep the sink clean (see Cleanup Tips, this chapter).

After removing the painted item from the drainer, fill the sink with soapy water. Immerse drainer (racks, colander, etc.) in the filled sink, soak about 10 minutes, then wash. Pour at least 2 quarts water down the drain.

I have been told that septic-tank owners will not have a problem unless they are using huge amounts of paint. Check with your septic-tank installer for additional information.

DRYING PAINT

See also Heat-Setting, this chapter.

Hair dryer. If you absolutely have to speed up drying time, grab your hair dryer. (Use a diffuser if you have one.) Use a setting of low or no heat, and keep the dryer moving. Consistent heat in one spot can do funny things to paint. Never let the dryer touch the paint.

Another word of warning: some manufacturers do not recommend using a hair dryer ever. That recommendation will be included on the paint bottle.

Before painting. It's wise to determine which drying method you're going to use before you start painting since drippy paint has a way of demanding instant attention.

Flat drying. Flat drying is usually the best method to use when fabric was saturated with paint, when dimensional paint types were used and when embellishments (acrylic jewels, lace, etc.) were attached with glue or paint.

The drying surface should be larger than the painted item. Paint can take as long as 24 hours to dry. So use either an out-of-the-way spot or a portable surface that is stable enough to easily move.

Tables or counters should be protected with plastic (old shower curtains are also great) or freezer paper. Don't dry painted items on newspaper or paper towels because paper sticks to wet paint.

For quick-dry projects, a table is fine. For projects requiring more than a couple of hours of drying time, it's more convenient if drying surfaces are movable. In other words, don't use the dinner table unless you're looking for an excuse to go out to eat!

Cut open a large box and cover it with several layers of newspaper. Then cover the newspaper with plastic food wrap or freezer paper. Wrap these layers around to the back and tape them so the top surface is smooth (Fig. 9-9). If the box is still floppy, cut strips of cardboard from another box and tape these across the back. Now you've got a stable, portable drying surface. (You can slide it under a bed for storage.)

I like to use a sweater drying rack. This is one of those collapsible gadgets with a nylon mesh platform supported by metal legs. It can be set up in the tub when used for drying, and then folded flat for storage. I love it!

If you have an old window screen lying around, you've got a great no-cost drying rack. Drying is faster on a mesh or screen rack since air circulates around the top and bottom layers. Cover the screening and frame with plastic food wrap or freezer paper if you don't want to spend time cleaning up this item.

For tinting and dyeing, the item must be wrinkle- and crease-free when drying. Every little lump and bump produces a dark streak. In these cases, *flat* drying means exactly that.

Fig. 9-9

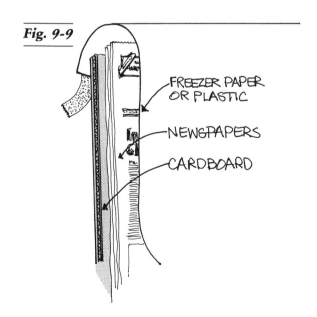

FREEZER PAPER OR PLASTIC

NEWSPAPERS

CARDBOARD

To prevent wet paint from leaking onto other areas, slide the freezer paper, parchment paper, or plastic food wrap between the layers. If you don't keep some type of nonporous layer between the painted and nonpainted areas, wet paint will soak into areas where you did not want paint.

If a shirt board was used during painting, leave it in place until all the paint has dried (see also Shirt Boards, this chapter).

Hanger. Clothing and yardage can, of course, be dried on hangers. This may be great, or it may be a disaster. Fabric saturated with paint has a way of sticking together in weird ways, and paint collects in these creases and folds. More paint means more color. And more color means dark streaks and lines when the paint dries.

You may like this effect. If so, you can create terrific shading by manipulating the fabric into folds, creases, and wrinkles. Rearrange the side areas of a shirt, fold the hem up, push the sleeves toward the front or the back, stuff the shirt with plastic bags (pin shirt bottom closed), and crunch diagonal lines or form peaks across yardage.

The weight of the wet fabric on the hanger produces a line across the shoulder of a shirt. There is an inflatable hanger on the market that's used for drying fine washables. These hangers don't produce "hanger line." Plastic bags (the kind stores use for bagging) can be wrapped around a metal hanger for padding as a substitute for the inflatable type.

Regardless of what type of hanger you use, insert the hanger into a shirt through the bottom hem. Sticking the hanger in at the neck does awful things to wet neck ribbing.

On the other hand, if the original plan was an even color, dry the item flat—no wrinkles, no creases, no folds.

Clothesline. When you're dealing with a 3-yard hunk of yardage, line drying is the practical solution. If possible, hang in a shady spot. But beware: clothespins have a way of leaving their marks by squeezing out the color. Place clothespins just in the selvage edge.

If you prefer an even color, use a lot of clothespins so the fabric is taut on the line. If you prefer an uneven color, let the folds, creases, and bunches do the job.

Clothes rack. Wooden or plastic drying racks are great. You can stick them outside during warm weather or in the tub during cold or rainy weather. (Be sure to cover the tub bottom with several layers of newspaper.) Racks produce the same good news/bad news that hangers do. When you want stripes across a shirt or yardage (up and down, straight across, diagonal), position the item on the bars of the rack in that direction. Dark stripes will occur on the top layer; light stripes on the bottom layer (the layer resting on the rack). If stripes were not the plan, dry flat.

EDGE FINISHES

These are a step up from a plain old hem. They function the same as a hem, with just a little more pizazz.

Cutting fabric.   Any type of edge finish requires a straight and even cut on the fabric. The best tool to use for cutting is a rotary cutter. Unless your scissors are very sharp and the cut is exactly on a marked line, cutting is a series of little ins and outs down the edge. Those ins and outs create problems when it comes time for fringing, stitching, fusing, or gluing.

If you don't have a rotary cutter, cut as carefully as possible. If possible, pull a thread on each of the four edges to use as a cutting guide. Check the cut edge; if you can see jigs and jags, recut. (See also Rotary Cutters; Scissors, both in this chapter.)

Resist.   Painting the edges of a scarf with Deka Colored Resist is about as painless an edge finish as possible. In this case, the edge is cut after the Resist has dried.

Bond the fabric to freezer paper or Totally Stable for painting. (If you didn't do so before painting, bond the painted fabric after the paint has dried.) Position the tape at least ⅝″ from the raw edge. Be sure the outer edges of the tape are square at the corners.

Use a flat scrubber or a soft flat brush to apply the Resist between the outer edge of the tape and the fabric (Fig. 9-10). Push the Resist into the fabric.

When the Resist is completely dry, remove the tape. Line the ¼″ marking of the ruler on the inner edge of the Resist. Either mark the line or cut with a rotary cutter (Fig. 9-11). Cut along the marked line if scissors are used. A rotary cutter is strongly recommended for this cutting. (See also Resist, this chapter.)

Self-fringe.   Self-fringe is another quick edge finish (Fig. 9-12). Threads are simply pulled from the exposed edges of the fabric. Depending on the use of the fabric, stitching may or may not be required before pulling threads.

A silk scarf that will be hand-washed infrequently will not need stitching before fringing.

Fig. 9-10

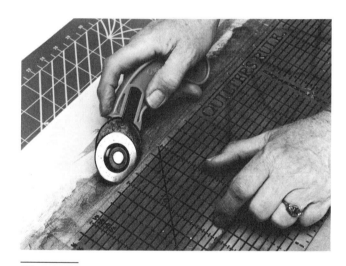

Fig. 9-11

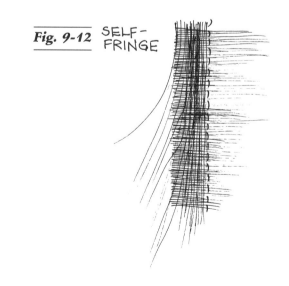

Fig. 9-12   SELF-FRINGE

Placemats that will be machine-washed frequently will probably require stitching before fringing.

Stabilize the fabric with either freezer paper or Totally Stable before beginning.

For nonstitch fringe, use a removable marker to note the depth of the fringe from the raw edge. Pull the threads from the raw edge to the marked line.

For stitched fringe, use a removable marker to note the depth of the fringe from the raw edge. Stitch a short straight stitch on the marked line. Then pull the threads from the raw edge to the stitched line.

Self-fringe should not be too long since the threads tangle and twist with use and laundering. If you'd like a fringe longer than ½″, tie the sections in bundles.

Machine-stitched edge finish. First change your needle, using the smallest size recommended for the thread and fabric you have selected. (Needles are just about the most inexpensive sewing supply used, and can be the determining factor in quality work. Frankly, I wouldn't use any needle but a Schmetz.)

For some reason, people have a tendency to use the same old needle week in and week out. Size and type are secondary concerns. Whenever your machine starts to skip stitches or stitches with a clunk-clunk sound, replace the needle. If you can't bear to throw needles out, use them for picture-hanging nails.

It's a little hard to remember the type and size of the needle that's in the machine unless you're sewing every day. Get one of those little pads of lift-off note papers. Then write the needle type and size on this note paper and stick it to the front of your machine.

If you have a computer machine, don't use a magnet to hold needles (or anyting else) on the machine. Magnets are bad news for any computer system.

If you need to change the needle for a different fabric or thread, stick the needle through the paper. That is, of course, if the needle isn't ready to be flung out in the trash.

Thread tension may also have to be adjusted. Stitch a test zigzag on scrap fabric. If the stitching creates either a tunneled or cupped edge, the thread tension is off.

Turning the thread tension knob to the left (or a lower number) loosens the top thread tension (Fig. 9-13). The top thread will be pulled to the back side of the fabric.

Turning the thread tension knob to the right (or a higher number) tightens the top thread tension

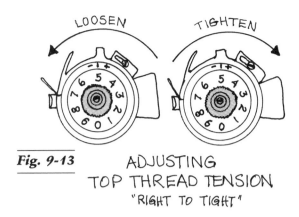

Fig. 9-13   ADJUSTING TOP THREAD TENSION "RIGHT TO TIGHT"

(Fig. 9-13). If tightened too much, the bobbin thread will be pulled to the top side of the fabric.

Using a different color thread for the needle and the bobbin will help you figure out if the tension is too loose or too tight. Use the same weight thread in both the needle and bobbin when adjusting tensions.

Do yourself, and your machine, a big favor. Don't use inexpensive low-grade thread. The money you save isn't worth the frustrations and problems caused by bargain-priced thread.

If the needle thread is clearly visible on the underside of the fabric, turn the thread tension knob to the right. If the bobbin thread is clearly visible on upper side fabric, turn the thread tension knob to the left.

When tension is correct, write the number of the thread tension knob and the needle size on that piece of scrap fabric. Then put the scrap fabric in your Stitch Directory (see Sewing Machine, this chapter).

Fabric should move easily under the presser foot. Be sure you are using an embroidery type foot (the kind with the groove on the underside; the groove slides over the stitches). The tension of the presser foot can be adjusted on most machines. Tighten it slightly if the fabric is not moving freely. On the other hand, if the foot seems to be catching on the stitches, the tension of the presser foot will have to be loosened slightly.

Eliminate surprises: pretest. Set the machine for a narrow width zigzag stitch. It should not be as close as a satin stitch. Test stitches on scrap fabric that has been bonded to the selected supply. (See Stabilizing Fabric, this chapter.) Widen the stitch slightly, then stitch over the first zigzag.

The second stitch should fill in the spaces left from the first stitch. Adjust the stitch width and/or length and tension, if necessary. On the back of the bonded supply, write the needle size and the numbers used for width, length, and tension of both the first and second stitching. Save this information in your Stitch Directory for future reference.

A tight, narrow satin stitch is always an excellent choice for an edge finish (Fig. 9-14). I do have an advantage when doing this type of stitching—it's called Viking #1, which zips around the edges in a flash. I also like my Viking "lightning stitch" (I reduce the width and length), which is delicate enough for the finest silk, but also very durable.

I did testing on other machines (mechanical and computer), and found the best results occurred when a stabilizer was used under the raw edges and stitching was done twice.

If your machine does not stitch a tight, narrow satin stitch, read about machine-stitched appliqués in Chapter 7 and use the two-stitch method.

If possible, use a rotary cutter to cut the edges of the fabric before stitching. If scissors are used, mark the cutting line with a removable marker. Do not take little snips. Instead, cut using the full length of the scissors.

Cut a piece of Totally Stable or freezer paper that is 2″ wider and longer than the edges of the fabric. Then bond the supply to the wrong side of the fabric.

It's best to use either a Teflon foot or a Teflon pad on the bottom of the presser foot. Teflon keeps the foot from sticking or catching on the plastic or glue surface of the supply.

Fill the bobbin with matching thread for scarves or other projects when the wrong side of the fabric will be seen.

Don't begin stitching at a corner, which is a guaranteed nightmare. Instead start at about the middle of the long side. When stitching is complete, tear the bonded supply away from the outer edge. (Use care when tearing since you don't want to disturb the stitches.) But leave the bonded supply covering the scarf in place.

Cut any excess fabric away from the stitched edge. Follow the grading procedures explained in Method One of Appliqué, Machine-Stitched, Chapter 7. The bonded supply will hold the fabric stable, making it easier to cut under the stitches.

SATIN STITCH

Fig. 9-14

If bits of the bonded supply are caught in the stitches, dip the fabric in water. Use tweezers to remove any pieces that did not dissolve in the water. Don't worry about the teeny pieces—they'll fall out as the scarf is worn.

If you'd prefer using your serger, the instruction book has complete details for this type of edge finish.

EMBELLISHMENTS

See also Beads, this chapter.

These are the goodies that add the special touches to painted clothing. They range from a small bead to yards of ruffles or lace. Really, anything goes—as long as it won't dissolve when it gets wet.

Embellishments can be attached to fabric with glue and paint, fusibles, tape, and pronged settings. Prewash washable embellishments before using since they are often coated with sizing (see Prewashing, this chapter).

Glue and paint. When using paint to attach acrylic jewels or beads to clothing, the glue or paint should squish up around the sides. Then the glue or paint forms a good bond and prevents the embellishment from falling off.

Dimensional paints are usually excellent glue substitutes. To avoid disappointment, pretest. Not all brands work the same with all embellishments.

Fusibles. These (both liquid and web fusibles) can be used to apply jewels (acrylic, rhinestone, glass, etc.) and sequin designs to clothing.

Use care when applying a fusible to the back of an embellishment. The heat needed for fusing can melt acrylic and sequin items. Heat 'n Bond requires a very low heat and works well with delicate embellishments.

Tape. Double-faced carpet tape can be used on the backs of many types of embellishments. (See also Lift-Off Appliqués, Chapter 7, and Tapes, Carpet, in this chapter.)

Pronged settings. If you don't care to use either glue or paint, use a setting that holds the bead and is attached through the fabric. Shafaii has snap-on stones and pearls. These embellishments are easily attached to fabric and are also removable.

FABRIC MARKERS

See Permanent Markers, this chapter, and Chapter 3.

FIBER CONTENT

See also Base Fabric, this chapter.

Modern fabrics being what they are, it's often very difficult to know exactly what type a fabric is. Those little tags sewn into clothing or the labels at the end of a bolt of yardage state the fiber content.

Take along a small roll of masking take when you go to a fabric store. Write the fabric content on a piece of tape and slap in on the fabric right there at the store.

You'll notice in Chapter 3 that some paints are limited to specific fabrics. And remember, acrylic fabrics of any type should not be used. Breaking the rules will result in unsatisfactory results. The paint will not be colorfast, and repeated launderings will wash out the paint.

FOAM BOARD

See also Print Blocks; Shirt Boards—both in this chapter.

This is one of those supplies that is better than sliced bread! You'll be able to purchase it in crafts or art supply stores. It's available in three thicknesses, although not all stores carry all three.

Foam board is a layer of dense foam with a paper covering on each side. It's easily cut, glued, and stapled. And it has dozens of uses—none the least of which is an excellent pin board. When possible, purchase scrap pieces. (You won't really need a 4' × 4' sheet!) The price is very reasonable.

FREEZER PAPER

See also Shirt Boards; Stencils, both in this chapter.

Freezer paper has multiple uses, and I really couldn't get along without it. I use it for iron-on stencils and stitching patterns, "shirt boards," stabilizing fabric for painting, tracing designs, and countless other uses. This stuff is great!

It can be bonded to itself, plastic to plastic, or plastic to paper when extra strength is needed. The paper side can be written or drawn on, and can also be used in a photocopier. Paint and glue don't stick to the plastic side.

The plastic coating bonds to a fabric when pressed with an iron. The bond is temporary, and the paper is easily removed without leaving a residue. If reasonable care is taken when removing the paper from fabric, it will not tear and is reusable.

When the iron will be against the plastic, cover plastic side with a layer of cooking parchment paper. Freezer paper doesn't stick to parchment paper, and you won't have a sticky mess on the iron. Cooking parchment paper can also be used to protect the ironing board (see Cooking Parchment Paper, this chapter).

Place the shiny side of freezer paper on the fabric (right or wong side, depending upon technique used). You iron on the paper side of freezer paper first. The iron is always dry when used with this paper. After bonding, turn over and press a second time on the fabric, if a tight bond is needed.

I have never figured out why crafts and fabric stores don't sell both freezer and cooking parchment paper. Maybe if we all pester them enough, they will.

Protecting tissue patterns with freezer paper. Bond freezer paper to the back of tissue paper pattern pieces to end the ripped and torn problem. First press pattern piece smooth and flat. Place freezer paper on board, shiny (plastic) side up. Next cover with pattern, right side up. Then cover with cooking parchment paper (Fig. 9-15). Press at wool setting, with a dry iron. When the pattern is cool, cut any excess paper away from the cutting line (Fig. 9-16).

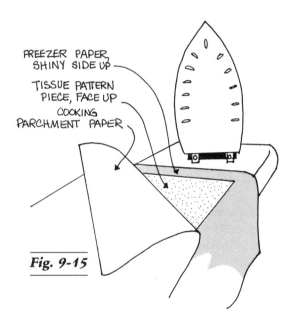

FREEZER PAPER, SHINY SIDE UP

TISSUE PATTERN PIECE, FACE UP

COOKING PARCHMENT PAPER

Fig. 9-15

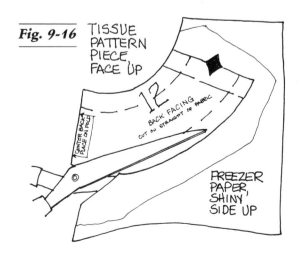

Fig. 9-16 TISSUE PATTERN PIECE, FACE UP

FREEZER PAPER, SHINY SIDE UP

Hang patterns on skirt hangers, or roll and place inside empty paper towel roll, plastic newspaper bags, or the leg of a panty hose for storage. (Don't cut all your nylons into nylon bands—save some for storage of rolled items.)

FUSIBLES

See also Fused Appliqués, Chapter 7; Cooking Parchment Paper, this chapter; and Appendix C, Fusibles.

I hate to be the one to tell you this, but 99% of any fusing problems you'll have are for one reason: the directions included with the fusible were not followed. Each brand and type has specific methods for application. What works for one type does not work for all types. Each type of fusible is limited to specific uses. Make sure you are using the proper fusible, in the correct weight, for the job.

A heavier weight fusible does have greater holding power, but it can add stiffness. A lighter weight fusible adds little stiffness, but it may not provide the sticking power needed for the project. Pretesting saves a lot of frustration (like finding all the appliqués on the bottom of the washing machine).

And, needless to say, a decent iron is the first requirement for success (see Pressing, this chapter).

GLITTER DRIFT

When your house starts looking like Tinker Bell has taken up residence, it's time to attend to Glitter Drift.

Fortunately, the washer doesn't seem to hang onto these little guys from load to load. The biggest problem is the dryer. Even if a glittered item was not in a drying load, you'll find those little sparklies sticking to everything. The solutions are easy—using one large pillow case and remembering to clean the dryer's lint screen.

Before you wash anything that has been sparkled with either glitter paint or glued glitter, place it in a large pillow case. Before drying, add a fabric softener sheet to the pillow case. Then tie the top closed with a nylon band so the glitter cannot roam. Some manufacturers do not recommend the use of softeners with certain paints. In these cases, simply do not add the sheet to the pillow case.

The item does wad up in the pillow case, so drying time is increased. I only half-dry the item in the dryer and then finish drying it on a hanger or clothes line. Before using the pillow case again, turn it inside out and give it a good shake. Check the corners for leftover glitter. (You'll be happier if you do this procedure outdoors.)

Use the Dritz Lint Pick-Up to pick up glitter that lingers on flat surfaces, like the ironing board. (The sticky side of Masking tape can also be used, but it takes longer to do the job.) This handy picker-upper also picks up the threads and fabric bits on your sewing and cutting table. Nothing cleans up cut threads and fabric snips faster from the wrong side of a quilt top. (And nothing is worse than seeing loose threads stuck between the top and batt, *after* everything is basted together!)

Spraying your broom and dust mop with End-Dust increases their glitter-grabbing power. A used fabric softener sheet also gets this stuff out of hard-to-reach corners. Use one sheet to wipe off the dryer's lint screen.

The kitchen or dining area should not be used as a work area when applying glitter. And always keep glitter stored in an out-of-the-way spot if young children are in the house. Glitter and colored sugars look exactly the same to a child.

GRADING

See Fused Appliqués; Machine-Stitched Appliqués (Method 1), both in Chapter 7.

HEAT-SETTING

See also Drying Paint, Manufacturer's Instructions; Cooking Parchment Paper; Stamp Pads—all in this chapter.

When you see "heat-set" on a paint bottle, do it! An iron must be used; clothes dryer heat is not enough. If the directions do not state the iron setting and length of pressing time, press for 60 seconds with an iron at a cotton setting. If that temperature is too hot, use a setting that will not damage the fabric.

Covering delicate fabrics with cooking parchment paper often allows you to use a higher temperature than normally recommended for a fabric. Pretest on fabric scrap before pressing your project.

Most paint manufacturers recommend pressing on the wrong side of the fabric. All recommend that paint dry completely before heat-setting. The heat of the iron bonds the paint to the fabric so your colors will stay bright and true. In fact, according to the experts, any paint (except dimensionals) benefits from heat-setting before the first laundering.

Tulip recommends that items painted with glitter paints be heated in a dryer set at regular heat for 10 minutes before the first laundering. Use the pillow case for this "drying."

"Puff"- or "swell"-type paints require heat to expand. Each brand has different requirements for iron-setting. The directions must be followed exactly.

When you need a damp pressing cloth, mist a fine layer of water over the cooking parchment paper (the top side, the one the iron will be on). The water will not go through the paper, but the steam will. It's the no-shine solution when pressing woolen fabric.

IRONING

See Pressing, this chapter.

KNOTS

See also Tying the Ties, this chapter.

The purpose of a knot is to secure a mass of fabric so paint does not coat it evenly. Twisting or rolling the fabric before knotting increases the strength of the knot. Results can be varied if both the knot and adjoining fabric are wet, if one is wet and the other is dry, if knots are left until paint has dried, or if knots are removed immediately.

Paint that is diluted with a large amount of water (as opposed to powder dyes) quickly migrates through the fabric. Even when knots are very tight, the fabric immersed in heavily diluted paint solutions will be evenly colored. For the best results, spray or mist those paint/water solutions directly on knots in the fabric (see Spraying and Misting, this chapter).

LAUNDERING

See also Manufacturer's Instructions, Prewashing, both in this chapter.

The best advice for laundering is to read the instructions right on the paint bottle or package. I find instructions given on the outside or cardboard packaging are usually more complete than those on the containers. So hang onto the outside packaging until the paint is gone.

Some manufacturers recommend not using detergents; others simply recommend not using citrus- or lemon-scented detergents.

If paint types are combined in one item, follow the most restrictive rules. If you've combined paint, fusibles, and glues in one item, read laundry instructions on each bottle or product packaging. And again, follow the most restrictive instructions.

Generally water temperature should be warm for washing and rinsing. Cold water can cause cracking of heavy paint application, and washing out of certain paint types. Warm dryer heat should be used, unless a bottle states otherwise. "Slick" or shiny paint types usually cannot be dried in a hot dryer. Be sure to read instructions.

Most glues, on the other hand, require cold-water wash. Glue often looks milky when the fabric is removed from the washer; usually it hardens again when completely dry. Any glue that requires heat-setting can be re-pressed when dry to strengthen the bond.

Another instruction that you have to follow is whether to turn the item inside out or right side out for washing and drying. Puff, Slick, Swell, and Shiny paints may stick together when they get warm, as in the dryer. Manufacturers' instructions will state whether or not paint can be dried in the dryer, and whether or not a garment should be right side out.

Glitter paints and glues require two weeks "curing" time before they can be safely laundered. Follow the advice from Tulip and stick the item in the dryer for 10 minutes before the first laundering. I go one step further and press the item with a warm iron. (Press on the wrong side of the fabric after covering with cooking parchment paper or a Teflon pressing sheet.)

Any tumbling action (washer or dryer) may be too much for an item with beads, "jewels," trims, or buttons attached with either glue or paint. That means washing by hand and drying on a clothesline or hanger. Follow the manufacturer's instructions exactly to protect your finished garment.

MANUFACTURER'S INSTRUCTIONS

See also Laundering, this chapter.

Each manufacturer has the same advice for users of its products: "Tell users to read and follow instructions."

Paint. The instruction most often ignored is prewashing (see Prewashing, this chapter).

The second most often ignored instruction is not following laundry recommendations for finished projects. Use correct washing and drying temperatures. Laundering before the stated period listed on the paint container causes all kinds of grief. Wait 2 weeks before laundering glitter paint.

The third most often ignored instruction is not allowing paint to dry completely before heat-setting—or even worse—wearing a garment before it's completely dry. *Feeling* dry is not the same as *being* dry!

Glue. Glue manufacturers listed exactly the same problems as paint manufacturers—with one exception. Some glues can be heat-set before completely drying. All glues need 2 weeks of drying time before laundering.

Markers. Even when not required by the manufacturer, heat-set items decorated with markers. It is usually best to wait 12 hours before heat-setting. (See also Heating-Setting, this chapter.)

MARBLING

Marbling is one of the more fascinating techniques used to apply paint to fabric or paper (Fig. 9-17). The swirls, lines, peaks, and valleys of different colors are beautiful. The finished results range from surprising to highly organized.

Marbling large pieces takes practice and patience—plus a large working area. It is best to start with smaller projects.

The following explanation of terms and techniques is greatly condensed. (Marbling is a book in itself!) See also the marbling instructions and accompanying illustrations in Chapter 4.

Size. Paint drops are floated on a thickened substance called size. The pan used to hold the size must be at least 2" deep. Minimum depth of the size in the pan is 1". Very deep pans make it hard to lay the fabric on the size properly. The pan also must be wider and longer than the fabric or paper being marbled.

Disposable baking pans are excellent to use for beginning marbling projects. Use disposable pans intended for wetting prepasted wallpaper, or use kitty litter pans, dishpans, disposable liners for planters, and even kid's swimming pools to hold the size. (Check yard sales for used baking pans.)

Size is usually the consistency of half-set gelatin. Professional marblers say the best consistency is that of slime. Thick paints can be used on thick size. But thick paints are not as easily manipulated for designs as thinner paints, and they tend to rinse off with the size.

Products for size are available in powder form (see Chapter 3, Appendix A, and Appendix B). These products are mixed with water. Some powders require blender mixing for smooth consistency of the size.

One ready-to-go product that works very well as size is liquid laundry starch. It is probably the best product for first projects. Another inexpensive prod-

uct excellent for first projects is unflavored gelatin. Dissolve 2 ounces in hot water, add 1 quart warm water, and mix well. This size thickens as it sits, which offers another design option: shapes can be formed (flowers are especially easy) on the thickened size. The instructions in Chapter 4, page 25, use these two products.

Before any paint is dropped on the size, the surface tension of the size must be broken. Bubbles on the surface must be broken or pushed to the edge of the pan. Strips of newspaper pulled gently across the top of the size handles these chores.

Cut strips of newspaper about 2" wide and long as the pan is wide. Use two or three layers of strips at a time. This method is also used to remove paint residue from the surface of the size. Size can be used until it is completely discolored by paint. But you don't want paint bits from the previous design floating on the top.

Fabric or paper which has been rinsed in an alum solution (mordant) is laid on the pattern or design visible on the size. The paint pattern or design is picked up by the fabric or paper.

Both size and alum solution can be poured down the sink drain. Pour at least 2 quarts water down the drain after the size and alum solution. Larger amounts can be flushed down the toilet, flushing at least twice. Septic-tank owners should check with their installer before disposing of any paint or paint-related products in drains.

Mordant solution (alum or aluminum sulfate). An alum solution is used to treat fabric or paper before marbling. This step can be eliminated, but the results will not be as satisfactory. (Colorfastness will probably be affected.)

Pickling alum (powder or granules) can be used, but the best results are obtained if aluminum sulfate is used. (See Marbling, Appendix A.)

If using pickling alum, mix 2 tablespoons in 1 quart warm water. Stir until completely dissolved. Directions for mixing aluminum sulfate are included with its purchase.

The alum solution (either pickling type or aluminum sulfate) acts as a mordant. It helps bond paint to the fabric or paper. Your colors will be brighter and more colorfast. To use, immerse fabric in alum solution. Be sure the fabric is completely saturated with the solution. Wring out and dry. Press to remove wrinkles.

When marbling paper, make a small pencil mark in one corner of the right side of each sheet of paper. Brush the alum solution over that side. (It's usually impossible to tell which side has been coated when the paper is dry.) Then, when the paper is dry, press the paper flat.

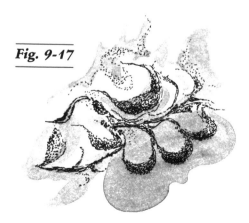

Fig. 9-17

Size. Powdered size is mixed with water. Some powders require mixing with a blender or food processor. Hand mixing produces a very lumpy size. Follow the manufacturer's directions when mixing.

Paints. Any fabric paint or liquid dye that will float on the selected size can be used. This is one time that pretesting is a required step. Launder the test fabric to check for colorfastness. (See also Marbling, Appendix A.)

For testing, I use a small aluminum pan, with about a ½″ depth of size. Ideally the paint will spread in a circle of ½″ to 2″ when a ¼″ drop is placed on the size. Too much spread means the paint is too thin. Too little spread means the paint is too thick. Neither miscalculation will produce good results.

Just keep in mind the maximum dilution rate for the paint you have selected. If you have to add more water than the recommended amount so the paint will float, you're probably not going to be too happy when all the paint washes out of the fabric.

Just so you'll know, the paint drops are referred to as "stones" in marbling. You'll understand why when all the paint drops sink to the bottom of the size. (There is a more sophisticated explanation for the term.)

Patterns/designs. Paint can be dropped on the size with eye droppers, tips of paint bottles, spoons—anything that will release paint. Bristles of toothbrushes create splatter designs. (Dip the brush in the paint, then pull a spoon across the brush's top.) Spray or mist bottles produce great overall effects (see Spraying and Misting, this chapter).

Tools used to manipulate paint for patterns or designs include anything that works! One of the most commonly used items is a hairpick or wide-toothed comb. Straight pins, tips of skewers, nails, and small paint brushes are some other suggestions.

Paint drops can be pulled across paint every which way: in back-and-forth motions, circles, zigzags, loops, or wavey lines. When manipulating paint, take care not to push it into the size. The paint must rest on the surface of the size in order to be picked up by the fabric or paper. If all the paint is pushed into the size, pretty soon all you will have is a very messy-looking pan of size. That mess will affect the look of the fabric or paper placed on it.

Duplicating designs and patterns. Duplicating marbled designs requires a great deal of practice. An easy way to duplicate designs is with the use of Deka IronOn Transfer Paint. Paper is marbled using the transfer paint, and the marbled design on the paper is transferred to the fabric.

Placing fabric or paper on size. The goal is to drop the fabric or paper on the size so the pattern or design is not disturbed and so as not to get air trapped under the fabric or paper. Air pockets keep areas of the fabric or paper off the size. The result is "white spots."

White spots are areas that do not get marbled. Even pieces of thread will prevent fabric from receiving paint. Lumpy size produces a maze of white spots.

Some manufacturers recommend dropping the fabric or paper in one single motion; others recommend dropping one end and "walking" the fabric or paper down the size. Do what works best for the fabric or paper you are using.

Fine wovens and larger pieces of fabric are hard to drop either way, so I bond them to freezer paper. This procedure may not be legitimate (from a professional marbler's point of view), but it does work.

Leave fabric on the size until you can see the paint coming through the fabric. That usually happens in about 5 to 15 seconds—longer if thicker paint was used. Don't worry about leaving it on too long, but 15 minutes is going too far! Paper usually is marbled in 5 to 15 seconds.

Your project is now ready to be rinsed off to remove the size and any excess paint.

Rinsing. If the combination of mordant solution, size, and paint was 100% correct for the fabric or paper you used, care is not required in rinsing. But the chances are that one element was slightly off. So do use care in handling the marbled piece.

You'll need a "rinsing platform"—another name I made up. The platform should be wider and longer than the marbled piece. With luck, it will fit in the sink. If not, use the tub or move to the back yard. Old cookie sheets, pieces of plywood, and foil-covered cardboard (use a double thickness of foil) can be used as rinsing platforms.

Lift the marbled piece off the size the way you would turn the pages of an enormous book. Grab each corner of one end and peel it back. Try not to let it stick together or drop back on the size. After removing the marbled piece from the size, place it—marbled side up—on the rinsing platform.

Pour lukewarm water over the marbled piece. Don't worry—the paint that is rinsing off didn't stick to the fabric anyway! Rinse until most of the size is removed from your piece.

Dry flat, heat-set if the marbled piece was fabric,

then launder to remove any remaining size. The paper may need pressing with a warm iron to flatten. (Don't press the paper if Deka Iron-on Transfer Paint was used.)

Problems. The following are causes for two common problems that occur in marbling.

1 *All the paint rinsed off with the size:* too much alum was in the solution; alum was not used; paint diluted too much; fabric or paper was not left on the size long enough.

2 *White spots appeared:* fabric or paper was not placed correctly on the size; lumpy size, throw it out and start over.

Chapter 4 has instructions for techniques using both liquid laundry starch and unflavored gelatin. Appendix A lists brand names for marbling supplies. Also detailed instructions for marbling techniques are given in the marbling books listed in the Bibliography. You owe it to yourself to look at these books—the pictures are gorgeous!

MEASURING

Try to be reasonably accurate when measuring paint, additives, or water—although a *few* extra drops of this or that won't mean disaster. A handy, no-cost measuring device for ounces is an empty, cleaned, paint bottle. Save all the paint bottles that have a wide top.

Plastic measuring spoons, cups, and funnels clean up more easily than metal ones. By the way, funnels really save time when transferring paint from one container to another.

MIST BOTTLES

See Spraying and Misting, this chapter.

NYLON BANDS

See also Tying the Ties, this chapter.

Kathleen Feehan came up with the following marvelous idea. I think it's one of the best tips I've ever gotten from anyone. For the best nonrubber band you can imagine, cut strips (2″ to 4″ wide) across the legs of panty or nylon hose. These bands won't melt, stick, or break. I haven't had any problems with discoloration since by the time they're old enough to be cut up, they've been washed dozens of times. Use the waistband when you need a large nonrubber band. (The toe is a perfect paint strainer.)

Don't limit the use of these bands to fabric painting, however. Nothing is better for tying plants to poles. Cut the circles and tie the ends together when you need more length. I once braided them to make a shoulder strap to carry my ski boots.

Also don't forget to save some legs for storing rolled items.

PERMANENT MARKERS

See also Chapter 3 and Appendix B.

It's best to use the markers labeled "Fabric Markers." Other types may work, but the results vary from brand to brand. Fabric markers are available in a variety of tip types, ranging from microfine to hard chisel to brush. Drying time of these markers ranges from fast to slow.

Microfine tips are hard and perfect for filling in small areas or refining a stamp print. A chisel tip is hard and is used whenever you want a definite line. It comes in different widths, flat and pointed. The brush tip is soft and can be used like a paint brush.

Colors of fast-drying markers cannot be blended with adjoining colors, unlike slow-drying markers.

Enamel markers contain enamel paint. They are excellent for items exposed to weather or heavy use (banners, canvas shoes, etc.).

Refillable markers have an empty barrel that you fill with fluid paint or dye as needed. The tip is usually a chisel type. Refillable markers are perfect when you can't purchase a marker in the color you want.

PINS, CLIPS, AND RINGS

I'm talking clothespins and bobbypins, paper clips and hair clips, curtain rings, and anything else that holds fabric together (Fig. 9-18). (Don't forget those clips used on opened bags of chips.)

All kinds of interesting designs happen when

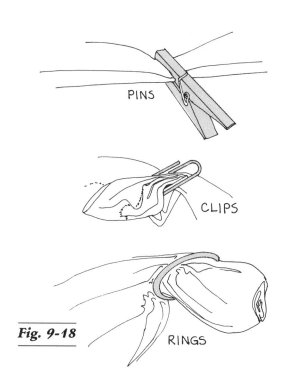

Fig. 9-18

fabric is held in a clump or wad and then sprayed, misted, or brushed with paint. And don't forget, resist can be applied to these clumps and wads too.

Use clothespins to hold pleats in sweatshirts, and bobby pins to hold "pinches" in T-shirts. Pull yardage through paper clips for speedy tie-painting. And pull sleeves, shirt fronts, or backs of sweats through various rings.

PRESSING

Think of pressing as the ups and downs of ironing. No more sliding the iron from one end of the board to the other. Pick up the iron to change position or direction. Whenever you see the term "pressing," this is what is meant.

Obviously you can't press without an iron. (Although folded sheets of a countertop can be substituted for an ironing board.) A good iron is the best gift you can give yourself.

I must qualify as an "Iron Killer." I can't tell you how many I've gone through—some became doorstops in less than a year! I kept going back to one I'd had for at least twenty-five years. It was big and heavy, and it did the job. The fact that it hadn't produced a drop of steam in years was a small price to pay.

I bought a Rowenta iron about two years ago and was finally able to retire my "oldie" to the shelf. Try as I can, I can't find a thing I'd like to change on the Rowenta iron.

Next time you buy an iron, think of the advantages of size and weight: bigger is better. Smaller lightweight irons just take longer to do the job—and often end up being doorstops!

PRETESTING

You're going to see this word a lot. It can't be stressed enough. Prestesting with yardage is easy. There's always extra fabric that can be used.

But pretesting with clothing can be a problem. It's a little hard finding an inconspicious spot on a T-shirt. I use old T-shirts, sweats, and jeans. (Find something else to use to wash the car.)

The only requirement for a tester is that it is of the same fiber content as the fabric that you will be painting. Testers let you try out an idea without the concern of ruining a new shirt or a piece of yardage. That takes away a lot of the "What if this doesn't work?" pressure. If it doesn't work, all you've done is ruin a good car-washing cloth.

Not being concerned about ruining something new (and the loss of money involved) gives you more freedom to experiment. And that's when the fun really begins. The best designs are always the ones we cook up on our own.

PREWASHING

See also Laundering, this chapter.

I think every paint container has a label instructing users to wash fabric before painting. It's not only important that you follow this direction, it's absolutely necessary. (See also Manufacturer's Instructions, this chapter.)

Fabric softeners (detergent, liquid, or sheets) coat fabric. Don't use them when prewashing.

Bleach should not be used, either before (in prewashing) or after painting. Detergents containing "whiteners" may contain bleach. Laundry detergents that remove every type of stain may alter the appearance and durability of paint or glue.

Don't use spray sizing or starch *before* painting. These sprays are the worst coatings because they have an uneven application. You'll end up with all kinds of funny shades of paint.

Spray sizing, however, is the best pressing aid to use *after* painting. It really speeds up pressing and doesn't leave a residue on the fabric. I also think it's far superior to spray starch.

Fabric has a coating of sizing. That's what makes new fabric (clothing and yardage) look so crisp and shiny. If that coating is still on the fabric when you apply paint, it will prevent the paint from coating the fabric, causing the paint to cover only the sizing. The sizing will wash out the first time you launder the fabric. And with the sizing out goes most of the paint.

Prewash the fabric in the same way it will be laundered after painting. After prewashing, 100% cottons should be dried in the dryer—even if the fabric will be line-dried after painting. The heat of the dryer will shrink cotton, but you won't have to worry about unexpected shrinkage after painting.

Any fabric that has a permanent coating (soil repellent, chintz, polished, permanent press, etc.) will not accept paint, glues, or fusibles. Information concerning finishes is on clothing labels or on the end of fabric bolts.

The heavy finishes used on muslin and denim don't wash out in one laundering. It's easy to tell when all the sizing has been removed from muslin. It'll come out of the dryer almost wrinkle-free since it's the sizing that causes all its wrinkles. Get the sizing out, and you've got a beautiful, soft, supple fabric. Always dry muslin in a hot dryer when prewashing. Then you won't run the risk of additional shrinkage. And this is the kind of surprise no one wants.

In addition to fabric, there's another group that requires prewashing. Any washable fabric trim or decoration that will be used in a project must be prewashed. Stick these items in a pillow case or one of those mesh bags used for fine washables before putting them in the washing machine. Launder in the same load with the fabric that they will be used with. If you have any question about the washability of these items, it's best to find out before you even begin.

Prewash test. There's an easy test you can do to determine if fabric is cleaned of all coatings. Sprinkle drops (*drops*, not cups) of water on the fabric. If the drops soak in immediately, the fabric is all set to go. If the water beads, launder again.

If the water beads after the second laundering, the coating is probably a permanent finish. Fabric with a permanent finish should not be used for painting, gluing, or fusing. This does not apply to muslin or denim—wash at least two more times before considering it a nonpaint surface. (Muslin and denim are often heavily coated with sizing.)

PRINT BLOCKS

See also Blockers; Reverse Blocks; Stamps—all in this chapter.

A blocker keeps paint off fabric; blocks put paint on fabric. The options available for blocks are literally endless (Fig. 9-19). The list begins with the edge of a 3 × 5 card and ends with purchased products. As long as the surface holds enough paint to leave the impression on the fabric, you've got a block (Fig. 9-20).

Blocks can do more than print fabric. Since a block holds paint, it will also hold washable glue resist. Think of the combinations—apply resist designs with a block, dye the shirt, then block print designs with paint.

Blocks that have larger raised surfaces can be dipped in permanent glue. Print the glue design on

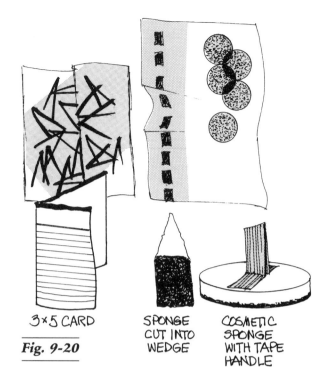

Fig. 9-20

3×5 CARD / SPONGE CUT INTO WEDGE / COSMETIC SPONGE WITH TAPE HANDLE

the fabric and sprinkle with glitter. Wait for the glue to dry completely before picking up excess glitter.

Printing surface. Fabric is placed on either a padded, soft, or hard surface for printing. The type of block, paint, and fabric determines which is the best surface to use.

The surface often used is a padded one, and for this type of surface nothing is better than an ironing board. The block is pushed into the fabric when a padded surface is under the fabric. The disadvantage of a padded surface is that care must be taken in applying paint to the block. Too much paint results in a smeared print. A sponge roller applies that very thin coating of paint often required for this type of printing.

Soft surfaces are midway between the padding of an ironing board and a countertop. Either four to five layers of newspaper or one of those tabletop ironing boards provides moderate cushioning.

Some types of blocks leave a better impression when the fabric is placed on a hard surface. Lighter weight fabrics usually print better on a hard surface.

Always pretest before beginning a project with block prints. A surface other than the one recommended may work better with your paint block/fabric combination.

General instructions. Always use an insert inside shirts when printing. Plastic food wrap,

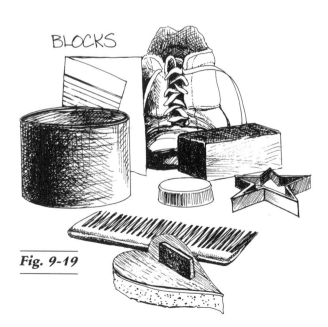

BLOCKS

Fig. 9-19

cooking parchment paper, or freezer paper are the best choices. The fabric must be wrinkle-free, and the surface under it must be smooth. Blocks don't print well on lumps and bumps. If blocks are to be placed on both the front and back of a shirt, let the paint dry before printing the second side.

Apply even pressure on the block when printing. Too much push on one side will cause an uneven print. If the block is large, or very soft, lay a piece of cardboard or foam core over it so you can apply even pressure across the entire block.

Blocks. I think everyone, at one time or another, has cut a shape in a potato, dipped it into paint, and stamped the painted shape on fabric or paper. Art Gum erasers are probably second in use as a paint block. Either of these methods are as good today as they were when first used (when Eve decided she had to do something to those curtains)!

The following items are a few more suggestions for print blocks. You can keep adding to the list.

Sponges. Don't overlook any size, shape, or type. The finer the grain of the sponge, the more definite the impression. (Cosmetic sponges are usually fine-grained.) Unless the sponge is very thin, you won't need a padded surface for printing.

Paint can be applied to a sponge in one of two ways. First is the obvious way. Dip one side of the sponge in a pan of paint and let it soak up the paint. The paint should be thick enough to stick to the sponge, but thin enough to be absorbed. If the paint is too thin, it oozes every which way all over the fabric when you're printing. The same thing happens if you get too much paint on the sponge. I call it the squish-squish sponge print.

The second way takes a little more time, but is more precise. Squeeze a heavy line of paint along the widest edge of the sponge. Use the edge of a paint spreader or plastic charge card to pull the paint across the sponge. The layer of paint should be even and not too heavy. You won't use quite as much paint with this method, and the impression will be even.

If you don't like painty fingers, make a tape handle to stick on the back of the sponge. Fold a 4″ strip of tape (strapping is best) in half, sticky sides together, but leave a 1″ tail at each end. Stick the tail ends to the sponge. That gives you a 1″ handle to hand onto when putting the sponge in the paint and picking it up from the fabric. Sometimes you can put a large safety pin in the back of the sponge for a handle (Fig. 9-21).

Banar Designs has a product called Stik 'N Puffs. They come in a variety of shapes, and their

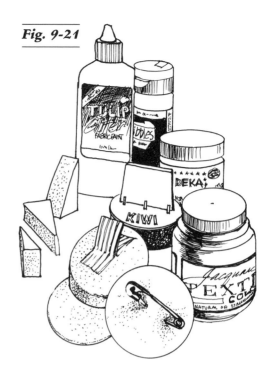

Fig. 9-21

intended use is to be covered with fabric. The combination of the cardboard back and the fine grain makes them a great sponge block. These little sponges have another plus—the cardboard backing has an adhesive back. Remove the paper covering the adhesive, and stick whatever you want on that adhesive surface (Fig. 9-22). Buttons, pieces of chenille, and small sticks are the types of things that stick on this surface—all make great block designs.

Plaid has a square sponge paint applicator called

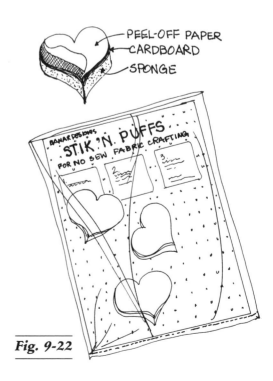

Fig. 9-22

Petifours. The back is split in half to form handles. These are great blocks for both paint and resist, and are very handy to use when you want a dabbled sponge print.

Grocery, hardware, and beauty supply stores are loaded with sponges. Cut the thinner ones into any shape you want. (Cookie cutters are great patterns.) Trace around the shape with a marker and cut away. Just don't try to cut out shapes with a lot of detail. Sponges are just too "spongy" for detail cutting.

Cookie cutters. The easiest way to get an even layer of paint on that skinny edge of a cookie cutter is with a sponge paint roller. Put a quarter-sized dab of dimensional paint on a piece of freezer paper and use a sponge paint roller to roll it out. This gets an even layer of paint onto the roller. Then roll the sponge roller over the bottom edge of the cutter (the one that cuts dough). Print on a hard surface (Fig. 9-23).

Don't forget the fat edge on open cookie cutters. It's less than a ¼″ wide and a great width for glitter paints. That edge can be either rolled with paint or dipped into paint. It's also perfect for dipping into both types of resist as well as glitter glue. Print on a hard surface with paint; on a soft surface with resist and glue. The cutter shape can be used alone, or the outline can be filled in with brushed paint or with fabric marking pens (Fig. 9-24).

I think plastic cookie cutters are a little easier to use than the metals ones. The open plastic ones have that wide ¼″ edge on the back. The closed plastic ones have a nice little handle on the back.

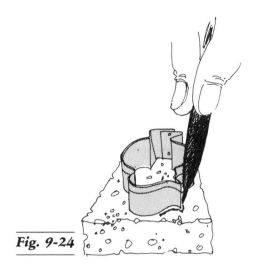

Fig. 9-24

Plastic blocks. Dizzle Paints has plastic print blocks (officially they're called Paint Blocks) in a variety of designs (Fig. 9-25). Pat the paint on the raised lines of the block with the side of a sponge brush or press the block on a stamp pad (see Stamps, this chapter). Print on a hard surface.

These blocks can also be used with washable glue resist, products labeled Resist, and glue. Sprinkle glitter on glue immediately after printing. Print on a soft surface when using these supplies. Glitter paint can be used with these blocks.

Supplies for making blocks. There are two products available that are great block makers. One is bought in a plumbing supply department or store; the other is ordered from Cerulean Blue, Ltd.

Gasket replacement is made from rubber. It can be bought by the yard or in 4″ squares. The surface of the rubber is either smooth or rough. It's easily cut in any design with scissors or a craft

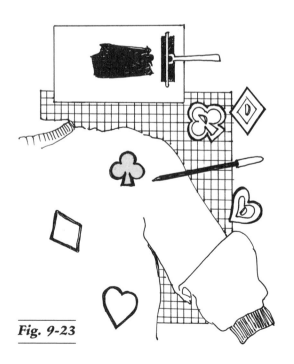

Fig. 9-23

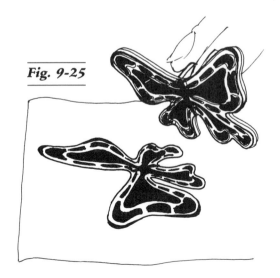

Fig. 9-25

knife. Glue the rubber gasket to a solid backing (wood, foam core, or Styrofoam) and print away.

Sure-Stamp is sold by the foot by Cerulean Blue, Ltd. It has an adhesive back, so you won't need glue to attach a solid backing. Designs are easily cut with scissors or a craft knife. Sure-Stamp is a softer density than the rubber gasket.

Both of these items are low in cost and hold up under repeated use. They work well with either washable glue resist or paint. Use them whenever you create designs that will be used on more than one project or for larger projects with several prints.

Foam board can be used as a substitute for either of these supplies. However, foam board does not cut as easily as the rubber gasket or Sure-Stamp, and it does not hold up under repeated use. Foam board usually works better if you roll the paint over the surface, rather than dipping it in paint (see also Foam Board, this chapter).

Found objects.   The paper or plastic core from calculator tape is a great block for circles. Use thread cones when you want larger circles, and the roller from paper towels for medium-sized circles. If the edge is thick enough, these are good blocks to use for glue and glitter. Print on a padded surface. Use corks, the bottoms or tops of jars and bottles, thread spools, etc., when you want a block for a solid circle.

Kiwi Shoe Polish Applicators are nice round sponge circles with a plastic handle on the back. Get them in grocery stores in the shoe polish display. The grain of the sponge is very fine, and it prints, both paint and washable resist beautifully.

The bottom of an egg carton has two rows of six almost-circles. Roll paint on these and print away. Cut the carton down to size if you don't want an even dozen. Stick a jewel in the center of the printed circle for a bit of jazz (Fig. 9-26). A soft surface is usually best for this type of block.

There are several types of paper that make good blocks. The edges of file cards, most greeting cards, posterboard, files, covers on spiral notebooks, foam board, cardboard—are all great surfaces to use for blocks. Bend them into angles, curves, squares, zigzags, or whatever you want. Then tape them to hold that shape.

Either roll paint over the paper's edge with a sponge roller or dip the edge into a paint pan. The layer of paint in the dip pan should be just enough to paint the edge. Too much paint, and the print will be smudged. Print on a hard surface.

Chore Girls are those silver-colored pan cleaners that look like a perm gone bad. I don't know why, but the silver-colored ones seem to

Fig. 9-26

print better than the copper-colored. They're great blocks for flower shapes (Fig. 9-27). (They have a faint resemblance to peonies.) Dip or brush soft dimensional paint on the surface. Sprinkle a layer of glitter on the wet paint for an added touch. A swipe of paint with a flat brush, and you've got the stem. (Instructions for this design are given in Chapter 5, page 36.)

Fig. 9-27

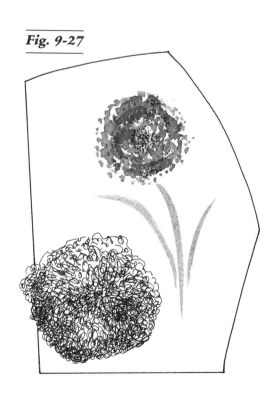

A friend of mine was given a sweatshirt that had the most original blocks possible. Her daughter painted the bottoms of the grandchildren's hands and feet and printed them on a shirt. She called it "The Handies and Feeties of My Sweeties." I have an idea that cleanup of those hands and feet was not too sweet!

You can also get fancy with blocks. Use a removable marker and trace around the outside edge of a block on fabric. Then lift the block. Stick a blocker (heart, circle, or square shape) in the center (side, bottom, or top) of the marking (Fig. 9-28). Print on a hard surface, then remove the blocker after the paint has dried. The shape of the blocker will be unpainted.

Pieces of wood are also great blocks. Use all four edges, top and bottom. Crafts departments have wooden forms used for decoupage painting. They're all sanded and ready to go.

Use a stamp pad (see Stamps; Stamp Pads, this chapter) or a sponge roller to apply paint to the wood. Push the square end of a triangular-shaped cosmetic sponge into a painted block. Print on the fabric. The cosmetic sponge will pick up the paint from the surface of the block. The print will have an unpainted area the size and shape of the sponge square.

I do get quite carried away on the subject of print blocks, but they are the most pain-free way to add designs to fabric. Blocks can be used with almost every type of paint, resist, or glue; you don't need a lot of paint; the prints can be plain or decorated to the hilt; and I just think it's fun finding weird things to use as blocks.

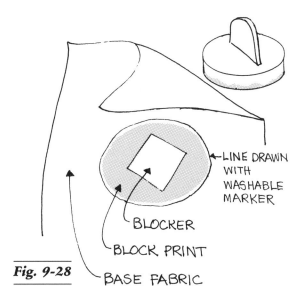

Fig. 9-28

LINE DRAWN WITH WASHABLE MARKER

BLOCKER

BLOCK PRINT

BASE FABRIC

REFILLABLE MARKERS

See Permanent Markers, this chapter; Chapter 3; Appendix C.

REMOVABLE MARKERS

See also Chapter 2 and Appendix D.

Nothing is worse than lingering markings. For some reason, they always seems to be smack dab in the front of a shirt for all the world to see. If wax or oil are included in the marker's ingredients, the markings will not be removable. (Not all markers and papers that claim to be removable are—pretest.)

Removable markers come in a variety of types, ranging from chalked and transfer papers to pencil-shaped containers with chalk to tubes holding powdered chalk to solid chalk to water- or air-erasable marking pens.

Clover has several marking supplies and tools: Charcopy is an excellent chalk transfer paper. Tolin' Station Transfer Paper completely removes on demand and wipes right off. EZ International Transfer Paper and Pressure-fax Transfer Pens also instantly remove. Clotilde, Inc., has removable marking pens that are both water- and air-erasable.

Water- and air-erasable markers are fast drying so be sure you follow directions. Marvy Uchida has one that is used with a rice transfer paper. The transferred design completely disappears.

A substitute for any of these products is chalkboard chalk. Use a chalk holder (which can be purchased in office supply stores) to keep the chalk off your hands. Sometimes plain old chalk lingers, but it should easily brush off the fabric. Sharpen the point in a pencil sharpener or by rubbing it on a used emery board.

The project often determines which is the best type of marker to use. Whichever product or type you select, just be sure you pretest before beginning your project.

RESIST

See also Chapter 3 and Appendix A.

A resist is used on fabric where you do not want paint. There are two types: solid and liquid. Some resists remain in the fabric. Others are rinsed out after the paint is dry and has been heat-set.

Solid (crayons). All techniques described in the book use crayons as a solid resist. Use either crayons labeled "Fabric" or children's boxed crayons, but fabric crayons will produce brighter colors.

Whenever you use crayons, protect your ironing board by covering the board with cooking parchment paper. And protect your iron by covering the crayon layer with a second piece of cooking parchment paper.

A hot dry (cotton setting, no steam) iron melts crayon wax into the fabric. Crayon wax is not removed after painting, so the color of the crayon becomes a feature of the design. Designs created with crayons can be free-form or specific shapes. A vegetable grater or pencil/crayon sharpener shaves crayons for scattered designs. Freezer paper bonded to the wrong side of fabric holds the fabric stable for crayoned lines and designs.

Wax is wax is wax. Don't get too heavy a layer of crayon on the fabric or it will stay stiff as a board. Also crayon really spreads when it melts, so keep the shavings fine.

Do not dry items with crayon resist in a heated dryer. The heat of the dryer may cause the crayon wax to soften and stain other items in the dryer.

Crayons can be used for reverse transfers. On paper, draw or trace the outline of a design with crayon. Just about any kind of paper can be used—sand paper, typing paper, Tolin' Station Vellum, etc. Pretest to make sure the paper will release the crayon on your fabric. Remember the design will be reversed when transferred to the fabric.

Color in the design, using crayon strokes that are heavy, even, and in one direction. (None of this scribble stuff!) Remove loose crayon particles from the paper with either tape or the Lint Pic-Up. (Those little flecks melt into the fabric if they're not removed.)

Place crayoned design on the right side of the fabric (Fig. 9-29). (The iron will be on the paper.) Press, applying even pressure. Peek under the transfer sheet to make sure that the design was transferred to the fabric—it usually takes two pressings. Allow the fabric to cool before removing from the board.

"Rubbing" is another method that uses crayons. It is described in Chapter 4, Fig. 4-21.

Liquid. Three types of liquid resist are used for the techniques in this book: washable glues, products labeled "Resist," and other products used as resist. All are described in Chapter 3.

Liquid resist can be applied to fabric in several ways: by dipping or block printing; or by using a brush, sponge roller, or fine-tipped applicator bottle. Results obtained from each method are different. But each method requires that resist soaks into the fabric and is dry before any paint is applied to the fabric.

Resist and resist. To help eliminate confusion about Resist and resist, it's time for an explanation of the two types. Whenever you see Resist (with a capital *R*) that means that a product labeled "Resist" is a suitable supply (Fig. 9-30). Whenever you see resist (with a small *r*) that means that washable glue is a suitable supply. You can substitute one for the other, but the results will not be the same.

Washable glue (resist) is very thick and not completely absorbed by the fabric. Also the definition of design lines will not be as sharp as with Resist. Yet resist is low-cost and is completely removed when laundered.

On the other hand, Resist is more fluid than resist and is completely absorbed by the fabric. When correctly applied, design lines are definite and sharp. It is available in clear and several colors, including metallics. Some types remain in the fabric after laundering, while other types wash out. Also Resist is more expensive than resist.

Another product—Presist (available from Cerulean Blue, Ltd.)—is a big favorite of mine. It can be used as a substitute for washable glue and does not require being pushed into the fibers of the fabric. It dries much faster than resist and easily rinses out of the fabric. The results are of a higher quality than those with glue. Presist can also be used for fine-line application, but the definition of the lines may not be as sharp as with Resist. It is more expensive than resist, but less expensive than Resist.

When you are coating tied bundles for a sweatshirt, the practical choice would be resist.

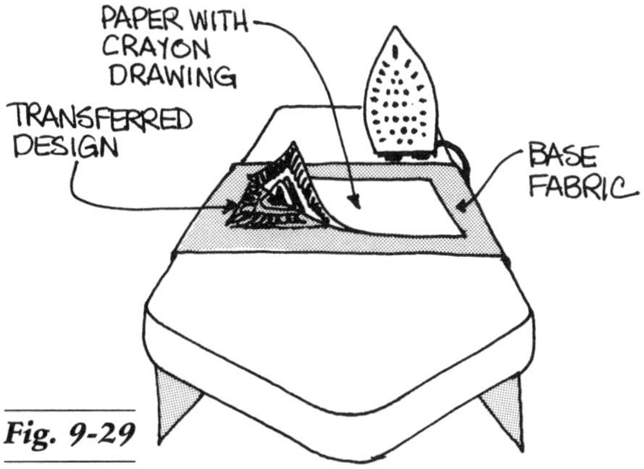

PAPER WITH CRAYON DRAWING

TRANSFERRED DESIGN

BASE FABRIC

Fig. 9-29

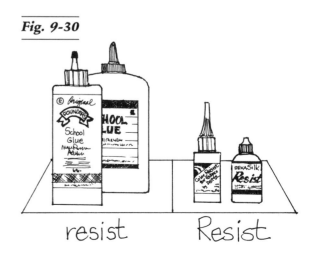

Fig. 9-30

resist   Resist

When you are painting a silk blouse, the practical choice would be Resist. And when you do not require sharp definition of a design line and do require a clear pattern shape, the practical choice would be Presist.

Resist. When fine-lined definite designs are desired, products labeled Resist produce more satisfactory results. Resist is most commonly used for painting silk and other fine wovens. It is not suitable for use on sweatshirt fleece or dense fabrics.

Instructions on a bottle of Resist tell you to scrape or drag the applicator tip on the fabric. Listen for a slight scratching noise, then you'll know you applied enough pressure to push the Resist into the fibers.

To determine that Resist did penetrate the fabric, look at the back of the fabric. The Resist should be clearly visible. (Hold the fabric up to a light source if necessary.) If it is not visible, additional Resist must be applied. If the fabric is heavy, it is sometimes necessary that Resist is also applied on the wrong side of the fabric.

When creating designs with Resist, you must connect the lines of the design. If they do not connect, paint colors will not be separated. Paint of one color will flow into any adjoining colors. Inspect the back of the fabric. You should be able to see the Resist. If the lines do not connect or if the amount of Resist is not even, redraw the lines.

Don't get too carried away with redrawing. If redrawing, or adding more layers, creates a buildup of Resist, it's better to rinse out all of the Resist and start over. You'll be a lot happier with the results if you do this. One caution: colored or metallic Resist may be difficult to remove. It's best to do your first project with clear Resist, which does rinse out completely.

Fabric must be taut and stable when Resist is applied. Freezer paper, bonded to the wrong side of fabric, works very well for some techniques. Hoops, frames, or stretcher bars also hold fabric taut. The depth of these items elevates the fabric above the work surface. Therefore Resist or paint will not "puddle," and drying will be faster.

Printed designs (either fabric or paper) can be placed under the hoop (frame or stretcher bars) and traced when light-colored fine wovens (silk, for example) are painted. The designs are used as patterns, for Resist lines and painting.

VisionARTS does not require the use of a frame for silk painting. Press freezer paper to the wrong side of the fabric, or follow the directions on the bottle for countertop painting.

Plastic food wrap can be used to cover the countertop, if you prefer. Wipe the counter with a damp cloth or sponge before putting down the plastic wrap. Then wipe off the food wrap with sponge to remove all wrinkles and creases.

Resist substitutes. Some softer transparent paints can be substituted for Resist. These paints can be either brushed, printed, or applied with a fine-line applicator. Two paints that work particularly well on silk are Tulip Soft Lite and Deka Flair. These paints remain in the fabric, as do colored Resist products.

Be sure to pretest. Remember that the purpose of a Resist is to prevent paint of one color from flowing into adjoining colors.

Washable glue and Presist. Dipping knotted, twisted, or tied fabric into any of these products produces marvelous designs. Allow the fabric to dry before painting. Each of these products is removed when the paint is dry and has been heat-set.

Use any of these products to coat the surface of a block for application of resist. Test (return to the handy "tester shirt") to ensure that the block will carry enough resist to penetrate the fabric.

The block must be pushed firmly into the fabric. Be sure the coating on the fabric is even. Check the back of the fabric to make sure that the resist did penetrate. Apply the paint to the fabric after the resist has dried. Heat-set the paint before rinsing fabric to remove resist.

These products can be applied to large areas with a brush—a flat scrubber brush is the best type to use.

If you'd like a crackled look (lots and lots of little lines), brush Presist over the entire surface of the fabric. Twist and wring the fabric after the coating is dry. The purpose is to create cracks in the coating. (Glue just doesn't "crack" too well.)

Brush or roll the paint over the fabric. When the paint is dry, heat-set. Rinse the coating out of the fabric. The original color of the fabric will be covered with a series of lines, caused when the paint seeps into the cracks of the coating.

REVERSE BLOCKS

See also Blockers; Print Blocks; Stamps—all in this chapter.

The nicest thing about writing a book is that I get to make up names for techniques and supplies. I'm sure there's a "real" name for the process that follows, but since the block is placed under the fabric, I think "reverse block" works fine. ("Under block" just didn't sound right.)

Anything with a texture or raised surface can be placed under a fabric when you apply paint with a roller or wide brush. The lumps and bumps of that surface create all kinds of interesting designs. Think of this as liquid "rubbings."

The more porous the item under the fabric, the more it will soak up paint. Any excess paint will be picked up by the fabric positioned on the reverse block.

Press a piece of freezer paper to the wrong side of your fabric. Take another piece of freezer paper or plastic food wrap and place it on a counter. Soak or coat porous items (thread, yarn, chenilles, pieces of sponge, paper, etc.) with paint, and position them on the freezer paper or plastic food wrap you are using to protect your counter. Now place your fabric right side down on the freezer paper with the painted items. (The paint on the items must be wet.)

Use either a rubber or sponge roller (without paint) to roll over the freezer paper on the wrong side of the fabric. The paint from the items will transfer to the right side of the fabric. After the paint has dried, remove the fabric.

ROLLERS

Rollers are available in foam (sponge), hard rubber (brayers), wood, and plastic. All types are handy to use for fabric painting.

There are some tasks that you can do with a roller that you just can't do with a brush. On the other hand, there are some tasks that you can do with a brush that you can't do with a roller. And there are still other tasks that you can do with either a brush or a roller.

Foam or sponge. The good news about foam or sponge rollers is their speed—paint goes on in a zip. The bad news is the amount of paint needed to saturate the roller. As far as I'm concerned, the advantage of speed overrides the disadvantage of the extra paint needed.

Hard rubber (brayer). This type of roller is often referred to as a brayer. The original use was (and still is) for rolling paint over wood or linoleum blocks. But it can also be used to roll paint directly onto fabric.

Wood or plastic. You have to go to the hardware or wallpaper store for these items, which are the little gadgets that you run down the seam of wallpaper to get a good seal. For this reason, they are called wallpaper seamers!

ROTARY CUTTERS

If you don't have a rotary cutter, consider getting one. Nothing reduces cutting time like these handy gadgets (Fig. 9-31). (They look like pizza cutters.) I

Fig. 9-31

prefer the Quilter's Rule brand since I think the curved shape of the handle makes it much easier to use—for both righties and lefties. And if you have any stiffness in your hands or fingers, this shape is far more comfortable than the straight-handle types.

Quilter's Rule has rulers specifically designed for use with rotary cutters. (You can use these rulers as regular ones too.) Quilter's Rule rulers are also my favorite. The back of the ruler has a raised cross-hatch design that really hangs onto the edge of the fabric. Therefore these rulers don't slip and slide when you're cutting.

The combination of cutter and ruler is perfect for anyone with limited vision. Use a strip of bright orange fluorescent tape on the line where the ruler will butt up to the fabric. Rotary cutters must be used on a mat specifically designed for cutting.

SCISSORS

First, always label your scissors with "old" or "new" written on a piece of tape stuck to the handle. "Old" labels mean that these scissors are fair game for any use. (What it really means is these scissors are shot.) "New" labels mean that these scissors are good and sharp. These scissors deserve care and consideration, including wiping off the blades each and every time they're used.

Contrary to what is usually believed, paper and polyester do *not* dull scissors blades any faster than plain old cotton. (Hair, however, is another story.) Scissors get dull from use and from not being wiped off after they're used.

When a "new" no longer does a good job, either change the label to "old" or sharpen the scissors. Nothing will drive you up the wall faster than scissors that chew away at fabric.

SEWING MACHINE

See also Edge Finishes, this chapter.

The combination of your machine and painted fabric offers unlimited creative options. Stitched and painted projects range from quickie place mats to original design garments.

Regardless of the age or type of machine you have, take the time to give it the care and cleaning it deserves. You'd never think of not cleaning out the lint trap in your dryer—yet I'll bet your machine rarely gets the de-linting it needs.

The feed dogs really get crammed with lint and thread bits. And inexpensive thread adds tremendously to lint buildup. If you use this thread, plan to do a lot of de-linting. (Better yet, don't use cheap threads.)

Also don't forget the bobbin case. Most important, remove the face plate and pick up all the lint that collects there. The instruction book that came with the machine tells you how and what to clean. (You still do have that wonderful little booklet, don't you?)

If you're concerned you'll never get parts back in place, call the dealer and arrange a 15-minute session so you can learn how to do this basic cleaning. Once you see how easy it is, you'll have no qualms about doing it on your own.

If oiling is a maintenance requirement of your machine, do it regularly. After oiling, put a small piece of fabric under the presser foot. Drop both the presser foot and the needle. The fabric will collect any excess oil. The only type of oil that should be used is sewing machine oil. Your dealer will have the one needed for your machine.

Buy one of those inexpensive photo albums with the plastic pockets to be your Stitch Directory. Every time you sew a speciality or decorative stitch, make a sample on a small piece of fabric for the directory. On the fabric write the numbers used for width, length, presser foot and upper (needle) thread tensions, needle size, and type. Include any information that would be helpful the next time you use this stitch.

I can't tell you how much time the directory saves me. It's silly to repeat the process of trying out different tensions, needles, and threads when you are duplicating a stitch on the same type of fabric for another project.

The directory offers another advantage too. For some reason, the directory encourages you to try new stitches and combinations. You won't be as intimidated by those machine knobs and numbers. Best of all, you'll find out the many wonderful tasks that your machine performs.

And follow Robbie Fanning's advice—hug your machine! (At the very least, do give it a love pat now and then.)

SHIRT BOARDS

This is the term I'm using for any layer placed under a fabric before painting. Since this layer is usu-

ally used when you're working on a shirt, "shirt board" seems to fit (Fig. 9-32). Use one of these nonporous layers whenever needed—regardless of the type of project.

Cooking parchment paper.   This is an excellent insert, since it's lightweight and easy to position. Pin or tape it in place if the area being protected is large. (See also Cooking Parchment Paper, this chapter.)

Foam board or cardboard (waxed/paint-proof).   These supplies can be used for a make-it-yourself shirt board. If you want a board to fit a specific shirt, make a paper pattern of the shirt with newspaper. Draw an outline on foam board or cardboard, then cut it out. (Arms can be attached, with tape.) Next cover one side of the board with wax paper and press it with a hot iron. The iron will melt the wax on the paper to the foam board or cardboard. Paint or glue won't stick to the waxed surface. Then turn it over and "wax" the second side. (The iron temperature may have to be reduced if you use foam core.) Be sure both sides have an even coating of wax. Waxing makes the board paint-proof and waterproof.

An advantage of this board is the thickness of the cardboard or foam core—it will hold a straight pin. Thus you can easily secure the shirt to the board so it doesn't move all over the place when you're painting. (See also Foam Board, this chapter.)

Nylon bands can also be used to attach the shirt firmly to the board. Use the bands just like you would use a wide rubber band around the board. (See also Nylon Bands, this chapter.)

Cushioned quilter's square.   (see June Tailor, Supply Sources). I found out quite by accident that this padded board intended for pressing quilt blocks is a wonderful shirt board. Bond freezer pa-

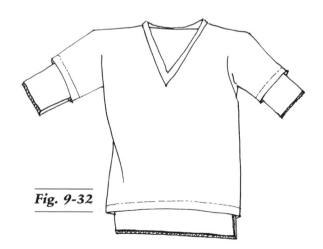

Fig. 9-32

per to the muslin cover to protect it from paint, glue, or marker stains, then slide the board inside the shirt. If you are using an iron-on transfer, you won't have to move the shirt from the ironing board to another surface for painting. Whenever pins are needed to hold the fabric stable, stick them into the padded surface. The unpadded back of the square is a perfect surface to use inside a shirt when you are stamping or using markers. I don't bond freezer paper to this side of the board, but I do bond it to the wrong side of the shirt.

Freezer paper. This can be used as an insert, or it can be bonded to the inside of a garment before you begin painting (Fig. 9-33). In order to do the job, freezer paper must completely protect the areas that you do not want in contact with wet paint. (See also Freezer Paper, this chapter.)

Plastic bags. Use bags to stuff the inside of shirts that are being dried on a hanger. Be sure to stuff the sleeves. Straight pins across the hem will hold the bags in position. (See Drying Paint, this chapter.)

Plastic food wrap. This can be used as an insert, though it's a little harder to use because it is so light and loves to stick to itself. I usually use it only when I'm working on a padded surface (ironing board) for detail or outline painting. *Caution:* Don't use an iron to bond the food wrap to the fabric because the plastic will melt into the fibers of the fabric.

Purchased shirt boards. These boards are available in almost every store that sells fabric paint, and they're very economical. The only problem is that they often come in just one size and without arms. If protection is needed for sleeves, use one of the other suggested materials in the sleeves.

Fig. 9-33

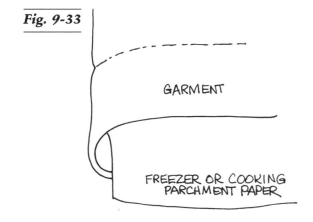

GARMENT

FREEZER OR COOKING PARCHMENT PAPER

Sleeve supporters. There are times when you need a solid object in sleeves (or socks) so you can apply resist, glue, or paint. All that you need is a smooth, rounded surface. An empty plastic bottle (soda, soap, bleach, etc.) will do the job (Fig. 9-34). But don't use your iron on a plastic bottle, or you'll end up with a plastic sleeve!

Fig. 9-34

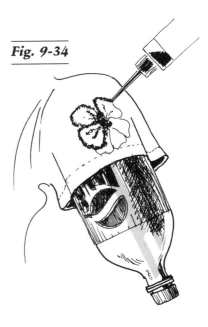

Super quickies. These shirt boards are quickly made with a piece of cardboard, posterboard, or one side of a cereal box. Slide the board into a plastic bag. Then tape down the bag so one side is smooth and wrinkle-free.

Wax paper. Wax paper is very limited in its use. Wet paint will stick to it, and this can really be a nuisance. If you do use wax paper, use a double layer.

SILK AND SILK PAINTING

Silk has gotten some bad press. All too often it's thought of as a slippery, wiggly, difficult-to-sew, expensive, dry-clean-only fabric. I have an entirely different opinion of silk. I think it's gorgeous, easy to sew, moderately priced, and I never dry clean it.

You do, however, have to be firm with silk. Press it to freezer paper or Totally Stable, and you're the boss. And as soon as silk is stabilized, it's a piece of cake to paint or sew.

I'll admit that some silks are knock-your-socks-off expensive. But blank scarves, ties, and blouses are not. In fact, they're very moderately priced (see Blank Clothing and Accessories, this chapter).

Hand-wash silk before painting or stitching, and that's the end of any dry-cleaning concerns. However, once dry-cleaned, *always* dry-clean.

Magic Wand is a solid stain remover that works like a charm on silk. I've used it on every spot from grease to blood with complete success. Rub Magic Wand into the stain and let it sit for a day or two before laundering the garment.

Most fabric paint (or liquid dye) can be used on silk. However, I don't think I'd want to use a heavy/stiff dimensional glitter. And a puff type paint hardly suits the fabric. But several softer transparent or translucent paints create beautiful results.

For your first project, purchase a blank scarf from one of the mail-order companies listed in Supply Sources. You'll be amazed to see how easy silk painting really is.

Use cooking parchment paper for a pressing "cloth." The paper takes care of any scorching concerns.

Chapter 5 has instructions for silk-painting projects that are very easy. The silk-painting books listed in the Bibliography include instructions for basic to advanced projects. One look at these books will convince you of the glories of silk painting.

SOFTENING STIFF PAINTS

Fortunately, soft paints are now on the market. When dry, these paints feel as soft as the fabric— well, almost! Always use soft paints when painting large designs. Otherwise your shirt ends up feeling like a bulletproof vest.

If a stiff drying paint is used, there's a cure that helps the "coat of armor" results. It's the same pillow case described under Glitter Drift, this chapter. (Make sure you've cleaned out all the glitter though.)

Wash painted shirt, using fabric softener in the final rinse. Place a fabric softener sheet and the shirt in the pillow case. If the shirt is really stiff, turn it inside out and put the softener sheet next to the paint. Tie the top of the case closed, and dry at regular cycle. (Drying time is extended because the shirt balls up in the case.) I usually complete drying on a hanger or clothesline.

Some manufacturers do not recommend using fabric softeners of any type, at any time. But if you can't wear the shirt because it's so stiff, it may be worth giving it a try anyway! You really don't have too much to lose.

SPOTS, STAINS, AND GOOP

Magic Wand is one spot remover that works, and it can be safely used on silk. (At least I've never had any discoloration or problems when I've used it on silk.) It's a solid stick in a push-up tube. Look for this product in grocery and fabric stores.

Goo Gone literally melts fiberglass tape residue from scissors blades. It is one of the few products that dissolves repositionable glue (liquid and spray). Keep Goo Gone away from children and use it in a ventilated area. Follow all manufacturer's instructions. Hardware stores are often the best place to find this product.

SPRAYING AND MISTING

Two methods 'spray" or "mist" paint on fabric. One method uses a bottle with either a pump or squeeze-type trigger. The other method uses a canister filled with a propellent. (The propellent is ozone-free, of course.)

Pump and squeeze trigger bottles.   These bottles have different types of nozzles (Fig. 9-35), and that means the paints come out in a different way for each container.

Spray bottles have squeeze-type triggers (the kind normally found on window cleaner bottles) and adjustable nozzles. Turning the nozzle changes the spray from a strong stream (a shot of paint) to a semi-fine mist. I've never seen a pump top on this type of spray bottle. I suppose too much force is needed for a pump to be effective.

Mist bottles produce exactly that (a fine mist that can cover an area up to 4″ across) when the bottle is held 6″ to 8″ from the fabric. These bottles have either a pump top or a squeeze-type level. The nozzle of a mist bottle with a pump top usually is not adjustable.

When you purchase mist or spray bottles, look for the ones with the longest hoses. Some hoses are ½″ shorter than the bottle, so there will be at least ½″ paint in the bottle that the hose can't reach. Also when the hose is not completely submerged, mist and spray suddenly changes to spits of paint. And that fine even mist becomes a mess of splots. Tilt the bottle, and the end of the hose usually pops out of the paint, producing more splots.

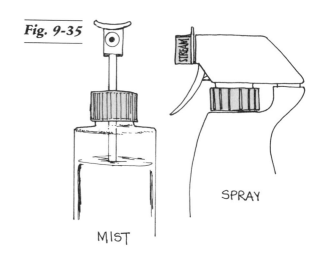

Fig. 9-35

MIST

SPRAY

When the fabric is flat, the bottle is tilted downward.

Before misting or spraying, prime the hose. It takes a few pumps or pulls on the level to get the paint up to the nozzle. Make sure the mist or spray is the intensity you want, using paper towels for pretesting.

Paint can be stored in the bottle for a day or two. Unscrew the top and put the hose into a bottle of water. Clean all the paint out of the hose and nozzle. Check the nozzle, you may have to use a pin to get all the paint out of that little hole.

Put the top back on the paint bottle and turn the nozzle to the closed position. Label and store the bottle in a cool place. If there are children in the house, store it in an out-of-the-way place. These bottles are the best squirt guns on the block!

Aerosol container. One aerosol product, Preval, is a canister filled with propellent that is used with either the bottle that comes with the propellent or any container holding paint. A short hose attaches to the bottom of the propellent container and is placed into the paint. Depress the lever on top of the canister and spray away! You have most of the advantages of air-brushing, without the expense of air-brush equipment.

Because the paint is dispersed in such a fine mist, you have far greater control of the amount of paint applied to the fabric. This feature makes shading very easy. You can also use Preval for stencils, both positive and negative (see Stencils, this chapter).

Paint must be stirred thoroughly. Strain paint (use the toes from nylon or panty hose) if it is not free of particles.

The paint container must be held in an almost upright position for good results. Clean all paint from the hose and nozzle when painting is completed.

Where to spray. The hassle of spray painting is having the bottle or paint container in as upright a position as possible. I use the bath tub as my "spray room." Read Cleanup Tips, this chapter, for ways to protect your tub and walls.

The shower head is a perfect hook for a hanger. The ledge at the back of tub is usually wide enough to hold cardboard or foam board. If you don't have a shower, pin the fabric to either cardboard or foam board and put it on the ledge of the tub.

If tub spraying doesn't appeal to you, surround fabric with shields (cardboard boxes or plastic sheets), or spray outdoors. Cleaning sprayed paint off the walls and floors is not much fun.

STABILIZING FABRIC

I'm a stabilizing fool! I use some type of stabilizer whenever I think it'll make projects easier, faster, or produce better results.

Having the fabric stable and held in position eliminates a lot of problems, such as fabric movement. For example pressure applied by a bottle tip, marker, stamp, block, brush, or roller moves fabric. This movement often results in unsatisfactory results—which can be eliminated with stabilizer.

Fabric can be stabilized by anchoring it to a surface with pins, bonding it to a surface, or coating it with a liquid stabilizer.

Foam board, cardboard, or a padded ironing board can be used as "pin boards" for fabric. Usually it will be necessary that a nonporous layer is placed under the painted area to serve as a shirt board (see Shirt Boards, this chapter).

Freezer paper or Totally Stable can be bonded to the back of the painted area for stabilization. Freezer paper also serves as a shirt board.

Liquid stabilizer (Perfect Sew) is applied to the back of the fabric. Its drying process can be speeded up with a hair dryer and pressing with an iron. Liquid stabilizer also completely rinses out. Just remember to heat-set the paint before rinsing out the stabilizer.

Depending on the technique chosen, pinning, bonding, or coating can be used for woven fabrics. Use a bonded supply or coating for knit and stretch fabrics since pins have a way of distorting these fabrics.

STAMPS

See also Print Blocks; Reverse Print Blocks, both in this chapter.

Technically stamps are blocks (or blocks are stamps). The intricate designs of a stamp require stamping on a hard surface. There are two types of stamps—fabric and paper (Fig. 9-36)—and one basic method of stamping.

The designs in a fabric stamp are deeply cut, producing a clear print on the fabric. The designs

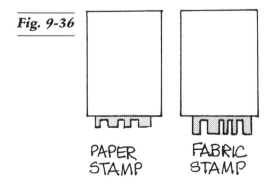

Fig. 9-36

PAPER STAMP   FABRIC STAMP

in a paper stamp are not deeply cut. Paper doesn't require a deep cut for a clear print, but fabric does. So when paper stamps are used on fabric, the print can be smeared and smudged.

Smears and smudges are a less common problem if a latex or foam pad is used. These pads can be purchased preinked or uninked.

Pelle's See-thru Stamps are clear and on a clear plastic base (plastic boxes). These stamps are excellent to use on fabric and paper, especially for repeat designs.

If you've ever tried to line up a series of prints, end to end, you're aware of the advantages offered by a clear stamp and base. Each print is exactly where you want it, because you can see where you're printing.

The polymer material used for Pelle's stamps is easily cleaned. And ink wipes off in a flash with a wet sponge.

Paints for stamping.   Ink is the term used for the coloring substance on stamp pads. Fabric paint or liquid dye used on a pad will also be referred to as ink.

Glitter, metallic, and most pearlized and dimensional paints usually won't print a clear impression. The paints that consistently print a clear impression are those used for air-brushing or marbling.

Remember that many paints can be diluted (see Appendix B for dilution rate of selected paint). Sometimes adding just a little water to a paint will give it a better impression—experiment time!

I've had wonderful results with fluid paints and liquid dyes on a foam or latex pad. (And they're supposed to be a lousy ink! Although they are lousy when used on a felt pad.) Pretest, with laundering, when experimenting.

STAMP PADS

A stamp pad is a flat, porous surface coated with ink. Felt is the supply most commonly used for self-made pads. The stamp is pushed into the inked pad, causing the design to be covered with ink. The stamp is then pushed down on fabric. The result is an impression of the inked design on the fabric. This method requires a deeply cut stamp for fabric use.

Now here's the change: don't use felt for the pads you make. Use a thin thickness of fine-grained foam (the finer the better) or latex. If you are unable to find sheets of this type of foam in an arts supply store, the next stop is a fabric store. The thin foam layer on the back of a plastic table covering is perfect.

Cut a piece of the table covering slightly larger than the stamp design. That will be the stamp pad.

Apply a line of paint across one end of the pad. Use a paint spreader, plastic charge card, or plastic putty knife to pull and push the paint across the pad. The layer of paint should be even and cover the surface of the pad.

Gently tap the stamp on the pad. No push-push, just a gently tap-tap. Look at the surface of the design. The stamp should be evenly coated with ink. (The wet ink will have a shine to it.)

If the entire design is not inked, or if one area has more ink than another, the pad was not evenly inked. Use the spreader (or a substitute) to pull the ink across the pad again. Add more paint if necessary.

When the design is evenly coated, stamp on scrap fabric. Gently position the stamp on the fabric. Apply steady, even, downward pressure on back of stamp. Rocking the stamp back and forth will produce a blurred image. If you get a good print on your scrap fabric, you're ready to begin stamping on your project (Fig. 9-37).

You must re-ink the stamp for each impression. Remember to look at the stamp each time to make sure it's evenly inked.

If you'd like to switch to another color of ink on the stamp, wipe off the first color with a wet kitchen sponge, stamping on dry paper towel to remove moisture. Then ink the stamp with another color.

Purchased stamp pads.   You don't have to make your own pads, Pelle's has foam pads ready for inking. Y & C also has multicolor inked pads. Just don't use a pad that contains alcohol because alcohol can eat the rubber used for stamps.

Be sure to try out the stamp pads inked with transfer ink. (Iron-On, by Ranger Industries is available in retail stores; both Fabric Transfer Ink by Inkadinkado and Stamp 'N' Iron by Co-Motion are

Fig. 9-37

available in retail stores and through mail order. Inkadinkado and Co-Motion are listed in the Supply Sources.) After stamping on paper, transfer design to fabric. Allow the transfer to cool before painting or coloring with markers.

Inking stamp with roller. This method works great if you're going to do only two or three impressions. But it's too time-consuming for multiple impressions.

On a piece of freezer paper, pour enough paint to ink a foam roller. Roll the roller through the paint until it is evenly covered. Then roll the roller over the surface of the stamp (Fig. 9-38). Remember to check to surface of the stamp before stamping to make sure it is evenly inked.

One paint that works very well for "roller inking" is Liquid Appliqué. The paint can be left as is after drying or it can be puffed with an iron or hair dryer. Works of Heart has stamps of embroidery stitches. These stamps, used with Liquid Appliqué create wonderful effects.

Uneven or incomplete prints. Regardless of how methodical we are, the stamped print sometimes is not even and areas or lines of the design are incomplete. Fixing incomplete prints is why markers were invented! Laura Pruit gave me a handy tip: use a fine-line marker to fill in designs that did not stamp clearly. I use Y & C Permawriter II markers, which have an extra-fine tip and come in several colors. Use these markers to draw over any areas or line of the design that did not print.

I press freezer paper or Totally Stable to the wrong side of a fabric before stamping. I seem to have fewer incomplete prints when a stabilizing layer is used. And print results are greatly improved when stamping on sweatshirt, fleece, or heavy wovens.

Coloring/painting stamped designs. If markers were originally invented to fix incomplete

Fig. 9-38

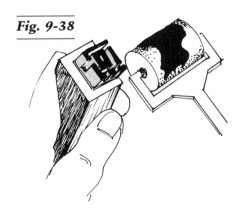

designs, they were invented secondly for coloring in the whole design. In the latter case, the stabilizing layer is a necessity. Use antifusant if necessary. (See Antifusant at the beginning of this chapter.) And always heat-set markers.

Transparent or translucent paint can be brushed over larger stamped designs. The ink used for the stamp shows through for an interesting effect.

Heat-setting designs. It's wise to heat-set stamped prints, even if the paint does not require it. If you're going to color the design with markers, both paint and markers can be heat-set at the same time. Both should dry 12 hours before heat-setting. (See also Heat-Setting, this chapter.)

Transfer paint as ink. Deka Iron-on transfer paint can be used as a stamp ink on either a felt or latex pad. Stamp on paper and transfer design to fabric. You can use Sulky Iron-on transfer pens to color in the design before transferring it to the fabric. Remember: Deka Iron-on is not colorfast on fabric that is not at least 60% synthetic.

Cleaning and storing stamps and pads. When you've finished stamping, stamp on a wet sponge (just a plain old kitchen variety) several times. You can use a soft toothbrush to remove every bit of paint from the surface of the stamp. Stamp on dry paper towels to remove excess moisture. Foam stamp pads (self-made or Pelle's) can be rinsed under running water to remove ink. These are reusable.

Store the stamp on its back out of sunlight. Store the inked stamp pads (self-made or Pelle's) in a tightly closed plastic bag. The ink will stay moist for two or three days. Don't let the ink dry out or the pad will be ruined.

STENCILS

See also Blockers; Tapes, both in this chapter.

There are stencils and there are stencils, and then there are more stencils! There are actually five kinds of stencils that can be used with fabric paint: (1) doilies, (2) fabric paint stencils, (3) make-it-yourself stencils, (4) quilt stencils, and (5) stencil tape.

You'll notice that stencils have small pieces connecting to larger areas, called bridges. Bridges define the design as well as provide stability. If bridges are removed, all you have is the exterior lines of the design.

Doilies. Doilies are a combination purchased and self-made stencil. Sometimes you'll use the entire design, and other times you'll only use portions of the design.

Doilies are great to use for stenciling (Fig. 9-39). Always use two or three thickness's since one thickness just doesn't do the job. Use metallic or treated paper styles. Wilton has several designs and sizes labeled "Grease Proof."

Before using a doily, punch out the paper bits remaining in the design areas. It's best to do this over a paper bag or sheet of newspaper. (Picking up all those little pieces is a chore.)

Use repositionable glue to secure the doily on the fabric. Liquid glue and glue sticks tend to goo up the little holes of the design.

Fabric paint stencils. These are available in dozens of shapes, sizes, and designs in plastic, coated paper, and press-on tape. Fabric paint stencils usually have a right and wrong side. Look at both sides of the stencil and you'll notice that the pieces of one side are slightly convex (or bulged up). This convex side is the top, or right side, of the stencil. Note that the slight bulge helps keep the paint from seeping under the stencil. The stencil can be turned over when you want a reverse of it—just use a little more care when painting the edges.

Make-it-yourself stencils. Make-it-yourself stencils can be created from either stencil plastic or an iron-on supply (freezer paper or Sulky Totally Stable). Designs can be traced on plastic with a crayon, plastic template marker, or china marker. Small lines are cut with a craft knife or an electric stencil cutter. Larger areas can be cut with scissors. Glues can be applied to the back in exactly the same way as for purchased stencils.

Stencils made from freezer paper or Totally Stable are ironed to the fabric. Either trace or photocopy designs on the nonbonding side. These materials are easily cut with scissors. Teeny cutouts, however, will require a craft knife. Both stencils and freezer paper are easily lifted off the fabric when the paint is dry. If reasonable care is used when removing, stencils are reusable.

Quilting stencils. Plastic quilting stencils have narrow channels cut into the plastic (Fig. 9-40). Quilters use these stencils to mark quilting patterns on blocks or quilt tops. The narrow channels are also perfect for lines of paint, glue, crayons, and fabric markers. Don't use paper quilting stencils, they have to be treated before using with paint.

Stencil tape. Fashion Tape (by DecoArt) is a press-on tape used for stenciling. It's a strip of stencil designs that is ready-to-use and has several designs available. Save the punch-out designs to use as negative stencils or blockers (see Blockers; Stencils, Negative Stencils, both in this chapter).

Positive stencils. If the stencil is positive, the design or shape is cut from the stencil material

Fig. 9-39

PAPER DOILY
USED AS STENCIL

Fig. 9-40

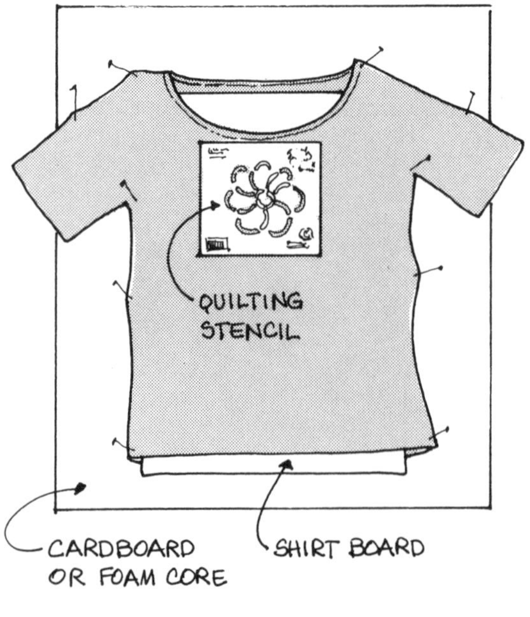

QUILTING
STENCIL

CARDBOARD
OR FOAM CORE

SHIRT BOARD

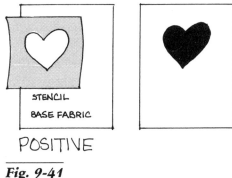

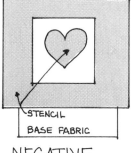

Fig. 9-41

(Fig. 9-41). Paint is applied in the sections that were cut out. When the stencil is lifted from the fabric, the paint has reproduced the cut designs or shapes.

Negative stencils. If the stencil is negative, the areas surrounding the design or shape are cut from the stencil material (Fig. 9-41). Paint is applied in the cut areas. When the stencil is lifted from the fabric, the paint surrounds the designs or shapes. Basically a negative stencil and blocker are the same thing (see also Blockers, this chapter).

Securing stencil to fabric. Stenciling requires two things: that the stencil be securely attached to the fabric and that the paint be thick enough so it does not leak under the stencil. A double disaster hits when runny paint is used with a shifty stencil. Instructions for securing and painting follow the descriptions of stencil types.

Personally, I think taping down a stencil is for

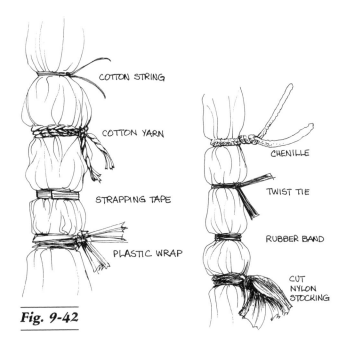

Fig. 9-42

the birds. I coat the back of a stencil with either liquid or spray repositionable glue, or a glue stick. I don't want to have to worry about a stencil moving hither and yon while I'm painting.

The glues are all easy to apply. Goo Gone removes liquid or spray repositionable glue. If you'd prefer not using this type of remover, cover the back of the stencil with duct tape (see Tapes, this chapter). Pull off the tape, and the glue is gone. Warm soapy water removes any glue stick.

After I put a stencil down on the fabric, I run the back of a plastic spoon or a wallpaper seam roller over the stencil. That poor stencil is stuck down like you wouldn't believe—it can't move.

Paints and painting. Regardless of the type of stencil or the method used to attach it to the fabric, be sure the paint is the correct consistency. (Time to return to the old test shirt.) Don't use stiff dimensional paint for large areas. And don't use thin, runny stuff for any stenciling.

Always brush from the cut edge of the stencil toward the center. Brushing or rolling paint into the edge produces blurred lines.

A stencil brush can be used to tap paint on the fabric. Tap the brush end in paint, then tap the excess paint on paper towel. The brush should only have a small amount of paint when applied to the stencil design. Hold the brush handle perpendicular to the fabric when applying paint with a stencil brush. Paint is applied along the edge of the design and lightly shaded toward the center area of the design.

Stencil Paint Creme by Delta is a solid paint product and usable on any surface you can paint on. Follow the directions on the wrapper.

If you enjoy using stencils, do give Preval (see Spraying and Misting, this chapter) a try. Then stenciling is done in a snap.

Cleaning and storing. Wipe all the paint from the stencil with a damp sponge or cloth as soon as you're finished painting. Wipe the stencil dry with paper towels. Then leave it flat on the counter until it's dry.

If a stencil has glue on its back, cover the back with freezer paper. Store stencils flat. (Those lumps and bumps that come from being stuffed into a too-small box make your next job difficult.) I use manilla file folders for storage. I also make foam board "folders" for the ones that are too big for the manilla folders.

TAPES

See also Basting Tape; Blockers; Stencils, Stencil Tape, both in this chapter.

I think tape was invented especially for fabric painting—all other uses are secondary.

Scissors blades have a way of getting pretty yucky if you're cutting a lot of tape, especially fiberglass tape. Goo Gone cleans all such junk off scissors blades. (See Scissors, this chapter.)

Masking. The bottom-of-the-line tape is masking tape. Use it only as a last resort. It doesn't stick that well to fabric, which means it'll leak if any paint is applied next to or over it.

Cellophane. Cellophane tape come in several sizes and three types: regular, lift-off, and double stick. Each type has a use, but my favorite is the lift-off type. It's great when you want a temporary attachment.

Sealing or package. These tapes have excellent holding powers and come in wider widths than cellophane tape. I prefer the clear variety, so I know what's going on under the tape.

Duct. Duct tape has a super hold. It's usually silver in color, but some brands are translucent with fiberglass strands running through it. Both brands have excellent sticking power.

Strapping. Strapping tape has an extra super hold. It's more expensive than duct tape and is hard to find in wider widths. You usually don't need the holding power of strapping tape.

Carpet (double-faced). Regular carpet tape is plastic and has moderate holding power. It can be used for lightweight lift-off embellishments.

The best indoor-outdoor carpet tape is fiberglass and water-resistant. This tape holds better than some glues, and nothing is better for lift-off embellishments.

Wall mount. This tape product is really a thin layer of foam encased between double-faced tape.

It's sold by the roll in hardware departments and is used for attaching lightweight objects to a wall. It's also available in floral departments, where it's sold in small cut squares and is used for attaching dried flower arrangements to the bottom of a container. The two sticky sides are perfect for making print blocks (see Print Blocks, this chapter).

TRACING, VELLUM, AND TRACING VELLUM PAPER

Tracing, vellum, and tracing vellum are semitransparent papers that can be used for tracing or photocopying designs and drawings. Each of these papers is slightly different in weight and strength, but all can be used for tracing or photocopying a drawing. They are available in both cut sheets and by the roll.

See also Cooking Parchment Paper (which is an entirely different product) in this chapter.

TRANSFERS AND TRANSFER SUPPLIES

See Chapter 2 for a more detailed explanation of transfer.

Iron-on. Transfers are available that are already tinted, shaded, painted, dyed, glittered, and veloured. There are literally hundreds of transfers that are line designs (outlines of specific shapes that are ready to be painted or embellished). The problem is not finding a transfer, but deciding which one to select.

Pretinted or shaded transfers are best used with transparent-type paints. A thin coating of paint over the shading enhances the transferred print. Paints are available specifically for these types of transfers.

Painted, glittered, and veloured transfers are ready-to-use. Adding additional embellishments is simply a matter of choice.

Cache Junction and Vignettes Transfers are dyed. They leave absolutely no texture on the fabric. Their appearance and feel is similar to a screened print.

Outline transfers have been used in needlework for ages. I know you've seen the designs used for embroidery, cross-stitch, and needlepoint. Fabric paint and markers can be used with these transfers. A fine-tip marker is perfect to use to color tiny floral designs.

Larger sizes of outline transfers, especially designed for fabric paint, come in every size, design, and type imaginable—including opaque. Combined with pens (transfer and permanent markers) and paints (transparent to heavy glitter), these transfers offer endless possibilities.

The great advantage of using transfers is that an iron is all that is needed to create the desired design. If I had to draw my designs I'd be limited to my capital *S* duck (see Fig. 1-1). That's the extent of my drawing talents!

Transfer paint and markers. I have more fun with these products. The paint (Deka IronOn) is applied to paper. Sulky IronOn Transfer Pens can be applied to either paper or fabric. When the pen is applied to fabric, it must be heat-set. Both the paint or pen can be applied to paper. When these products are dry, you've got an iron-on transfer that can be used repeatedly.

You can even paint or color designs found in the newspaper. (Florist and garden shops have great floral designs in their ads.) Photocopy the design of your dreams and apply paint or pen to the back of the paper. (Then it won't be reversed on the fabric.) Tolin' Station Vellum and Sure-Fit Tracing Vellum work like a charm for this method.

Transfer paper (wax and chalk). The first decision you have to make is whether you want the transfer paper to leave permanent markings. If you do, then use a paper that contains wax. An iron is used to melt the wax into the fabric. If you do not want to leave permanent markings, use a paper that has a chalk coating. Chalk should easily remove from the fabric.

TYING THE TIES

See also Knots, this chapter.

I recommend that you read this entire section before beginning a tie-painted project.

A long list of items can be used for ties (Fig. 9-42) each producing a slightly different effect. The tighter the wrap, the lesser the amount of paint that reaches the inner area of the tied fabric bundle. And as with knots, fabric can be twisted, folded, rolled, or pleated before tying.

Diluted paint that's been used as a tint or dye solution quickly migrates through the fabric. Diluted paint can be used only as a spray or mist application on tied bundles (see Spraying and Misting, this chapter).

There's no such thing as *the* perfect tie material; there are over a dozen perfect tie materials. Some are better for a continuous wrap that goes from the base of the tied fabric bundle to the tip. Others are better for spaced ties that are placed at intervals along the length of the tied bundle.

Porous materials (chenilles) soak up the paint, which is absorbed by the bundle. Nonporous materials (rubber bands) block the paint where they are placed. The amount of fabric included in the bundle can be very small (the size of a dime) to very large (an entire shirt front).

Types (continuous and spaced), materials (porous and nonporous), and sizes (large and small) can be combined in one project.

Many tie materials are reusable. Covered floral tape, garden twist ties, and rubber bands can be removed without cutting. Usually the string, yarn, and thread types take too long to unwind to bother saving. If you do cut ties for removal, carefully clip them with scissors. One little snip can ruin a shirt. I use an old bandage scissors, although children's blunt-tip scissors also work well.

Press the fabric after the paint has dried. Heat-set if the paint was diluted. If tie "peaks," don't flatten, lightly spray the fabric with water or sizing and press a second time. Usually laundering takes care of the remaining peaks.

Methods for bundling fabric and types of placement are as varied as the kinds of tie material. Directions in Chapters 4 and 5 are just the beginning.

The most important thing to remember about ties is that anything that will do the job can be used. Here are just a few suggestions.

Chenilles. These items look like long pipe cleaners. The fuzzy covering really soaks up paint, so paint goes into the bundle. They're better used for medium- and large-sized bundles. Check for colorfastness since chenilles often bleed. But if the bleeded color is right, that may be what you want to use. In this case, heat-set the bleeded color. (Pipe cleaners themselves can be used as ties, but their use is limited because they're so short.)

Cotton string. This is the old standby, although it does have a tendency to break when pulled tight. I prefer Pearl Cotton or crochet thead when I need a tie material for small bundles.

You can, of course, use any inexpensive thread (cotton or spun poly) you've got in a drawer. It's better to use inexpensive thread for a tie than for sewing!

Cotton yarn. This has little stretch, soaks up a lot of paint, and is especially good for medium-sized bundles. It can be used spaced or as a continuous wrap.

Covered floral wire. This is good for spaced and continuous wrap. If pulled tight enough, the color does not seep under the wire. There will be tiny lines of the original color when the tie is removed. Be careful if you use covered floral wire for tiny bundles in T-shirts. The wire may leave peaks that are difficult to flatten. I like the fact that the color of the covering bleeds. It adds an additional color line to the fabric, another line that will need heat-setting.

I prefer the type of covered floral wire that comes on a spool. I think it's easier to use.

Embroidery floss. This is an interesting tie that is good for small- and medium-sized bundles. Use all six strands for strength.

Garbage bag bands. These are those plastic ties with teeth. You stick one end of the band into the hole at the other end, and pull tight. The teeth grab, and the bag stays closed. Use nylon bands to close the tops of your garbage bags, and use the plastic closures for your ties. They're easy to pull tight and they stay that way. The band is tight enough so that paint does not seep under it. There'll be ¼" bands of the original color wherever there was a band.

And don't forget those little plastic tabs used to close plastic bread bags!

Garden twist ties. These come on a continuous roll, which I cut it into 24" to 36" lengths for easier handling. I like these ties for spaced and intermittent wrap. They form a partial block when pulled very tight.

Nylon (hosiery) bands. These can be cut open or used in the circular shape. When the band is cut wide (4") and opened, it can be pulled very tight for excellent spaced ties. Nylon bands do not block paint.

If you are concerned that the nylon's original color may stain your fabric, run the nylon through a wash cycle. Nylon bands used for ties should not be reused since residue from previous use may bleed. (See also Nylon Bands, this chapter.)

Nylon twine. This is strong and does not absorb paint. It can be used as an intermittent continuous wrap for a different type of spaced wrap. It's not too good to use on T-shirts. And it really distorts knit fabric when pulled tightly. This drawback is also true of nylon fishing line.

Plastic food wrap. This is the recycled tie. If you've been wondering what you're going to do with all that plastic food wrap you've been sticking everywhere, use it for ties. Cut the plastic food wrap into strips 2" to 4" wide. Twist each strip so that it's narrow, then wrap it around the bundle. Plastic food wrap can really be pulled tight and tied in a knot for spaced ties.

Polyester yarn. This sometimes has quite a stretch, so it's better to use as a spaced wrap. Polyester yarn doesn't hold paint, being one of the semiporous types.

Rubber bands. These are great for spaced placement. Paint will not seep under the band if you get them good and tight. Be careful: the ones used around newspapers have a tendency to leave black marks.

Tape. This comes in all sizes and weights that provide a variety of uses. Masking tape doesn't bond well, so paint seeps under it. Strapping tape, on the other hand, hangs on like glue. One tied bundle could have a variety of tape types and widths. (See also Tapes, this chapter.)

Twisted paper ribbon. This can be used twisted or untwisted. Twisted is fun to use as a spaced continuous wrap. Untwisted can be used as a loose continuous wrap. Check for colorfastness since some brands of paper ribbon bleed. When you're finished using this item as a tie, you've got painted paper ribbon! (Doesn't everyone want ribbon to match a T-shirt?)

WORKTABLE

Don't overlook the handiest worktable you've got—your adjustable ironing board. The padded surface is perfect for some types of block printing and a great substitute for a pin board. Protect the top of your board with an old sheet, plastic covering, cardboard, or foam board.

Sit in a chair and adjust the board to the height you like for cutting out appliqués, painting designs, attaching embellishments on shirts, or any handwork activity you do. (You'll find a slight difference in height for each activity.)

But don't just use your ironing board for sit-down work. It's great for use for handwork activities that require you to stand. No more of this bending over a too-low table.

If you have one of those adjustable lamps that attach to a tabletop, attach it to the wide end of the board. Once you use an ironing board with a light, you'll never want to take off the lamp.

However, ironing boards do have a way of wrecking the carefully planned decor of a living room. Fortunately there's a floor frame (Morgan's Universal Craft Stand) with adjustable features that adapt to about every crafts and needlework activity. It takes up very little floor space and can be left in a corner when not in use. I've even used it as a display easel!

Recommended Paint Types or Brands for Techniques in Chapters 4 and 5

Some techniques require use of specific paint types or brands for satisfactory results. Substitute any brand you're familiar with that you feel would give satisfactory results.

Manufacturers and brands are listed alphabetically in Appendix B.

JUST A REMINDER: Always follow the Unbreakable Rules of Fabric Painting (Chapter 1) and the Unbreakable Rules of Painting (Chapter 3).

TINTING

Reduce water amount when darker color is desired. Heat-setting is recommended for all diluted paints; pretest for colorfastness.

Deka Silk: 18 ounces water to 2 ounces paint
FabricArts: follow directions on bottle
Jones Tones: 40 ounces water to 2 ounces paint
Just Enough: dilute to desired shade
Galacolor: 3 ounces water to 1 ounce paint
Tumble Dye: dilute to desired shade
Versatex Air-Brush Ink: 1 ounce water and 1 ounce isopropyl alcohol to 6 ounces Ink (alcohol optional)
VisionARTS: highly concentrated liquid fabric dye; follow directions on bottle; not suitable for cotton or cotton/polyblends

ANTIQUE PATINA (CHAPTER 4)

These paints or dyes leave no texture on fabric when diluted. Fabrics are easily hand- or machine-quilted. Heat-setting is recommended.

Deka Silk: suggested color, #715 Cinnamon; 18 ounces water to 2 ounces paint
FabricArts: suggested color, Raw Umber; follow directions on bottle
Just Enough: suggested color, Burnt Umber; dilute to desired shade
Versatex Air-Brush Ink: suggested color, Brown; 6 parts ink, 1 part water, 1 part isopropyl alcohol (alcohol optional)

DYEING (CHAPTER 4)

Use the brands listed in this appendix under Tinting; reduce water for darker color. The following brands can be used as well:

Delta Fabric Dye: 2 ounces water to 2 ounces paint; do not rinse following application; spraying with StaSet recommended
Delta Starlight Fabric Dye: 2 ounces water to 2 ounces paint; do not rinse following application; spraying with StaSet recommended
Tulip Brush Top: 2 ounces water to 2 ounces paint; do not rinse following application; may leave slight texture on surface

PAINT IN A BAG (CHAPTER 4)

Use the brands listed in this appendix under Dyeing and Tinting.

TIES USED WITH LIQUID RESIST (CHAPTER 4)
Paints

Use brands listed for Tinting, Dyeing, or Misting/Spraying.

Glues

Aleen's Budget School Glue: usually requires two launderings for complete removal
Plaid Founder's School Glue: washes out completely in one laundering

See also Other Liquid Resist (Chapter 5)

SOLID RESIST WITH TINT OR DYE (CHAPTER 4)
Paints

See brands listed for Tinting or Dyeing.

Solid Resist

Crayola Crayons (fabric or standard type).
Substitute: children's crayon box

MARBLING (CHAPTER 4)

Size is a gelatin-like solution (slightly thinner than half-set gelatin dessert) on which paint is floated. The density of the size determines the thickness of the paint.

Non-Traditional Size

Liquid laundry starch
Unflavored gelatin

Traditional Size

Createx Marble Powder (Size): requires mixing in blender
Deka Marbling Medium (Size): hand mix
Delta MarbleThix (Size): requires mixing in blender

(Distilled water may be required for mixing size.)

Solution for Pretreating Fabrics (Mordant)

Alum (found in spice department of grocery store): powdered or granules; results not as satisfactory as with aluminum sulfate
Createx Marble Fabric Size
Jacquard (aluminum sulfate)

Marbling Paints

When laundry starch or unflavored gelatin is used as size, paint should have consistency of light to heavy cream; manipulation of thicker paints may be limited. When traditional size is used, paint should have consistency of light cream; test paint on small amount of size before beginning.

Createx Marbling Colors: do not dilute
Deka-PermAir Fabric Paint: dilute 2 ounces paint to 1½ teaspoons water, if necessary.
Versatex Air-Brush Ink: dilute 1 part water to 6 parts paint, if necessary
Liquid Appliqué: squeeze drops on size, do not dilute
Tulip Soft Top: replace brush top with long tip top; squeeze drops on size; usually does not need diluting
Fluid paints, dyes (Deka-Silk, FabricArts, Just Enough, Tumble Dye, etc.): spray or apply drops on size; pretest

Be sure to pretest any type you feel like trying.

MISTING AND SPRAYING (CHAPTER 5)

Dye-Namite, Webbing, or Glitter Webbing
Preval Power Unit with paints suitable for pump or trigger bottle

You can also use brands listed for Tinting or Dyeing which have a dilution rate of at least 3 teaspoons water to 2 ounces paint. You can also use all fluid paints or dyes. Pretest diluted paints; heat-set when dry.

FABRIC STAMPS (INK FOR PAD) (CHAPTER 5)

Glitter, textured, or metallic paints will not give satisfactory results; fluid or very thick paints must be pretested prior to use; additives may be required; purchased pads must not contain alcohol.

PRINT BLOCKS (CHAPTER 5)

Paint selection is determined by type of block and fabric. Glitter or textured paints are usually not suitable for sponge or porous blocks and may require being "patted" on plastic block surface; pretest before beginning project.

FOUND OBJECTS PRINTING (CHAPTER 5)

See Print Blocks, above.

PAINTING WITH A BRUSH (CHAPTER 5)

Use paints labeled "soft" or "brushable." Do not use paints noted as "not suitable for large painted areas" (see Appendix B). Pretest.

PAINTING SILK AND FINE WOVENS (CHAPTER 5)

Crayons: see Solid Resist with Tint or Dye
Paints: use all fluid paints and dyes; brands listed for Tinting or Dyeing; brushed paints noted as "dries soft" or "dries very soft" (Appendix B), or labeled "Soft"; pretest

TRADITIONAL LIQUID RESIST (CAPITAL R) (CHAPTER 5)

Cerulean Blue, Ltd.
Deka-Silk Resist
Delta Color Resist
FabricARTS Water-Based Resist
Jacquard Resist

OTHER LIQUID RESIST (CAPITAL R) CHAPTER 5)

Cerulean Blue, Ltd. Presist

Although similar to Resist, this product offers more options in its use, is easy to use, and rinses out completely. Apply with sponge, brush, roller, syringe, or fine-line applicator bottle. It can be substituted for washable glue resist techniques.

NONTRADITIONAL LIQUID RESIST (LOWERCASE R) (CHAPTER 5)

Many fabric paints can be used as substitutes for Resist. I've listed only a few. The list would be too long if all were included! Use either a fine liner or soft flat brush for paints that are more fluid; an applicator bottle with a metal tip for those with more density. Experiment. Pretest (include laundering).

Cerulean Blue, Ltd: Cloud Cover, Luminère, Neopaque
DecoArt: Metallics Light (excellent as edge finish)
Deka Flair
Fashion-Show: Soft Fabric Paint
Jacquard: Textile Colors
Tulip: Soft Lite Paint
Versatex: Textile Paint

ROLLER PAINTING (CHAPTER 5)

Glitter and textured paints are difficult to apply evenly with rollers; avoid paints "not suitable for large painted areas." Liquid paints and dyes are suitable only when applied to porous items (fabric, sponges, chenilles, etc.). Application with roller will require more paint than brushing.

STENCILS (CHAPTER 5)
Brushed or Rolled

Paint should be at least as thick as heavy cream; thin paints will seep under stencil. Pretest for satisfactory results. Heat-set when required.

Permanent Markers

Apply antifusant to fabric before using marker to eliminate marker bleeding under stencil; heat-set before rinsing antifusant from fabric.

Solid

Delta Stencil Magic Stencil Paint Creme

Spraying

Carnival Arts DyeNamite or Webbing; bottled paints limited to use with Preval Power Unit. Use paints labeled "Air Brush" or diluted paints (see Tinting or Dyeing, this appendix). Attach stencil securely to fabric; block adjoining areas (tape, freezer paper, etc.). Pretest; heat-set when dry.

Brands and Manufacturers of Paint, Resist, Fabric Coatings, and Permanent Markers

Dilution amounts and recommended laundry procedures given for a paint were provided to me by that paint manufacturer and were current as of March 1, 1993. Always read and follow directions printed on each paint container before use.

In this appendix paint brands and manufacturers are given first, followed by paint-related supplies such as Resist, fabric coatings, and permanent markers, beginning on page 122. Listings are alphabetical, by brand name. A cross-reference of manufacturers' names that differ from brand names is also given at end of this appendix.

Mail-order sources are listed in the Supply Sources at the end of this book. If a mail-order source is not given, contact manufacturers for retail outlets or mail-order sources.

How to Use This Appendix

Listings in this appendix appear in alphabetical order by paint brand name. Following is an explanation of terms used in this appendix.

Brand names: names of products made by the manufacturer. NOTE: Space does not allow listing of all products made by each manufacturer.

Mail-Order source: Sources given have been suggested by the manufacturer; see Supply Sources at the end of this book.

Suitable fabrics: The following categories are given for suitable fabrics. NOTE: *Do not use acrylic or acrylic blends.*

All fabrics: fine, medium, and heavyweight wovens; knits; and sweatshirt fleece (silk, rayon, cotton, and cotton/poly blend).

Poly/cotton: fine, medium, and heavyweight wovens; knits; and sweatshirt fleece. (Usually the blend is 50% polyester, 50% cotton.)

Stretch fabrics: athletic wear with high stretch. (Usually blended with either Spandex or Lycra.)

Silk and wool: use only pure silk or wool fabrics (see Visionarts).

Maximum dilution. Follow manufacturer's recommendations. Adding more water than recommended may cause

unsatisfactory results. Follow these guidelines as you measure:

2 ounces = 4 tablespoons or ¼ cup
3 teaspoons = 1 tablespoon or ½ ounce
1½ teaspoons = ½ tablespoon or ¼ ounce

Additives. Use additives as directed by manufacturer. Do not mix additives from one brand with paints of another brand.

Heat-set required. Follow directions on paint container.

Heat-set recommended. Unless directed to the contrary by manufacturer, follow these guidelines:

1 Press on wrong side of fabric.
2 Do not heat-set until paint has dried.
3 Do not heat-set dimensional paints.
4 Do not apply high heat to glitter paints (iron temperature should not exceed synthetic setting).

Press for 60 seconds at cotton setting, or highest setting allowed for fabric (cover fabric with cooking parchment paper). Heat-set glitter paints in dryer for 10 minutes, or press on wrong side with warm iron (extreme heat has a way of melting glitter). If you heat-set glitter paints in the dryer, place your item in a pillow case and tie it closed before drying (see Glitter Drift in Chapter 9).

Features. Here you will find a partial listing of features and uses of types or names of paint of that brand; not every type of brand is suitable for all techniques listed.

NOTE: This is a partial listing of manufacturer's recommendations. Consult container and packaging for additional information before beginning projects.

Paints

CLOUD COVER
Cerulean Blue, Ltd.
P.O. Box 21168
Seattle, WA 98111-3168
Customer service: 206-323-8600; orders: 1-800-676-8602
Brand name: Cloud Cover

Mail-order source: Cerulean Blue, Ltd.
Suitable fabrics: all fabrics
Maximum dilution: 1½ teaspoon (¼ ounce) water to 2 ounces paint
Additives: Clear Extender
Heat-set: not required
Features: dries soft; semi-transparent; colors mix, wide color range; can be sprayed with water after application; suitable for techniques not requiring heavy dilution.
Note: Not dimensional; do not mix with other brands of paint; do not launder for 2 weeks.

CRAYOLA CRAFT
Binney & Smith
1100 Church Lane
Easton, PA 18044
1-800-CRAYOLA
Brand names: Glossy, Ritzy, Splashy, Glitzy
Suitable fabrics: poly/cotton blends
Maximum dilution: do not dilute
Additives: not required
Heat-set: not required
Features: colors correspond to Crayola Crayons; bottle shaped for easy outlining; suitable for techniques not requiring dilution of paint.
Note: Not suitable for large painted areas; launder inside out, cold or warm water, low heat dryer.

CREATEX COLORS
ColorCraft, Ltd.
14 Airport Road
East Granby, CT 06026
1-800-243-2712
Brand names: Createx Textile Colors, Createx Colors Marble, Createx Pearlized Colors
Mail-order source: ColorCraft, Ltd.
Suitable fabrics: all fabrics, except slick and smooth types
Maximum dilution: Textile and Pearlized Colors, 3 teaspoons (½ ounce) water to 2 ounces paint; Marbling Colors, do not dilute
Additives: Pearl White (Extender)
Heat-set: required
Features: dries very soft; excellent for large painted areas; wide range of Pearlized Colors; Textile Colors and Pearlized Colors mixable; can be sprayed with water after application; suitable for techniques not requiring heavy dilution.
Note: Not dimensional; avoid thick buildup of paint, brush into fibers; launder in cold water, inside out; machine drying not recommended; not dimensional; do not launder marbled fabric for two weeks.

DECOART
P.O. Box 360
Stanford, KY 40480
1-800-367-3047
Brand names: DecoArt Heavy Metals Light, DecoArt Dazzling Metallics, Hot Shots, DecoArt Shimmering Pearls, So-Soft, DecoArt Dimensions

Mail-order source: Craft King; Creative Wholesale Distributors
Suitable fabrics: all fabrics
Maximum dilution: Hot Shots, 3 teaspoons (½ ounce) water to 2 ounces paint; all other paints, do not dilute
Additives: Fabric Painting Medium; Transparent Medium; Glo-It Luminescent Paint Medium; White So-Soft
Heat-set: not required
Features: Heavy Metals Light: subtle glitter, very soft. Dazzling Metallics: colors range from translucent to opaque. Hot Shots: fluorescent colors. Shimmering Pearls opaque: mixable with Transparent Medium for transparency. So-Soft: mixable with Transparent Medium for transparency. Dimensions colors coordinate with Brush-On Paints. Dimensions suitable for stretch athletic wear. DecoArt also makes several paint-related products. DecoArt paints are suitable for techniques not requiring heavy dilution; some techniques may require additives.
Note: Do not use lemon-scented detergents; do not use softeners with Hot Shots; do not use additives with Dazzling Metallics.

DEKA
Decart, Inc.
Box 309
Morrisville, VT 05661
802-888-4217
Brand names: Deka-Silk, Deka-Silk Resist, Deka Colorless Extender, Deka Silk Stop-Flow Primer, Deka-Permanent Fabric Paint, Deka-PermAir, Deka-IronOn Transfer Paint, Deka-Fun, Deka-Flair
Mail-order source: Dick Blick, Dharma Trading Co., Sax Arts and Crafts
Suitable fabrics: Deka-Silk, Deka-Permanent Fabric Paint, Deka-PermAir, Deka-PermGlitter, all except acrylics; Deka-IronOn, 60/40 synthetic blend to 100% synthetic (not acrylic)
Maximum dilution: Deka-Silk, 18 ounces water with 2 ounces paint; Deka-Permanent Fabric Paint and Deka-PermAir, 3 teaspoons (½ ounce) water to 2 ounces paint; Deka-IronOn, Deka-PermGlitter, Deka-Fun, Deka-Flair, do not dilute
Additives: Deka Colorless Extender; Deka Covering White; Deka Silk Stop-Flow Primer (antifusant, fabric coating)
Heat-set: required, follow manufacturer's instructions; do not heat-set Deka-Fun
Features: IronOn: unique transfer paint is suitable for stamp pad ink, marbling, brush techniques. Deka-Silk: leaves no texture, suitable for all techniques not requiring thick paints. Deka-Permanent and Deka-PermAir: very soft, suitable for techniques not requiring heavy dilution. Deka-Permanent and Deka-PermAir can be mixed together. Deka-PermGlitter: very soft, suitable for areas up to 4" square. Deka-Flair: soft dimensional, suitable as resist. Deka-Fun: dimensional glitter, suitable as glue substitute. Deka Stop-Flow Primer prevents paint and fabric markers from spreading.
Note: IronOn cannot be used on 100% natural fabrics. Deka-PermAir should be applied in a light coat, not

dimensional, allow to dry overnight before heat-setting. Deka-PermGlitter not dimensional. Deka-Fun requires cool dryer and iron. Stop-Flow Primer is a permanent finish, leaves slight texture on fabric.

DELTA
Delta Technical Coatings, Inc.
2550 Pellissier Place
Whittier, CA 90601-1505
1-800-423-4135

Brand names: Delta Fabric Dye, Delta Starlight Dye, Delta Liquid Stars, Delta Liquid Hearts, Stencil Magic Paint Creme, Ceramcoat, Gleams, StaSet, Swell Stuff

Mail-order source: Grason's, Inc.

Suitable fabrics: all fabrics

Maximum dilution: non-dimensional paints, 3 teaspoons (½ ounce) water to 2 ounces paint; Fabric Dyes and Starlight Fabric Dyes, 2 ounces water to 2 ounces paint; Dimensional, Glitter, Ceramcoat, do not dilute

Additives: Textile Medium StaSet; Swell Stuff #1200 (use only with Ceramcoat Acrylic)

Heat-set: Fabric Dye, Starlight Fabric Dye, Swell Stuff required; non-dimensional paints, recommended not required; glitter, recommended not required; dimensional paint, do not heat-set

Features: Fabric Dye and Starlight Fabric Dye mixable. Delta Starlight is opaque. Fabric Dye and Starlight are suitable for techniques not requiring heavy dilution, can be sprayed with water after application. Liquid Stars and Hearts are textured iridescent. Stencil Creme solid applicator is suitable for "rubbings." Gleams Ceramcoat is suitable for paper jewelry. StaSet improves colorfastness for diluted paints. Dimensionals are suitable as glue substitute.

Note: Ceramcoat requires additive for fabric use (Swell Stuff #1200).

DIZZLE
Colortex Co.
One Cape May Street
Harrison, NJ 07029
201-482-5500

Brand names: Dizzle Soft Paints, Dizzle Brights, Dizzle Magic Sticker Paint, Dizzle Slick, Dizzle Puff, Dizzle Sparkling Tints

Suitable fabrics: all fabrics

Maximum dilution: non-dimensional paints, 3 teaspoons (½ ounce) water with 2 ounces paint; dimensionals, Glitters, Magic Sticker, do not dilute

Additives: Soft Paint Extender (increases transparency of paints)

Heat-set: dimensional paints, do not heat-set; non-dimensional paints, recommended not required; Glitter paints, recommended not required

Features: Dizzle makes a wide selection of paint types and paint-related products, a soft tube container for easy outlining, several soft paints, and transparent Brush-on Soft Paints and Sparkling Tints. Transparent shades are excellent for all types of transfers. Soft Paint Extender increases transparency, lightens color. Sparkling Tint has subtle glitter effect. Slick is suitable as glue substitute.

Magic Sticker Paints used to make removable stickers. Various products are suitable for techniques not requiring heavy dilution.

Note. Read instructions on cardboard packaging for each paint type.

DYLON USA
101 Wheaton Drive
Youngsville, NC 27596
919-556-2977

Brand names: Dylon Color Fun Fabric Paints

Mail-order source: Dylon USA, Attention: Customer Service

Suitable fabrics: all fabrics

Maximum dilution: 3 teaspoons (½ ounce) water to 2 ounces paint

Additives: Extender

Heat-set: required

Features: paints dry soft; colors mix for wide range of colors; suitable for techniques not requiring heavy dilution.

Note: Not dimensional.

DYE-NAMITE
WEBBING
GLITTER WEBBING
Carnival Arts
P.O. Box 4145
Northbrook, IL 60065
1-800-527-4700

Brand names: Dye-Namite, Webbing, and Glitter Webbing

Mail-order source: Craft King

Suitable fabrics: all fabrics

Maximum dilution: cannot be diluted

Heat-set: follow directions

Additives: none

Features: instant spray application; fast drying. Dye-Namite dries soft with no texture; Webbing and Glitter Webbing are usable on several surfaces

Note: Follow instructions on can; limited to spray and mist techniques.

FABRICARTS
Ivy Imports
12213 Distribution Way
Beltsville, MD 20705

Brand names: FabricARTS Liquid "All-Fabric" Paints, FabricARTS Dilutant, FabricARTS Thickener

Mail-order source: Textile Colors

Suitable fabrics: all fabrics

Maximum dilution: must be diluted with FabricARTS Dilutant/water solution; lighter shades obtained with White

Additives: Dilutant, White, Thickener

Heat-set: required

Features: fluid fabric paint; very easy to use; usable in refillable marker; colors mixable; suitable for all techniques, additives may be required.

Note: Use Thickener for techniques requiring thick paints; use dilutant to ensure colorfastness.

FASHION SHOW
Plaid Enterprises, Inc.
1649 International Boulevard
P.O. Box 7600
Norcross, GA 30091-7600
　Brand names: Fashion Show Sparkle, Fashion Show Fabric Soft Paint, Fashion Show Fabric Soft Paint Extender, Fashion Show Jewel Dimensional Paint, Fashion Show Metallic Dimensional Paint
　Suitable fabrics: all fabrics; some types may require Fabric Soft Paint Extender for use with fine wovens
　Maximum dilution: do not dilute
　Heat-set: Fabric Soft Paints, required; dimensionals, do not heat-set
　Additives: Soft Paint Fabric Extender
　Features: flexible bottle tip for easy outline, detail and "dot" painting. Fabric Soft Paint dries very soft. Extender increases transparency, allows spraying with water after application. Fashion Show Sparkle has subtle glitter effect. Several metallic shades; suitable for techniques not requiring heavy dilution.
　Note: Cool water wash, gentle cycle.

GALACOLOR
Galacraft, Inc.
1760 East 15th Street
Los Angeles, CA 90021
1-800-BUY-GALA
　Brand names: Galacolors, Ultra Soft 2000, Galafetti, Gala Color Extender, Plexi
　Mail-order source: Galacraft, Inc.
　Suitable fabrics: all fabrics
　Heat-set: do not heat-set
　Additives: Gloss Extender; Gel; Plexi, #34
　Maximum dilution: 3 ounces water to 1 ounce paint; Extender and Gel, 1 ounce water to 1 ounce additive
　Features: variety of types; all types and additives intermixable; colors range from transparent crystals to metallic opaque. Plexi 34 or Gel: excellent for clear outlining. Galafetti: textured suitable for spreading over large areas. Diluted Extender is suitable as seam sealant. All paints and additives suitable as glue substitute; suitable for all techniques.
　Note: Do not use hair dryer to dry; do not launder for one week; launder in gentle cycle, remove from dryer while still damp.

GRUMBACHER
30 Engelhard Drive
Cranbury, NJ 08512
　Brand names: Grumbacher Galaxy, Grumbacher Permanent Fabric Paint, Grumbacher Fab Fixative, Grumbacher Permanent Fabric Dye
　Suitable fabrics: all fabrics
　Maximum dilution: do not dilute
　Additives: Textile Medium; Fab Fixative
　Heat-set: follow manufacturer's instructions
　Features: Galaxy: subtle glitter. Permanent Fabric Paint: soft dimensional. Suitable for techniques not requiring heavy dilution.

　Note: Hand-wash, do not wring, line-dry; do not use softeners or detergents.

JACQUARD
Rupert, Gibbon & Spider, Inc.
P.O. Box 425
Healdsburg, CA 95448
1-800-442-0455
　Brand names: Jacquard Textile Colors, StarBright, No Flow
　Mail-order source: Rupert, Gibbon & Spider, Inc.
　Suitable fabrics: all fabrics
　Maximum dilution: 1 ½ teaspoons (¼ ounce) water to 2 ounces paint
　Additives: Colorless Extender; White; Super Opaque White; Metallic Pearl White; Colorless Starbright; No Flow (antifusant, fabric coating)
　Heat-set: required
　Features: dries soft; extensive range of basic, metallic, and neon colors. Starbright has subtle glitter effect. Colorless Starbright mixable with Textile Colors. Several additives enhance properties. Can be sprayed with water after application; suitable for techniques not requiring heavy dilution. No Flow excellent antifusant for paint and markers, removed in laundering.
　Note: Not dimensional. Starbright can be heat-set in dryer or with warm iron; do not use hot iron.

JONES TONES, INC.
68743 Perez Road, #D-16
Cathedral City, CA 92234
619-321-9665
　Brand names: Jones Tones Stretch Fabric Paint, Jones Tones Plexi 400
　Mail-order source: Craft Stop
　Suitable fabrics: all fabrics
　Maximum dilution: 40 ounces water to 2 ounces paint
　Additives: Plexi 400 (extender, creates translucent colors)
　Heat-set: recommended, not required for tinting, antique patina, dyeing techniques; not required for other techniques
　Features: multi-use product, tinting to dimensional; colors mixable; suitable as dimensional or brush-on paint for stretch fabrics; all colors, including Plexi 400, suitable as glue substitute; machine dryable; suitable for all techniques.
　Note: Dilute, 2 teaspoons water to 2 ounces paint, when painting large areas; texture increases when dilution rate decreases.

JO SONJA'S ARTIST'S COLORS
Chroma Acrylics, Inc.
P.O. Box 510
Hainesport, NJ 08036
1-800-257-3278
　Brand names: Jo Sonja's Artist Colors, Jo Sonja's Textile Medium
　Mail-order sources: Chroma Acrylics, Inc.; Sax Arts and Crafts

Suitable fabrics: poly/cotton blends
Maximum dilution: 3 teaspoons water (½ ounce) to 2 ounces paint
Additives: Textile Medium
Heat-set: required
Features: tube container; can be used on fabric, furniture, wood; wide range of colors, including metallics and Folk Colors; suitable for techniques not requiring heavy dilution.
Note: Jo Sonja's Textile Medium required when painting fabric, pretest before using as dimensional or for large painted areas.

JUST ENOUGH
Carnival Arts, Inc.
See Dye-Namite
Suitable fabrics: all fabrics
Maximum dilution: unlimited; product is dye, fabric retains smallest amount of color
Additives: not required
Heat-set: required
Features: liquid dye, unlimited dilution with water for desired shade; dries soft, with no texture; colors mixable; suitable for all techniques except those requiring thick paints.
Note: Not dimensional; test before using for stenciling, stamps or block prints.

LIQUID APPLIQUÉ
Marvy Uchida of America, Corp.
See Permanent Markers section of this appendix.

LIQUITEX
Binney & Smith
1100 Church Lane
P.O. Box 431
Easton, PA 18044-0431
Consumers Affairs Department: 215-253-6272
Brand names: Liquitex Concentrated Artist Color, Liquitex Liquigems, Liquitex Marble Ease
Suitable fabrics: poly/cotton blends
Maximum dilution: Concentrated Artist Color, 14 ounces water with 2 ounces paint; Liquigems, do not dilute
Additives: Liquitex Marble Ease
Heat-set: Concentrated Artist Color, required; Liquigems, do not heat-set
Features: wide color range. Liquigems are dimensional. Artist Color is suitable for all techniques. Marble Ease is an additive for marbling paint.
Note: Launder in cold water, right side out. Artist Color has moderate texture when diluted, not suitable for fine wovens; not suitable for large painted areas when not diluted. Liquigems not suitable for large painted areas.

LUMINÈRE
NEOPAQUE
Cerulean Blue, Ltd.
See Cloud Cover

Suitable fabrics: all fabrics
Maximum dilution: do not dilute
Additives: not required
Heat-set: required
Features: dries very soft. Luminère and Neopaque can be mixed together for endless color possibilities, several metallic and opaque colors. Can be sprayed with water after application; suitable as Resist; suitable for techniques not requiring heavy dilution.
Note: Not dimensional; heat-set both sides of fabric at cotton setting; gentle action wash and dry.

PALMER FABRIC PAINT
Palmer Paint Products, Inc.
Troy, MI 48083
1-800-521-1383
Brand names: Palmer Acrylics, Paint Pots, Palmer Shaded Transfer Paints, Palmer Medium, Palmer Fabric Paint
Mail-order source: Aleene's
Suitable fabrics: all fabrics except silk and acrylics, best results on 50/50 poly/cotton blends
Maximum dilution: Fabric Paint, do not dilute; Shaded Transfer Paint, 2 parts paint to 1 part water
Additives: Medium, used as extender with Fabric Paints; used as textile medium with Acrylic Paint, 1 part Acrylic Paint to 2 parts Medium)
Heat-set: required, Fabric Paint and Acrylics/Medium mix; recommended not required, Shaded Transfer Paint
Features: Paint Pots snap-on tops prevent paint from drying out. Available in packaged color assortments, fluorescent and metallic colors. Primary and pastel color sets in Shaded Transfer Paints. Shaded Transfer Paint dries soft; dilute with water or medium for desired thickness and shade. Medium added to Palmer Acrylics reduces stiffness. Suitable for techniques not requiring heavy dilution.
Note: Not dimensional; do not apply heat directly on paint, heat-set on wrong side of fabric, protect painted area with cooking parchment paper, do not heat-set until completely dry; heavy layers of paint may crack; wash/dry instructions on package, wait at least 3 days to launder.

POLYMARK
Polymerics
24 Prime Park Way
Natick, MA 01760
508-650-4500
Brand names: Glitter, Sparkles, Iridescent
Suitable fabrics: poly/cotton blends
Maximum dilution: do not dilute
Heat-set: do not heat-set
Features: 1-ounce bottle; all types suitable as glue substitute. Glitter excellent for thick-line application. Sparkles and Iridescent can be applied with spreader to small areas (2" square). All types suitable for dimensional techniques.
Note: Not suitable for large painted areas; wait one week before laundering; launder in warm wash and rinse, low heat dryer.

SCRIBBLES

Duncan Crafts
5673 East Shields Avenue
Fresno, CA 93727

Brand names: Matchables, 3-Dimensional Fabric Writers, Brush 'n Soft Fabric Paint, Soft Fashion Paint, Glittering, Shiny, and Crystals

Suitable fabrics: poly/cotton blends

Maximum dilution: 3-Dimensional Fabric Writers and Brush 'n Soft Fabric Paint, 2 ounces water to 2 ounces paint; Glittering, Crystals, do not dilute

Additives: not required

Heat-set: dimensional, do not heat-set; soft, recommended not required; Glittering, recommended not required

Features: Soft Fashion Paint Matchables and 3-Dimensional types are color-coordinated. Available in dimensional iridescent colors. Soft Fashion Paint is transparent. Dimensional paints suitable as glue substitute. Matchables are suitable for all techniques not requiring heavy dilution.

Note: Shiny not suitable for large painted areas; Soft Fashion Paint texture softens with laundering. Launder garments inside out, warm water wash and rinse, gentle cycle, low heat or air-dry; turn right side out immediately after drying.

TULIP

Tulip Productions
24 Prime Park Way
Natick, MA 01760
508-650-4500

Brand names: Tulip, Easy Flow, Pearl, Sparkles, Puffy, Crystals, Slick, Glitter, Color Switch, Soft Lite Paint, Soft Sparkling Tints, Soft Brush Top, Soft Covers All, Soft Glitter, Soft Metallic, Fiber Fun, Fashion Suede, Color Switch, ColorPoint

Suitable fabrics: all fabrics

Maximum dilution: non-dimensional paints, 3 teaspoons water (½ ounce) water to 2 ounces paint; BrushTop, 2 ounces water to 2 ounces paint; dimensional, glitter, Color Point, Fashion Suede paints, do not dilute

Additives: not required

Heat-set: non-dimensional, recommended, not required; glitter, recommended, not required; Puff, Fashion Suede, Lite Soft, Jumpin'Jeans Denim, Color Switch, follow directions; dimensionals, do not heat-set

Features: comprehensive range of paint types. Easy Flow bottle designed for easy outline and detail painting. 4-ounce bottles with Paint Writer tip. ColorPoint bottle designed for paint "dot" technique. Several soft dimensional and non-dimensional paints; soft translucent and opaque paints. Most dimensional types suitable as glue substitute. Soft Brush Top suitable for marbling. Soft Lite Paint suitable as resist. Various types suitable for all techniques except those requiring heavy dilution.

Note: Launder items in warm water wash and rinse, do not use cold water; follow laundry instructions on bottle; some paints require line dry; do not use Soft Sparkling Tints or Soft Glitter with dimensional paints. Puffy Paints not suitable as glue substitute. Tip should not touch fabric when you apply Color Switch Paints.

TUMBLE DYE

Seitec: Sew Easy Industries
2701 West 1800 S
Logan, UT 84321
1-800-333-3279

Mail-order source: Seitec: Sew Easy Industries

Suitable fabrics: all fabrics

Heat-set: required

Maximum dilution: unlimited

Additives: none

Features: liquid dye; packaged in pump (mist) bottle; dries soft, no texture; colors intermixable; can be used in refillable marker; suitable for all techniques, except those requiring thick paints.

Note: Salting technique does not alter appearance.

U.TEE.IT

Dupey Management Corporation
9015 Sterling Street
Irving, TX 75063
214-929-4676

Brand names: Pearlescent, Glitz, Gloss

Mail-order source: Dupey Management Corporation; Rainbo Productions, Inc.

Suitable fabrics: poly/cottons

Maximum dilution: do not dilute

Additives: not required

Heat-set: not required

Features: improved formula, smooth, even flow from bottle; flat bottle for easy outline and detail painting; economical 4-ounce bottle. Pearlescent and Gloss can be sprayed with water after application. Glitz (glitter) easily applied in fine line; Glitz dries soft if thinly applied with spreader. All types suitable as glue substitute; suitable for techniques not requiring dilution.

Note: Launder inside out, gentle cycle, warm water wash and rinse, low heat or line dry; fabric softener recommended.

VERSATEX TEXTILE PAINT

Siphon Art
P.O. Box 150710
San Rafael, CA 94915
510-236-0949

Brand names: Versatex Textile Paint, Versatex Textile Air-Brush Ink

Mail-order source: Dharma Trading Co.

Suitable fabrics: all fabrics

Additives: Textile Paint Opaque White; Textile Paint Extender; isopropyl alcohol

Heat-set: required

Maximum dilution: Textile Paint, 4 ounces water plus 1 ounce isopropyl alcohol to 1 ounce paint; Air-Brush Ink, 1 ounce water plus 1 ounce isopropyl alcohol to 6 ounces Ink; (alcohol is optional additive, ensures bright colors)

Features: Textile Paint and Air-Brush Ink can be mixed together. Textile Paint dries soft, has little texture; available in several frosted colors; all colors intermixable; suitable for all techniques. Air-Brush Ink has thinner consistency than Textile Paint, dries very soft, has no texture; available in several fluorescent colors; all colors intermixable; not limited to air-brush use, suitable for all techniques except those requiring thick paints.

Note: Textile Paint and Air-Brush Ink non-dimensional; avoid heavy buildup, push paint into fabric; pretest Air-Brush Ink before using as stencil paint; mild detergent recommended, dry at low heat, tumbling increases softness of Textile Paint.

VISIONARTS
See FabricARTS
Brand names: Visionarts, Visionarts Catalyst
Mail-order sources: Textile Colors
Suitable fabrics: limited to silk, wool, rayon, and nylon
Maximum dilution: rate depends upon color, follow instructions on bottle
Additives: Visionarts Catalyst, required
Heat-set: not required
Features: non-toxic, liquid dye; absorbed by fabric; dries very soft, texture of fabric not altered; usable in refillable marker; easy painting method for fine wovens, frame not required; suitable for techniques requiring heavy dilution.
Note: Use catylst as directed.

Paint-Related Supplies

Refer to brand name in Paint section for address and mail-order information if not included in these listings.

RESIST BRANDS
Traditional (Products Labeled Resist)

Traditional Resist may not give satisfactory results on heavyweight wovens, knits, and sweatshirt fleece. Use of fine-line applicator bottle required. Clear Resist is removed in laundering. Colors and metallics are colorfast. Pretest before beginning project. See Resist section, Appendix A.

Use of Gutta is not recommended for beginners.

Cerulean Blue, Ltd. RESIST: clear, colors, metallics
Deka-Silk Resist: clear, color, metallics
Delta Color Resist: clear
FabricARTS Water-Based Resist: clear, colors, gold
Jacquard Resist: clear, colors, metallics

Other Resist Product
PRESIST
Cerulean Blue, Ltd.
Features: liquid paste starch; apply with fine-line applicator, stamp, block, brush, roller; easy to use; rinses out completely in water.
Note: May not provide sharp definition of detail obtained with Resist; water-soluble, not suitable for dipped or immersed techniques.

Washable Glues Used as Resist
BUDGET SCHOOL GLUE
Aleene's (see Supply Sources)

FOUNDER'S SCHOOL GLUE
See Plaid Enterprises, Inc.

Paints Used as Resist
See Appendix A

FABRIC COATINGS
Antifusants
NO FLOW
Jacquard
Suitable fabrics: all fabrics
Features: easily applied with brush, roller, block; prevents bleeding and spreading of marker or paint; removed in laundering
Note: Heat-set marker or paint before laundering.

STOP-FLOW PRIMER
Deka
Suitable fabrics: all fabrics
Features: easily applied with brush, roller, block; prevents bleeding and spreading of marker or paint; leaves slight texture on fabric.
Note: Permanent finish, is not removed in laundering; heat-set marker or paint before laundering.

Textile Medium

Use only as directed by paint manufacturer. Can be used with markers. Heat-setting usually required. Permanent finish, texture depends upon brand. Pretest.

PERMANENT MARKERS

Application of antifusant to fabric recommended before using markers.

Apply stabilizing layer (see Stabilizing Fabric, Chapter 9) to wrong side of fabric before using markers. Leave in place until after heat-setting.

Allow marker to dry minimum 12 hours before heat-setting.

Replace marker cap immediately after use.

Decorator Marking Pen
LIQUID APPLIQUÉ
Marvy Uchida of America, Corporation
1027 East Burgrove Street
Carson, CA 90746
Suitable fabrics: all fabrics, stabilize
Maximum dilution: do not dilute
Antifusant: not required
Heat-set: required
Features: puffs with heat; barrel container has applicator tip; easy application of fine line or dots; suitable for stamp or block prints, outlining designs, small brushed areas (squeeze paint from barrel on non-stick surface when used with brush or roller); available in several colors.

Note: Not suitable as glue substitute; must dry minimum 12 hours before puffing; stabilize fabric to eliminate puckering; store with tip down.

Enamel Markers
GLOSS PAINT MARKERS
The Testor Corporation
620 Buckee Street
Rockford, IL 61104-4891
815-962-6654
Mail order: J. R. Hennis Wholesale
   Suitable fabrics: heavy, tightly woven fabrics; stabilizing usually not necessary
   Antifusant: usually not required
   Heat-set: not required
   Features: dries soft; soft wedge tip; excellent for canvas shoes, banners, items receiving heavy use or subjected to weather
   Note: Use in well-ventilated area; do not launder for 1 week; clean up with odorless turpentine or substitute

Fabric Marking Pens
BANAR FABRIC FUN PENS
Banar Designs
P.O. Box 483
Fallbrook, CA 92028
   Mail-order source: Banar Designs
   Suitable fabrics: all fabrics, stabilize for best results
   Antifusant: recommended
   Heat-set: required
   Features: pointed brush tip; wide range of colors; slow drying; apply gray or black under lighter shades for shading; suitable for coloring iron-on transfers, stamp prints, small designs.
   Note: Do not launder for one week; store horizontally.

DYLON COLOR FUN PENS
Dylon USA
   Suitable fabrics: all fabrics, stabilize for best results
   Antifusant: recommended
   Heat-set: required
   Features: wedge tip; fast dry; variety of colors; suitable for coloring larger designs.
   Note: Fast dry, not suitable for blending adjoining colors; store horizontally.

FABRICMATE
Y & C
490 Eccles
South San Fransico, CA 94080
415-737-8888
   Mail-order source: Dick Blick; Cerulean Blue, Ltd.; Dharma Trading Co.; Ruppert, Gibbon & Spider, Inc.; Sax Arts and Crafts
   Suitable fabrics: all fabrics, stabilize for best results
   Antifusant: recommended
   Heat-set: recommended
   Features: comprehensive range of colors, tip sizes and types, including calligraphy and extra fine-tip Permawriter II. Slow drying; colors can be blended for water-color effect. Suitable for coloring iron-on transfers, stamp prints, large and small designs.

Note: Heat-set fabric projects; do not launder for one week; store horizontally.

MARVY MARKER
Marvy Uchida of America, Corporation
See Liquid Appliqué (this section)
   Mail-order source: Dick Blick, Sax Arts and Crafts
   Suitable fabrics: all fabrics, stabilize for best results
   Antifusant: recomended
   Heat-set: recommended
   Features: comprehensive range of colors, tip sizes and types, including very soft brush tip and DecoColor metallics with extra fine tip; fast drying, except Brush Marker; suitable for coloring iron-on transfers, stamp prints, large and small designs.
   Note: Heat-set fabric projects; do not launder for one week; store horizontally.

Refillable Marker
FABRICARTS
   Mail-order source: Textile Colors
   Suitable fabrics: dependent upon paint or dye used in marker
   Antifusant: dependent upon desired effect
   Heat-set: dependent upon fluid paint or dye used in marker
   Features: marker barrel can be filled repeatedly with any fluid paint or dye in desired color; wedge tip.
   Note: Store marker horizontally when filled; must be used with fluid paint or dye.

Transfer Pens
SULKY IRON-ON TRANSFER PEN
Sulky of America
3113 Broadpoint Drive
Harbor Heights, FL 33983
1-800-874-4115
   Mail-order source: Clotilde, Inc.; Nancy's Notions, Ltd.; Speed Stitch
   Suitable fabrics: all fabrics; stabilize for best results
   Antifusant: rarely required (pretest)
   Heat-set: required
   Features: transfer pen usable on paper for repeat patterns, or on fabrics as marker; dries rapidly on fabric; wide range of colors, including opaque white for dark fabrics; suitable for coloring iron-on transfers, stamp prints, small designs.
   Note: Must be heat-set when used directly on fabric; do not launder for one week. White ink pen may not produce good results when used directly on fabric. Store pens horizontally; follow directions on packaging.

Cross-Reference

Manufacturer's names that differ from brand names of their products:

   Binney & Smith: see Crayola Craft or Liquitex
   Carnival Arts: see Dye-Namite, Webbing, Glitter Webbing, or Just Enough
   Cerulean Blue, Ltd.: see Cloud Cover or Lumière and Neopaque

Chroma Acrylics, Inc.: see Jo Sonja's Artist's Colors
ColorCraft Ltd.: see Createx Colors
Colortex Co.: see Dizzle
Decart Inc.: see Deka
Duncan Crafts: see Scribbles
Dupey Management Corporation: see U.tee.it
Galacraft, Inc.: see Galacolor
Marvy Uchida: see Liquid Appliqué or Marvy Marker

Plaid Enterprises, Inc.: see Fashion Show
Polymerics: see Polymark
Rupert, Gibbon & Spider, Inc.: see Jacquard
Seitec: Sew Easy Industries: see Tumble Dye
Siphon Art: see Versatex Textile Paint
Sulky: see Sulky Iron-On Transfer Pen
Y & C: see FabricMate

Tools for Applying Paint, Resist, and Glues

Many of these products are available by mail order. See Supply Sources at the end of this book.

BOTTLES
Fine-Line Applicator

Fine-line applicators are soft plastic bottles with removable metal tips. They are available in ½-ounce to 16-ounce sizes; tips can be used on other paint or glue bottles.

Cerulean Blue, Ltd.
Createx
Dharma Trading Co.
Embossart
Textile Colors
Rupert, Gibbon & Spider, Inc. (The 16-ounce bottle is a gem; use the large metal tips available from Rupert)
Wilton Enterprises (decorator tips used for cake frosting, disposable plastic frosting bags, connector collars for bags)

Pull Top/Squirt-Type

Rupert, Gibbon & Spider, Inc.
Substitute: cleaned mustard bottles

Flat-Sided Squeeze Bottle

Cerulean Blue, Ltd.
Substitute: empty paint bottle

Empty Paint Containers

All you have to do is clean them out! use pliers to remove tip for cleaning and filling

BRUSHES
Disposable Sponge or Foam

Sizes from 1″ to 4″ are available in hardware, crafts, some grocery stores and all crafts supply catalogs.

¼″ Size (Daubers)

Textile Colors (both pointed and flat-end daubers)
Substitute: foam applicators for eye makeup; foam swabs used to clean computers

Bristle

Purchase bristle brushes intended for acrylic or fabric paint. A starter collection would include a fine liner, soft flat or soft round, and flat hard scrubber. Don't waste money on poorly made brushes. With care, brushes last for years.

Cerulean Blue, Ltd.: Y & C brushes

BRUSH CLEANER

After testing numerous brands of brush cleaners, I found I still prefer the one I've used for years—Brush Plus, a Plaid Enterprises, Inc., product. It's economical and has many uses. It cleans brushes and removes goofs and mishaps. Available in crafts stores and arts and crafts catalogs. (Chapter 3 has instructions for cleaning brushes.)

DROPPERS, PLASTIC, AND GLASS

Textile Colors (both plastic and glass)
Rupert, Gibbon & Spider, Inc. (glass)
Substitute: dropper from children's vitamin bottle

FABRIC PAINTING SUPPLIES AND TOOLS

See also Arts and Crafts Supplies, Appendix D

Cerulean Blue, Ltd.
Dharma Trading Co.
Textile Colors
Rupert, Gibbon & Spider, Inc.

PRINT BLOCKS
Cookie Cutters

Wilton Enterprises

Cookies cutters are also widely available in variety/discount and grocery stores.

Plastic

Dizzle Paint Blocks

Sure-Stamp (adhesive-backed rubber)

Cerulean Blue, Ltd.

Sponges

Banar Designs (adhesive cardboard backing, several shapes)
Cerulean Blue, Ltd. (Petifours)
EZ Crafts (wood-backed, with handle)
GICK Crafts (several shapes)
Plaid Enterprises, Inc.

Sponges are also availabe in grocery, hardware, discount/variety, drug, crafts stores.

Rubber Gasket Material

Look in the plumbing department of your hardware store.

Wood Shapes

Look in crafts stores (unpainted products used for home decor projects).

Foam Board

This can be found in crafts and arts supply stores.

Found Objects

Whatever works!

REFILLABLE MARKERS

Textile Colors

ROLLERS

Foam

Cerulean Blue, Ltd.
DecoArt
Dick Blick
Sax Arts and Crafts

Rubber Brayers (Hard)

Dick Blick
Sax Arts and Crafts catalog

Wood or Plastic Wallpaper Seam Rollers

These are available in hardware or paint stores.

SPRAY/MIST BOTTLES

See also Spraying and Misting, Chapter 9

Pump or Trigger Type

These are available in craft, grocery, and hardware stores.
Substitutes: empty hairspray bottles, plant misting bottles, empty window cleaner bottles

Aerosol

Preval Spray Gun (removable pressurized unit, placed on paint container): available in most Napa Auto Parts Stores and Standard Brands Paint Stores

SPREADERS

Tulip
Substitutes: expired charge card, plastic knife, card stock

STAMPS

Daisy Kingdom
Pelle's See-Thru Stamps
Works of Heart

Stamp Pads

Do not use pads containing alcohol.

Co-Motion
Inkadinkado
Pelle's
Ranger Industries
Y & C Multi-Color Stamp Pads
Substitute: plastic table covering with thin foam backing; felt

STENCILS

Refer to Stencils section, Appendix D

SYRINGES

These can also be used to apply glue.

Aleene's
Cerulean Blue, Ltd.
Rupert, Gibbon & Spider, Inc. (my favorite has a snap-on tip cover)

TIE-PAINTING SUPPLIES (RINGS AND WIRE)

Plastic Rings

Wrights/Boye: several sizes, labeled Cabone Rings
Clover Needlecraft, Inc.: teeny and small sizes, labeled knitting markers
EZ International: several sizes

Metal Rings

EZ International: several sizes

Cloth Covered 30-Gauge Wire

EZ International: labeled Spool Wire

Non-Paint Supplies and Tools

Addresses and mail-order information for companies and manufacturers are given in Supply Sources at the end of this book.

APPLIQUÉS
Fabrics (printed fabrics suitable for fused appliqués)
Daisy Kingdom
Hoffman California Fabrics

Iron-On Transfers
Banar Designs: over 36 design packets, each containing several transfers
Dizzle: every type from prepainted to glitter to opaque for dark fabrics
Seitec: Cache Junction Impressions and Vignettes, dyed transfers; Dimensional Velour Designs, heavy velour
Tulip: every type, including those with coordinating stencils and those with a chalkboard-like surface

Leather
Tandy Leather Company

Patterns/Designs (patterns or designs suitable for appliqué and painted designs)
Art of Sewing (magazine)
Country Handcrafts (magazine)
Crafts (magazine)
Creative Needle (magazine)
Dover Publications, Inc.
The Hand Maden
Kwik Sew
Mary's Productions
Quilt (magazine)
Sew-Art international
Sew News (magazine)
Speed Stitch
Treadleart (magazine)
Wearable Wonders (magazine)

Stick On (adhesive backed)
Back Street, Inc.

Stitch, Glue, or Fuse Down
Daisy Kingdom
Shafaii
What's New
Wrights/Boye

ARTS AND CRAFTS SUPPLIES
See also Fabric Painting Supplies, Appendix C
Aardvark Adventures
Dick Blick
Craft Catalog
Craft King
EZ Crafts/Division EZ International
Factory Direct Craft Supply
Home-Sew
Kirchen Bros.
Nancy's Notions, Ltd.
Sax Arts and Crafts
Suncoast Discount Arts & Crafts

BASTING TAPE (⅛″, WATER-SOLUBLE)
The Hand Maden
J & P Coats

BATTENBERG LACE (TAPE AND INSERTS)
Barrett House
Sew Art International
Seitec: Sew Easy Industries

BEADS, STONES, AND JEWELS
Acrylic
Art's International
The Beadery Craft Products

Cross-Locked and Glass
Clotilde, Inc.
EZ International
Nancy's Notions, Ltd.

Glass, Crystal, and Semi-Precious

These companies also carry complete supplies and findings used for beading.

The Bead Shop
Beadworks
Garden of Beadin'
Optional Extras, Inc.

Iron-On Rhinestones

Seitec: Sew Easy Industries

Snap-On Stones and Pearls

Shafaii

BUTTONS

Buttons to Cover

Dritz
EZ International

Button Covers

EZ International
Home-Sew

Clay Buttons

A Homespun Heart

CHRISTMAS SHIRT (CHAPTER 6)

Lights

Craft King

Music Box

Craft King; Home-Sew

CLOTHING AND/OR YARDAGE (BLANK AND PRINTED)

Blueprints Printables
Cerulean Blue, Ltd.
Cotton Express
Daisy Kingdom
Dharma Trading Co.
Gohn Bros.
The Hand Maden
Hoffman California Fabrics
Ivy Imports
Max e.b.
Qualin International
Rupert, Gibbon & Spider, Inc.
Sax Arts and Crafts
Textile Colors
Thai Silks

CLOTHING AND ACCESSORY PATTERNS

Clotilde, Inc.
The Crowning Touch, Inc.
Daisy Kingdom
Great Copy Patterns
The Hand Maden
Mary Production's
Nancy's Notions, Ltd.

Simplicity Pattern Company
Speed Stitch
Stretch & Sew, Inc.
Sure-Fit Designs
Tandy Leather Company
Treadleart (catalog)

COOKIE CUTTERS

Wilton Enterprises

COOKING PARCHMENT PAPER

This can be found in the grocery store (usually near wax paper).

James River Corporation (allow 6–8 weeks for delivery)
Wilton Enterprises

FABRIC PAINTING SUPPLIES

See Appendix C and Arts and Crafts Supplies in this appendix.

FRAME (ADJUSTABLE, FLOOR)

Morgan and Associates

FREEZER PAPER

This can be found in grocery and variety/discount stores.

James River Corporation

FUSIBLES

Products are listed by manufacturer's name, followed by brand name.

Paper Backed

Aleene's: Hot Stitch Fusible Web
Dritz: Magic Fuse
HTC: TransWeb, Stitch Witchery Plus, and Transbond
Pellon: Wonder-Under and Heavy-Duty Wonder-Under
Sew-Art international: AppliHesive
Therm O Web: Heat'n Bond Original, Heat'n Bond Lite

Without Paper Backing

HTC: Stitch Witchery
Pellon: Wonder-Under
Solar-Kist: Fine Fuse, Tuf-Fuse

Liquid

Beacon Chemical Co.: Liqui Fuse

GLUES/ADHESIVES

Products are listed by manufacturer's name, followed by brand name.

Glues for Jewels, Gems, and Stones

You can use paints listed "suitable as glue substitute" (Appendix B) or the following:

Aleene's: Jewel-It
Beacon Chemical Co.: Gem Tac; Liqui Fuse (heat-setting required for Liqui Fuse)
Delta/Slomons: Stitchless Fabric Glue (heat-setting required)

Glues for Fabric (permanent, will not wash out)

Aleene's: OK To Wash It
Beacon Chemical Co.: Fabri Tac; Liqui Fuse (heat-setting required for Liqui Fuse)
W. H. Collins, Inc.: Unique Stitch
Delta/Slomons: Stitchless Fabric Glue (heat-setting required)
Jones Tones, Inc.: Plexi 400 Stretch Adhesive

Glaze Solutions

Use glaze solutions when protection is needed for iron-on transfers or glitter after glue has dried; apply with soft brush or by spraying.

Galacolor: Gel—dilute 50/50 for glaze. Extender—dilute 50/50 for glaze. Plexi 34 Clear—dilute 50/50 for glaze.
Jones Tones Inc.: stretchable, dilute 3 parts Plexi to 1 part water for glaze

Glues Used with Glitter

Use paints listed "suitable as glue substitute" (Appendix B) or the following:

Aleene's: Jewel-It
Beacon Chemical Co.: Gem Tac
Distlefink Designs, Inc.: Sequin Art Glue
Duncan: Foil 'n Accent
Galacolor: Gel

Lift-Off or Pressure-Sensitive

Aleene's: Tack-It Over & Over, liquid
Clotilde, Inc.: Sticky Stuff, liquid
W. H. Collins: Basting Glue, solid, removed in laundering
Createx: Foil Adhesive Pressure Sensitive, liquid
Delta: Stencil Magic Repositionable spray
Dritz: Glue Stick, solid, removed in laundering
Plaid Enterprises, Inc.: Founder's Stikit Again & Again, liquid

Note: Magic Goo Gone removes glue residue from plastic stencils.

MARKERS
Permanent

See Appendix B

Removable

See Sewing Supplies; Fabric Painting Supplies

NEEDLEWORK/STITCHERY SUPPLIES

Aardvark Adventures
Clotilde, Inc.
Clover Needlecraft, Inc.
House of White Birches
Nancy's Notions, Ltd.
Sax Arts and Crafts
Sew-Art international
Speed Stitch

Suncoast Discount Arts & Crafts
The Hand Maden
Treadleart (catalog)
Yo's Needlecraft

PILLOW COVERS (FORMS)

Putnam Company, Inc.

PRESSING AIDS

Dritz
June Tailor

PRESSING AND DRYING SHEETS (TEFLON SHEETS)

Note: Can often be used as substitute for cooking parchment paper.

Solar-Kist Corporation: Easy-Way Pressing Sheet; Fabric Painters Drying Sheet

ROTARY CUTTER/RULERS

See also Sewing Supplies
Quilter's Rule International

SEAM SEALANT

See also Sewing Supplies

Aleene's: Stop Fraying
Dritz: Fray Check
Galacolor: Extender (can be diluted with water, 50/50)

SEQUINS
Cross-Locked, Regular Size

EZ International

Cross-Locked, Hologram/Oversized

Craft Stop
Jones Tones, Inc.

Kits, Bagged Sequins

Distlefink Designs, Inc.
Jones Tones, Inc.

Premade Designs

Art's International

SEWING MACHINE SPECIALITY FEET

See also Sewing Supplies
The Crowning Touch, Inc.

Sewing Supplies

Clotilde, Inc.
Gal Friday Sewing Notions
Gohn Bros.
The Hand Maden
Home-Sew
Nancy's Notions, Ltd.
Sew Art international
Sew/Fit Company
Speed Stitch
Treadleart (catalog)

STABILIZERS
Water-Soluble Sheets
See also Sewing Supplies

Clotilde, Inc.: Amazing Solvy
Sew-Art international: Aqua-Solve
Sulky of America: Solvy

Iron-On
See also Freezer Paper; Sewing Supplies

Sulky of America: Totally Stable

Liquid
Palmer Pletsch: PerfectSew

Tear Away
See also Sewing Supplies

H&C: Armo
Sew-Art international: Stitch & Tear and Tear-Away

STENCILS, STENCIL PLASTIC, AND MARKERS
See also Arts and Crafts Supplies; Fabric Painting Supplies; Sewing Supplies (check catalogs for quilting stencils)

W. H. Collins Inc.: vinyl plastic sheets (plain and grid marked), non-smear markers (Template Marking Pencil)
EZ International: stencil plastic, quilting stencils, markers
DecoArt: Fashion Tape
Quilting Creations by D. J., Inc.: comprehensive selection of quilting stencils
Tulip: stencils included in Secret Recipes iron-on transfer packets

STUDS/NAILHEADS/TOOLS FOR ATTACHING
Art's International
EZ International
Distlefink Designs, Inc.: also has Bedazzler (tool for attaching)
Dritz: also has tool for attaching

TAPE MEASURE (FIBERGLASS WITH HOLE AT END)
Dritz: Lifetime Tape Measure

THREADS
Bobbin (White, extra fine)
Sew-Art international: Sew-Bob

Decorative
See also Needlework/Stitchery Supplies; Sewing Supplies

Maderia Marketing, Ltd.
Sew-Art international
YLI

Fusing
Coats: Stitch 'n Fuse

Invisible (fine nylon)
Dritz
Sew Art International

Silk
YLI

TRANSFER SUPPLIES
See Sewing Supplies.

Cooking Parchment, Tracing, Vellum, Tracing Vellum Paper
Dick Blick: tracing and vellum paper available in rolls
James River Corporation: cooking parchment paper available in rolls
Sax Arts and Crafts: tracing and vellum paper available in rolls
Sure-Fit Designs: tracing and vellum paper available in rolls, two widths
Tolin' Station Vellum: available in cut sheets
Wilton Enterprises: cooking parchment paper available in rolls

Note: Cooking parchment paper is a non-stick surface for paints, glues, and fusibles and is usable as a pressing cloth and stitching aide.

Transfer Mediums
Aleene's Transfer-It
Delta: Photo-to-Fabric Transfer by Delta; Stitchless Fabric Glue and Transfer Medium
Fashion Show: Picture This transfer medium for fabric
Galacolor: Magic Transfer Medium

Transfer Paint
Deka IronOn: see Deka in Appendix B

Transfer Papers and Tools
Clover Needlecraft, Inc.: chalk markers, Charcopy; "Hera" Marker; blunt edge tracing wheel
EZ International: Pressure-fax transfer pen; transfer paper
Marvy Uchida: Fabric Pattern Transfer Kit
Sulky: Iron-On Transfer Pen
Tolin' Station: transfer paper; vellum; marking stylus
Yo's Needlecraft: Chalk markers and transfer paper

Supply Sources

Most supplies, tools, and equipment are available in local crafts or fabric stores. Also many shop owners will order items for you. Chain stores are good local sources as well.

To make sure you'd be able to purchase any product mentioned, I asked each manufacturer to recommend the best mail-order source for its products. And that's why Supply Sources ended up the size it did!

Rather than have one section for manufacturers and another for mail-order companies, I have combined the two sources in one alphabetical listing.

A mail-order source for a manufacturer's products is often included in the manufacturer's listing. If no mail-order source is given, contact the manufacturer for local retail outlets and mail-order sources. Manufacturers will also answer any questions you have about their products.

NOTE: Paint manufacturers that do not have mail-order services are not listed in Supply Sources. See Appendix B for names of these manufacturers.

Catalog price is given, along with minimum order information. (Price may change, due to ever-increasing postal rates.) LSASE means you should include a large, self-addressed, stamped envelope with your request for information.

Contact magazines publishers for subscription rates.

Terms Used to Describe Contents of Catalogs

Arts and crafts supplies: tools, supplies, equipment used for numerous creative activities, including fabric painting

Fabric painting supplies: tools, supplies, equipment used for fabric painting

Fiber art supplies: tools, supplies, equipment used for fiber-based activities, ranging from needlework to weaving

Sewing supplies: tools, supplies, equipment used for hand- and machine-stitching and fabric-painting projects

Classifications: comprehensive, extensive, numerous, assorted (*comprehensive* indicates just about everything used for an activity; *assorted* indicates limited selection of items used for an activity)

Items of interest found in a catalog are noted.

Warning: These catalogs could be damaging to your budget!

Manufacturers and Mail-Order Companies

A HOMESPUN HEART
2223 F Street
Iowa City, IA 52245
1-800-336-3490
Catalog $1.00; minimum order required; comprehensive selection of clay buttons

AARDVARK ADVENTURES
P.O. Box 2449, Dept. FP
Livermore, CA 94551-2449
1-800-388-2687
Catalog $2.00; extensive crafts and fiber art supplies; unusual, hard-to-find items; information-filled catalog

ALEENE'S
Division of Artis, Inc.
85 Industrial Way
Buellton, CA 93427
1-800-825-3363
Free catalog; comprehensive selection of glues and adhesives; Hot Stitch Fusible Web; syringe; books; videos

ART'S INTERNATIONAL
Retail Division
3306 83rd Street
Lubbock, TX 79423
806-792-2136
Free catalog; comprehensive selection of premade sequin designs (including bridal); acrylic jewels, rhinestones; nailheads

BACK STREET, INC.
P.O. Box 1213
Athens, GA 35611

BANAR DESIGNS
P.O. Box 483
Fallbrook, CA 92028
619-728-0344
Free catalog; comprehensive selection of iron-on transfers; permanant markers

BARRETT HOUSE
P.O. Box 54085
North Salt Lake, UT 84054-0585
801-299-0700
    Catalog $2.00; comprehensive selection of Battenberg lace items, inserts, yardage, decorator items, kits

BEACON CHEMICAL CO.
Signature Marketing
P.O. Box 427
276 Sycamore Street
Wyckoff, NJ 07481
    Mail-order source: House of White Birches

THE BEADERY CRAFT PRODUCTS
105 Canonchet Road
P.O. Box 178
Hope Valley, RI 02832

THE BEAD SHOP
177 Hamilton Avenue
Palo Alto, CA 94301
1-800-99-BEADS
    Catalog $3.00; comprehensive selection of beads, supplies, books

BEADWORKS
139 Washington Street
South Norwalk, CT 06854
203-852-9194
    Catalog $10.00; minimum order required; comprehensive selection of beads and findings

DICK BLICK
1-800-447-8192
    Catalog $3.00; comprehensive arts and crafts supplies; sponge (foam) rollers; wooden jewelry; permanent markers; transfer supplies; block printing supplies; adjustable stretcher frame

BLUEPRINTS PRINTABLES
71504 #7 Industrial Way
Belmont, CA 94002
1-800-356-0445; CA 415-594-2995
    Comprehensive selection of sun print fabrics and clothing

CERULEAN BLUE, LTD.
P.O. Box 21168
Seattle, WA 98111-3168
Customer service: 206-323-8600; Orders: 1-800-676-
    8602
    Free catalog; minimum order required; extensive fabric painting supplies; numerous blank fabrics, ready to paint; scarves; Sure Stamp; foam rollers; kits (paint, fabric, brush) for all levels; books

CLOTILDE, INC.
1909 S.W. First Avenue
Fort Lauderdale, FL 3315-2100
1-800-772-2891

Free catalog; comprehensive sewing supplies; numerous crafts supplies; Sticky Stuff; fusibles; removable markers (pens and chalk); Quilter's Rule rotary cutter; fabric crayons; patterns; books; videos

CLOVER NEEDLECRAFT, INC.
1007 East Dominquez Street, Suite L
Carson, CA 90746
1-800-233-1703
    Mail-order source: Yo's Needlecraft

COATS: See J.&P. Coats

W. H. COLLINS, INC.
Whippany, N.J. 07981

CO-MOTION
4455 South Park Avenue
Tucson, AZ 85714-1669
(602) 889-2200
    Catalog $3.00; comprehensive selection of rubber stamps and stamping supplies; Stamp 'N Iron Fabric Transfer Ink and preinked pads

COTTON EXPRESS
1407 Queen Anne Road
Wilson, NC 27893
919-399-7639
    Free catalog; numerous woven and knit cotton fabrics

CRAFT CATALOG
6095 McNaughten Centre
Columbus, OH 43232
1-800-777-1442
    Catalog $2.00; extensive arts and crafts supplies; Founder's School Glue; color iron-on transfers; crafts videos, discounted prices

CRAFT KING
P.O. Box 90637
Lakeland, FL 33804
813-686-9600
    Free catalog; extensive arts and crafts supplies; 20-gauge wire; plastic rings; (tie-painting); music boxes and lights (Christmas shirt)

CRAFT STOP
68733 Perez
Cathedral City, CA 92234
619-321-8877
    LSASE; all Jones Tones products; Glitter, Sequin Jewels, larger size cross-locked hologram sequins, foil iron-on transfers

CREATIVE WHOLESALE DISTRIBUTORS
4898 Jonesboro Road
Forest Park, GA 30050
404-363-9097
    Catalog $2.00, minimum order required; complete assortment DecoArt Paints and products

THE CROWNING TOUCH, INC.
2410 Glory C Road
Medford, OR 97501
503-772-8430
Catalog with LSASE; complete selection Fastube and Fasturn products, patterns, books, specialty foot for machine, videos

DAISY KINGDOM
134 Northwest 8th Avenue
Portland, OR 97209
1-800-234-6688
Catalog $2.00 each (there are four); comprehensive selection of iron-on transfers and no-sew appliqués; rubber stamps; fabrics; clothing

CY DECOSSE INCORPORATED
5900 Green Oak Drive
Minnetonka, MN 55343
1-800-328-3895
Free catalog; *Singer Sewing Reference Library*, excellent series of books for sewing (hand and machine) and serger techniques, instructions applicable to all machine and serger brands

DELTA
2500 Pellissier Place
Whittier, CA 90601-1505
1-800-423-4135
LSASE: free project sheets, include request for specific designs Mail-order source (paints, glues, Marble Thix): Grason's, Inc.

DHARMA TRADING CO.
P.O. Box 150916
San Rafael, CA 94915
1-800-542-5227; 415-456-7657
Free catalog; comprehensive fabric painting supplies, blank clothing (infant and adult sizes), accessories, shoes, fabrics; Magic Transfer Paper; catalog loaded with advice and instructions

DISTLEFINK DESIGNS, INC.
P.O. Box 358
Pelham, NY 10803
914-738-4807
Free catalog; comprehensive assortment loose sequins, sequin design kits; sequin glue; BeDazzler; Dye Ties

DOVER PUBLICATIONS, INC.
31 East 2nd Street
Mineola, NY 11501
Free catalog; comprehensive assortment of design and pattern books for all crafts and needlework activities

DRITZ
P.O. Box 5028
Spartanburg, SC 29304

DUNCAN CRAFTS
5673 East Shields Avenue
Fresno, CA 93727

DUPEY MANAGEMENT CORPORATION
9015 Sterling Street
Irving, TX 75063
214-929-4676
LSASE: complete selection U.tee.it Paint products

EMBOSSART
5215 South 550 West
Hooper, UT 84315
1-800-344-7603
Free catalog; extensive assortment fine-line applicator tools (used for either paint or glue)

ENTERPRISE ART
P.O. Box 2918
Largo, FL 34649
813-536-1492
Free catalog; complete assortment Tulip Paints and products; arts and crafts supplies

ERIC'S PRESS
P.O. Box 5222
Salem, OR 97304
LSASE; all books by Diane and Lois Erison

EZ CRAFTS/DIVISION EZ INTERNATIONAL
95 Mayhill Street
Saddle Brook, NJ 07662

EZ INTERNATIONAL
See EZ Crafts

FACTOR DIRECT CRAFT SUPPLY
440 Conover Road
Franklin, OH 45005
513-743-5855
Free catalog; assorted crafts supplies; numerous laces

GAL FRIDAY SEWING NOTIONS
79 West Genesse Street
Baldwinsville, NY
Cataog with LSASE; numerous sewing supplies; books

GALACOLOR
See Galacraft

GALACRAFT
1760 East 15th St.
Los Angeles, CA 90021
1-800-BUY-GALA
Free catalog; complete assortment Galacolor and Galacraft paint and paint-related products

GARDEN OF BEADIN'
P.O. Box 1535
Redway, CA 95560
1-800-BEAD LUV, CA 707-923-9120

Free catalog; comprehensive selection of beads and bead-related supplies; assorted books

GICK CRAFTS
9 Studebaker Drive
Irvine, CA 92718
714-581-5830
Free catalog; comprehensive selection of glitter, iron-on transfers (books and single designs), sponge blocks, stencils, beads

GOHN BROS.
111 105 South Main Street
Middlebury, IN 46540
Catalog 50¢; extensive fabric selection (no silk), swatches on request; unusual sewing notions

GRASON'S, INC.
31143 Via Colinas
#508
West Lake Village, CA 91362
818-707-6008
Free catalog; complete line Delta, Delta/Slomon products; extensive arts and crafts supplies; Beacon Chemical Co. adhesives

GREAT COPY PATTERNS
P.O. Box 85329
Racine, WI 53408-5329
414-632-2660
Catalog with LSASE; extensive selection clothing patterns; knit and woven fabrics; ribbing; Ultrasuede

H. T. CHANDLER TEXTILE CORPORATION
450 7th Avenue
New York, NY 10123
212-695-0990

THE HAND MADEN
318 Grand Avenue
Pacific Grove, CA 93950
408-373-5353
LSASE with list of requested information; extensive sewing, needlework supplies, woven fabrics (Hoffman, P & B, etc.), no silk; numerous crafts supplies; laces; trims; decorative threads; patterns; books

J. R. HENNIS WHOLESALE
4619 Luna Drive
Machesney Park, IL 61111
815-654-0179
Free catalog; complete line Testors products

HOFFMAN CALIFORNIA FABRICS
25792 Obrero Drive
P.O. Box 2009
Mission Viejo, CA 92691-3140
714-770-2922

HOME-SEW
Bethlehem, PA 18018
215-867-3833

Free catalog; extensive sewing supplies; assorted crafts items; fusible thread; muslin; laces; trims; buttons; transfer supplies; sequins

HOUSE OF WHITE BIRCHES
Berne, IN 46711
1-800-347-9887
Catalog $2.00; Liqui Fuse; Fabric Tac; Gem Tac; magazines; books; kits

INKADINKADO
76 South Street
Boston, MA 02111
617-338-2600
Catalog $2.00; comprehensive selection of rubber stamps and stamping supplies; Fabric Transfer Ink pre-inked pads

J. & P. COATS
Dept. CO1, Dept. 27067
Greenville, SC 29616
803-234-0331

JONES TONES, INC.
68743 Perez Road, #D-16
Cathedral City, CA 92234
619-321-9665
Mail-order source: Craft Stop

KIRCHEN BROS.
Box 1016
Skokie, IL 60076
708-647-6747
Catalog $2.00; extensive crafts supplies; metallic elastic thread; chenilles; beads; cloth covered wire; discounts

KWIK SEW
3000 Washington Avenue North
Minneapolis, MN 55411-1699
1-800-328-3953
Catalog $5.00; comprehensive selection of clothing patterns; appliqué patterns (single designs and books)

LARK BOOKS
50 College St.
Asheville, NC
704-253-0467
Free catalog; numerous crafts and stitchery books

MADERIA MARKETING, LTD.
600 East 9th Street
Michigan City, IN 46360
219-873-1000

MARY'S PRODUCTIONS
P.O. Box 87
Aurora, MN 55705
218-229-2804
Catalog with LSASE; books by Mary Mulari; appliqué designs and embellishments for sweatshirts and accessories

MAX E.B.
255 West Broadway
Paterson, NJ 07522
   Catalog $1.00 and LSASE; extensive selection cotton clothing blanks, infant and adult sizes

MORGAN AND ASSOCIATES
P.O. Box 58
Blue Springs, MO 64013
1-800-272-3899
   Catalog with LSASE; Morgan's Universal Craft Stand, multi-use floor stand, adjustable for most crafts and needlework activities; video

NANCY'S NOTIONS, LTD.
333 Beichi Avenue
Beaver Dam, WI 53916-0683
1-800-883-0690
   Free catalog; comprehensive sewing supplies; numerous crafts supplies; Rowenta irons; Teflon plate for iron; Sulky products; fabrics; ribbing; heirloom laces; books; videos to rent

NATIONAL THREAD & SUPPLY
695 Red Oak Road
Stockbridge, CA 30281
1-800-847-1001
   Free catalog; minimum order required; extensive sewing supplies; zippers; zipper parts; Magic Wand; Singer Sewing Reference Library books

NETWORK FOR WEARABLE ART
P.O. Box 10936
Napa, CA 94581
   Information with LSASE; national organization with local chapters for individuals with interest in wearable art

OPEN CHAIN PUBLISHING, INC.
P.O. Box 2634
Menlo Park, CA 94026
415-366-4440
   Free catalog; comprehensive selection of sewing and crafts books

OPTIONAL EXTRAS, INC.
P.O. Box 1421
150A Church Street
Burlington, VT 05402
1-800-736-0781
   Catalog $1.50; comprehensive selection of beads, stones, supplies

PALMER PLETSCH
P.O. Box 12046
Portland, OR 97212-0046
1-800-728-3784
   Free catalog; PerfectSew (wash-away liquid fabric stabilizer); comprehensive selection of sewing and serger books; videos

PELLE'S SEE-THRU STAMPS
P.O. Box 242
Davenport, CA 95017
408-425-4743
   Catalog $2.00; comprehensive selection of fabric stamps with clear plastic base; quilt block designs in four sizes; custom stamps, made to your order; stamp pads; stamp ink

PLAID ENTERPRISES, INC.
1649 International Boulevard
P.O. Box 7600
Norcross, GA 30091-7600

PREVAL
Precision Valve Corporation
P.O. Box 309
Yonkers, NY 10702

PUTNAM COMPANY, INC.
P.O. Box 310
Walworth, WI 53184
1-800-338-4776
   Free catalog; pillow covers; pillow forms; batting; fiberfill

QUALIN INTERNATIONAL
P.O. Box 31145
San Francisco, CA 94131-0145
415-647-1329
   For catalog, send LSASE with 52¢ postage; comprehensive selection of silk yardage, blank silk clothing, scarves, accessories, and covered jewelry; silk painting supplies and tools; Milsoft (makes silk almost wrinkle-free), books

QUILTER'S RULE INTERNATIONAL
2322 N.E. 29th Avenue
Ocala, FL 32670
1-800-343-8671

QUILTING CREATIONS BY D. J., INC.
P.O. Box 508
Zoar, OH 44697

RAINBO PRODUCTIONS, INC.
8206 Santa Clara
Dallas, TX 75218
214-324-3338
   Catalog with LSASE; complete assortment U.tee.it paints

JAMES RIVER CORPORATION
Consumers Affairs
P.O. Box 6000
Norwalk, CT 06856-6000
1-800-243-5384
   Contact for ordering form: Kitchen Parchment® Paper and/or Paper Maid™ 20 Below Freezer Wrap® (allow 6–8 weeks for delivery)

SAX ARTS AND CRAFTS
2405 South Calhoun Road
P.O. Box 51710
New Berlin, WI 53151
1-800-558-6696; WI 1-800-242-4911
Catalog $4.00; minimum order required; comprehensive arts, crafts, and fabric-painting supplies; extensive fiber art supplies; fabrics, blank clothing; art tissue; transparencies for sun print fabrics

SEITEC
Sew Easy Industries
2701 West 1800 S
Logan, UT 84321
1-800-333-3279
Free catalog; iron-on dyed transfers, large and small designs; iron-on rhinestones; battenberg lace, inserts and yardage; Tumble Dye

SEW-ART INTERNATIONAL
145 South Main Street
P.O. Box 550
Bountiful, UT 84011
1-800-231-2787
Catalog $2.00; comprehensive sewing supplies and threads; Renaissance thread (30% wool/70% acrylic), books and machine needles; fusibles; stabilizers; transfer supplies; patterns; books

SEW/FIT COMPANY
P.O. Box 397
Bedford Park, IL 60499
1-800-547-4739
Free catalog; extensive sewing supplies; books; self-covering earrings; iron-on transfers; Maderia thread; fusibles; worktables

SHAFAII
1000 Broadway
Houston, TX 77012
713-923-5366
Catalog with LSASE; comprehensive selection ready-to-use appliqué designs, lamé, satin, puffed; snap-on stones and pearls; Penny Pins; iron-on studs; conchos

SINGER SEWING REFERENCE LIBRARY
See Cy Decosse Incorporated

SOLAR-KIST CORPORATION
Craft and Fashion Division
P.O. Box 273
LaGrange, IL 60525

SPEED STITCH
3113 Broadpoint Drive
Harbor Heights, FL 33983
1-800-874-4415
Catalog $3.00; comprehensive stitchery and sewing supplies; comprehensive assortment of books; all Sulky products; stabilizers; decorative threads; transfer pens; appliqué patterns; Speed Stitch kits

STENCILS & STUFF
5198 T. R. 123
Millersburg, OH 44654
Catalog $2.00; comprehensive selection of stencils made by Quilting Creations by D. J., Inc.; stencil adhesives and supplies

STERLING/LARK BOOKS
50 College Avenue
Asheville, NC 28801
704-253-0467
Free catalog; numerous crafts and stitchery books

STRETCH & SEW, INC.
3895 East 18th Street
P.O. Box 185
Eugene, OR 97440
1-800-547-7717
Free catalog; comprehensive selection of clothing patterns

SULKY OF AMERICA
3313 Broadpoint Drive
Harbor Heights, FL 33983
1-800-874-4415

SUNCOAST DISCOUNT ARTS & CRAFTS
9015 U.S. Highway 19 North
Pinellas Park, FL 34666
813-576-0835
Catalog $2.00; comprehensive crafts supplies; numerous stitchery supplies; discounted prices; books; wooden shapes; cookie cutters

SURE-FIT DESIGNS
P.O. Box 5567
Eugene, OR 97405
503-344-0422
Free catalog; tracing vellum, rolls in two widths; master clothing patterns; custom-fitting, designing book; pattern fitting video

TANDY LEATHER COMPANY
1400 Everman Parkway
Fort Worth, TX 76140
Catalog $2.50; comprehensive assortment of leather and supplies; leather appliqués; leather fringe; leather conchos; iron-on transfers

THE TAUNTON PRESS
63 South Main Street
P.O. Box 5506
Newtown, CT 06470
1-800-888-8286
Free catalog; numerous sewing and stitchery books

THE TESTOR CORPORATION
620 Buckee Street
Rockford, IL 61104-4891
815-961-6654
Mail-order source: J. R. Hennis Wholesale

TEXTILE COLORS
P.O. Box 887
Riverdale, MD 20738
1-800-783-9265; D.C. metro. area 301-403-1072
Catalog $2.00; complete assortment Visionarts and FabricARTS dyes and paints; extensive selection fabric painting supplies; silk yardage; blank ties, scarves; books; videos

THAI SILKS
252 State Street
Los Altos, CA 94022
1-800-722-SILK; Calif., 1-800-221-SILK
Free catalog; comprehensive selection of silk fabrics; scarf blanks; necktie blanks

THERM O WEB
112 West Carpenter Avenue
Wheeling, IL 60090
1-800-992-9700

TOLIN' STATION
P.O. Box 8206
Greensboro, NC 27409
919-855-8932
Free catalog; extensive transfer supplies; jewelry findings

TREADLEART (CATALOG)
25834-I Narbonne Avenue
Lomita, CA 90717
1-800-327-4222
Catalog $3.00; comprehensive sewing supplies and books; appliqué patterns; iron-on transfers; pressing aids; Quilter's Rule rulers; see Bibliography for magazine

UPDATE NEWSLETTERS
PJS Publications, Inc.
308 Hitt Street
Mt. Morris, IL 61054
Catalog with LSASE; comprehensive selection of booklets detailing machine and serger sewing techniques

WHAT'S NEW
3716 East Main Street
Mesa, AZ 85202
1-800-272-3874
Free catalog; no-sew lamé appliqué kits

WILTON ENTERPRISES
2240 West 75th Street
Woodridge, IL 60571
1-800-772-7111
Catalog $5.95 (catalog is also an instructional manual and is available in some stores stocking Wilton products); parchment paper by the roll; cookie cutters; decorator tips, bags; treated paper doilies

WORKS OF HEART
P.O. Box 15007
Portland, OR 97215
503-231-3774
Catalog $2.00; comprehensive selection rubber fabric stamps, numerous stamps of embroidery stitches; ink

WRIGHTS/BOYE
West Warren, MA 01092
413-436-7732

YLI
P.O. Box 109
482 North Freedom Way Boulevard
Provo, UT 84603-0109
801-377-3900
Catalog $2.50; comprehensive selection of decorative threads, including silk; accurate color chart included in catalog; silk ribbons

YO'S NEEDLECRAFT
940 #P East Dominquez Street
Carson, CA 90746
310-515-6473
Catalog with LSASE and two first-class stamps, include list of requested product information; complete selection Clover Needlecraft products

Bibliography

PERIODICALS

I recommend all of these magazines. Each is loaded with ideas. Call or write for subscription rates.

Country Handcrafts
5400 S. 69th Street
Greendale, WI 53129
1-800-344-6913

Crafts
PJS Publications, Inc.
News Plaza
Box 1790
Peoria, IL 61656
1-800-727-2387

Crafts 'n Things
Clapper Publishing, Inc.
701 Lee St., Suite 1000
Des Plaines, IL 60016-4570
1-800-CRAFTS; in Illinois, 708-297-7000

The Creative Machine
Open Chain Publishing, Inc.
P.O. Box 2634-FP
Menlo Park, CA 94026
415-366-4440

Creative Needle
Needle Publishing, Inc.
1500 Jupiter Rd.
Lookout Mountain, GA. 30750
404-820-2600

Fiberarts Magazine
50 College St.
Asheville, NC 28801
704-253-0467

Ornament
P.O. Box 2349
San Marcos, CA 92079-2349
619-599-0222

Quick & Easy Crafts
House of White Birches
Berne, IN 46711
1-800-829-5865

Quilt
Harris Publications, Inc.
1115 Broadway
New York, NY 10010

Sew News
P.O. Box 1790, News Plaza
Peoria, IL 61656
1-800-289-6397

Threads Magazine
63 S. Main St.
P.O. Box 5506
Newtown, CT 06470-5506
1-800-888-8286

Treadleart
25834 Narbonne Ave., Suite I
Lomita, CA 90717
1-800-327-4222

Wearable Crafts
306 East Parr Road
Berne, IN 46711
1-800-888-6833

BOOKS

I know these books will be as inspirational to you as they have been for me. Include each one on your 'must read' list.

Beaney, Jan. *The Art of the Needle*, Pantheon Books, 1988.

Chambers, Anne. *A Guide to Making Decorated Papers*, Thames and Hudson, 1989.

Ericson, Diane and Lois. *Print It Yourself*, Eric's Press. The Ericsons have written several excellent books. Write for information to Lois Ericson, P.O. Box 5222, Salem, OR 97304.

Hatch, Sandra, and Ann Boyce. *Putting on the Glitz*, Chilton, 1991.

Kennedy, Jill, and Jane Varrall. *Silk Painting*, Chilton, 1991.

Maurer, Diane Vogel with Paul Mauer. *Marbling*, Crescent Books, 1991.

Taylor, Carol, with Patty Schleicher, Mimi Schleicher, and Laura Sims. *Marbling Paper & Fabric*, Sterling/Lark, 1991.

Tuckman, Diane, and Jan Janas. *The Complete Book of Silk Painting*, North Light Books, 1992.

SERIES PUBLICATIONS

Creative Sewing Ideas, Singer Sewing Reference Library, Cy DeCosse Inc., 1990.

O'Connel, Barbara Weiland. *Beyond Straight Stitching*, Update Newsletters, PJS Publications, 1988.

PUBLICATIONS SUGGESTED FOR DESIGNS (CHAPTER 2)

Dover Publications, Inc.
313 East 2nd Street
Mineola, NY 11501
Free catalog

Kwik.Sew Books and Patterns
3000 Washington Ave., North
Minneapolis, MN 55411-1169
Appliqué the Kwik.Sew Way, by Kerstin Martensson
Pattern #2039, Appliqués and Designs

Mary Mulari
Mary's Productions
Box 87
Aurora, MN 55705
Send LSASE for catalog. Mary has written several books that are excellent sources for designs and ideas. Look for her new book, *Glorified Sweatshirts*, to be published by Chilton.

Index